## Also by Gavin McInnes

*Street Boners: 1,764 Hipster Fashion Jokes*
*Dos and Don'ts: 10 Years of "Vice" Magazine's Street Fashion Critiques*
*The "Vice" Guide to Sex and Drugs and Rock and Roll*

# THE DEATH OF COOL

## From Teenage Rebellion to
## the Hangover of Adulthood

# Gavin McInnes

Previously published as *How to Piss in Public*

Scribner
New York   London   Toronto   Sydney   New Delhi

Scribner
A Division of Simon & Schuster, Inc.
1230 Avenue of the Americas
New York, NY 10020

First Scribner trade paperback edition July 2013

Previously published as *How to Piss in Public* by Scribner

SCRIBNER and design are registered trademarks of The Gale Group, Inc.,
used under license by Simon & Schuster, Inc., the publisher of this work.

For information about special discounts for bulk purchases,
please contact Simon & Schuster Special Sales at
1-866-506-1949 or business@simonandschuster.com.

The Simon & Schuster Speakers Bureau can bring authors to your live event.
For more information or to book an event, contact the Simon & Schuster Speakers Bureau
at 1-866-248-3049 or visit our website at www.simonspeakers.com.

Designed by Carla Jayne Jones

Manufactured in the United States of America

1   3   5   7   9   10   8   6   4   2

Library of Congress Control Number: 2011034596

ISBN 978-1-4516-1417-6
ISBN 978-1-4516-1418-3 (pbk)
ISBN 978-1-4516-1419-0 (ebook)

All photographs courtesy of the author except where noted.

# WARNING

With the exception of this warning and a few minor tweaks, the book you're holding in your hands is essentially the same as the original hardcover edition entitled *How to Piss in Public*. Why the title change? Good question.

I always wanted this book to be called *The Death of Cool* because it's ultimately about the party years of your life and all that dies when you become a grown-up. You can't be cool when you're old, and that's a good thing, because there's nothing more pathetic than a dad trying to be a teenager. However, due to its lack of catchiness, the publisher wasn't jazzed about that title. They wanted something that showed how "balls out" the book is, so when I produced a viral video called "How to Piss in Public" (that was viewed over a million times), they took it as a sign.

I fought it at first but eventually realized it followed suit with everything else I've done. It's punk rock to the point of being ostracizing. That's kind of the point of the book, too: Don't compromise or try to appeal to the masses—be yourself, even if you're insane. In the '80s, I was in punk bands called Anal Chinook and Leatherassbuttfuk. Before cofounding *Vice Magazine,* I published an autobiographical comic called *Pervert.* After *Vice* I founded a site called Street Boners and TV Carnage and published a book by the same name. Even my new company, Rooster, is another word for cock. *How to Piss in Public* made sense so we went for it.

However, when sales weren't what I had hoped they'd be, I decided to blame everyone else. I shat on my publisher for insisting on the title and convinced my agent he's terrible at his job. I noticed, while doing press for the book, that journalists had removed the dust jacket so they wouldn't be seen reading it on the train. I told my wife this when she asked how the book was doing. My brother told me his friend said he felt like a paraplegic with a small bladder when he was seen reading the book. I told my wife that, too. Hosts refused to say the title on television when I tried to promote it. That must be why the book wasn't the next *Fifty Shades of Grey*. It couldn't have had anything to do with the fact that mostly women buy books, and writing a collection of alpha-male stories about fighting and fucking and getting paid isn't exactly a moneymaker. Thinking this way is a great coping mechanism that I highly recommend.

Unfortunately, when the publisher was ready to do a paperback, they called my bluff and said we could use my title. This is sort of like when I was told I should be circumcised. I had always loved my foreskin, but when presented with the opportunity to chop it off, I realized I could stop pretending it looked like an elephant trunk and be a Darth Vader helmet like everybody else. So I actually considered circumcision, but, ultimately, I realized I truly do love my foreskin, just like I love this title.

Of course, if this doesn't change anything and the book still doesn't meet expectations, I'll have nobody to blame but . . . um . . . YOU.

To Blobs
Please make sure our family never sees this, especially the kids.

# Contents

# Contents

# Contents

# THE DEATH
# OF COOL

# Where No Man Has Gone Before
# (1984)

"**M**y girlfriend has no vagina," said the voice behind me. I was fixing my shitty Mohawk in the reflective windows by the principal's office and turned around. It was my friend Lawrence McCallister, a big-nosed geek covered in zits who always had some kind of catastrophe on his hands.

"How can she have no vagina?" I asked, continuing to preen.

"I know, I know," he responded, "but trust me. I'm positive."

I consoled him with a pat on his shoulder and said, "That sucks, man," but I was secretly thrilled. I thought I was the only one in school who had felt around down there and got nothing. I was worried it was some kind of *Sword in the Stone* thing where if you don't feel an opening, it means you're gay.

I went to the Earl of March High School in a rural Canadian suburb called Kanata. In 1984, I was a punk fourteen-year-old and knew as much about sex as you know about the early eighties Kanata punk scene. This was before the Internet but after *Playboy*, so everything we understood about naked ladies came from *Hustler*, an almost medical porn mag that always featured women with their slutty high heels up by their slutty ears and their pink pussies splayed wide open. They held their legs up so high and so spread, a generation of young men grew up assuming the vagina was a bazooka-sized hole located right below the belly button.

To make matters worse, girls in the eighties wore jeans so tight, they had to use a bent coat hanger to pull up the zipper. Heavy petting back then involved cramming your hand into a vacuum-sealed denim space and desperately writhing around in search of an opening. You'd force your fingers across some sparse pubes, go right, then left, go farther down than humanly possible, and if you didn't feel an opening, you'd assume it wasn't there. It didn't help that teenage boys are too horny to do anything properly.

Girls didn't share this libidinous curse but really enjoyed kissing, so we made an unspoken truce that involved lying around in a negligent parent's basement listening to Led Zeppelin. The boys would oblige the girls with hours and hours of Frenching and the girls would oblige the boys with maybe a third of the underside of one tit.

A few months after hearing of Lawrence's lost hole and resigning myself to the fact that I might never find one, I found one. I was kissing a half-black girl named Megan Franklyn in Mark Donnelly's basement listening to "Stairway to Heaven" and I'd been rooting around in her skintight drawers for so long, my wrist felt broken. Out of nowhere, I had a huge surge of frustrated confidence and thought, "Let's just fucking give 'er and go where no man has gone before." (The phrase "give 'er" is a Canadian's way of saying "Git-R-Done.") I plunged my aching hand so deep into the abyss I wouldn't have been surprised if it had popped out in China. Then I went even farther. Finally, about half a foot lower than I could have ever imagined, my virgin fingers finally touched beef curtains. "What the what?" I thought. "It's basically in the asshole."

After discovering pussy, I dropped acid, started a band, got beat up, ripped my foreskin, went to jail, planted trees, dealt drugs, got tattoos, squatted Europe, got hustled, had some threesomes, farted, watched my friends die, lived in China, played some pranks, started a multimedia global empire, got on TV, gave myself gonorrhea, got beat up again, invented hipsters, went broke, got rich, got married, got knocked out, and had some kids. If I could go back in time and tell Young Me one thing, it would be the same thing I'd tell all young men.

> *Dear fourteen-year-old boys,*
>
> *First, stop reading this. This book is for older people. Second, if you are fourteen, here's a tip from someone with so much experience, gynecologists call me Mister: Her hole is way farther down than you think. You know when you hear directions and they say, "Keep driving, and when you think you've gone too far, keep going"? That's where it is. And once you find it, your life will never be the same.*
>
> > *Sincerely,*
> > *Your Pal,*
> > *Me*

# Zapped by Space Guns into a Shit Hole on Acid (1985)

I would never do acid in New York City—it's too dirty and claustrophobic—but when you're stuck way out in Buttfuck, Ontario, it's your only escape.

First, let me tell you how Buttfuck this place was. Canadian developers back then were busy creating cookie-cutter housing communities in the middle of nowhere. They had slogans such as "Tomorrow's city . . . today" and names such as New Granada and Bridlewood. They were far from the city and had no drugs, bars, gangs, sluts, or crime—just trees, houses, and the local school.

My parents were educated but working-class Scots who wanted to get as far away from their shitty past as possible. Like all ex–poor people they wanted a better life for their kids and this seemed like a great opportunity. They tried England but it wasn't working. Canada was brand-new back then. It had just settled on a flag in 1965 and was yet to choose a national anthem (they chose "O Canada" in 1980). In the 1970s, they were building their lower middle class from scratch and pouring British immigrants into the mold like pancake mix.

In 1975, five years after a breathtakingly gorgeous baby Me was born, the Glaswegians who created me gave up on their new home in England and stuck the whole family in a mass-produced Canadian suburb surrounded by farmers' fields. Kanata is a half hour from Canada's tiny capital, Ottawa, and had houses that were so prefab and generic, I would often get lost trying to figure out which one was mine.

On my first day of school, I was asked to say a few words and after using my posh English accent to say, "Well, hellowe, I simply cannot tell you how chuffed I am to be here in Canad-er and have brought along my park-er for the occasion," I got the shit pounded out of me so badly, I was saying, "Maggie Longclaws is pregnant, eh?" like Bob and Doug McKenzie within the week. This began my life role as a misfit always adapting to uncomfortable situations. Whether it's an Englishman in Ontario, an English speaker in French Canada, a Canadian in New York, or the only dad at the family resort covered in tattoos, I've always been most comfortable when I'm out of place.

Can you blame them for kicking my ass? (1975)

It was fun, though. Rural seclusion is great when you're a little kid. We shot at each other with BB guns, chased cows, and would make jumps for our bikes that were so intense, anyone who landed wrong was guaranteed a broken wrist. This was in the pre-safety days when not only did we not wear helmets, we didn't even wear shoes, and if your bike didn't have brakes, you'd have to stop the front tire with your bare foot. We swung off tire ropes into swimming holes in the summer and had snowball fights in the winter, but when the testosterone kicks in, so does the need for more. The seclusion goes from "groovy times" to a pressure cooker that makes you want to start a nuclear war. So, the day our teenage years began, we took our cold, bleak, lame environment and magically converted it into Funtown by using drugs. We also started a club that we pretended was a gang.

Steve (hat), Dogboy (curly hair), and
me in a photo booth where we'd try
to not laugh for as long as possible.
(1986)

Half the students at my high school were the children of British expats, and the other half were Canadian farmers' kids. Our crew consisted of about a dozen ornery misfits from both sides. We called ourselves the Monks because we were loosely divided into mods (a now-esoteric subculture that was like punk but based more on neatly dressed, working-class 1960s British soul fans) and punks, though there were quite a few hosers (Canadian rednecks). Our crew ran the gamut. There was a huge basketball player with a harelip named Marty, a male-model-looking kid we thought was ugly so we called him Dogboy, and the Fonzarelli of the group, Steve Durand. Lawrence McCallister was a mod and so was his buddy John. We called John Pukey Stallion because he always threw up at parties and never got laid. We weren't part of the school's social hierarchy and had carved our own niche as the weird kids.

Being fucking idiots was very important to us. If anyone farted or burped without saying "safety" before someone else called "slut," everyone in the gang got to beat the poo-stuffings out of him until he could name five breakfast cereals. Unfortunately, guys started memorizing cereal lists, so we were forced to switch it to chocolate bars to keep things interesting. This was the early stages of a career devoted to troublemaking. Our motto was, "It ain't shit 'til it hits the fan" but the bully from *The Simpsons* later said it much better when he asked Bart, "If no one gets mad, are you really being bad?"

Drugs enhanced this lifestyle, especially acid. We'd drop a tab around eight o'clock at night and go walk around a boring landscape that had blissfully transformed into a place worth visiting. I acquired X-ray vision to see through houses and observe how people lived when they didn't know they were being watched. We stole hovercrafts and walked through trees. One time, Pukey's head was a chicken.

My favorite LSD trip happened when I was fifteen. It was me, Steve, Dogboy, and Marty. We met after dinner behind our high school, and Steve pulled a sheet of about ten tabs from his wallet. As we each put one of the tiny square papers on our tongues, Dogboy said to Steve, "Let me see your driver's license." Steve pulled it out and Dogboy fell to the ground laughing. Steve always went cross-eyed in his ID pictures and eventually we made it a tradition—even for the yearbook. Soon we were all sharing our driver's licenses and laughing at them, but I noticed something strange about Marty when he saw his. He looked disturbed. Marty's harelip was obvious, but we'd known him for so long we couldn't see it. Now I was seeing it. It was more than a single harelip; it was a full, lustrous, head-of-harelip. "That's kind of a bad trip," Marty said after quietly looking at the picture on his license. Then he put it back in his wallet and decided to move on.

We wandered over to a big hill by the football field where we used to punch each other in the nuts and we lay down to stare up at the night sky. It was a beautiful spring night, and the moon was so bright, we could see all the clouds perfectly. I realized I was tripping balls. "Holy shit," I said to Marty as Steve and Dogboy continued to laugh at their licenses. "Do you see octagons?" The entire sky was made up of eight-sided geometry-defying shapes all turning in the same direction like cogs. It was a mosaic honeycomb of shapes that seamlessly rotated in unison, and I wanted to know if it was just me.

"Yes!" Marty said. "I see it, too."

Now I was really confused. "Whoa," I said. "Now, that is a fucking trip and a half. I get how I can be hallucinating something, but how can *you* be seeing the same thing? That's like us having the same dream."

Then he asked, "You know those weird desk toys where there's a plastic board made up of steel pins, like a bed of nails kind of but they move?"

"Er, kind of?" I replied.

"You push your hand on one side," he explained further, "and then your hand imprint is on the other side."

I finally got what he was talking about. "I think it's called Pin Art," I said.

"That's it!" he said excitedly. "And if you put your face on one side, the pins appear on the other side as an imprint of your face." I didn't know where he was going with this and I was getting nervous. Then he said, "That's what I see in the sky. Only it's God doing the impressions of your face." Then he fucking turns to me and says, about a foot away

9

from my ear hole, "Whatever face comes out the other end, that's your face. Do you understand?"

I was desperate to get off this topic and nervously said, "Yeah, yeah, I get it. Hey! That cloud looks like Garfield taking a shit. You see that?"

He wasn't having it, and he got up on one elbow so we were face-to-face. "No, man, I'm serious," he said. "I'm going to ask you tomorrow if you really do get it, because it's important." I could feel a bad trip starting to bubble from my toes and surge up my body, so I sprang upright and said, "Let's sneak onto the golf course," to which Steve and Dogboy yelled, *"Yeah!"*

Those guys usually got all Beavis and Butthead on acid, and I envied that. For me, acid was like having a thousand eyes and twenty million ears that could hear every conversation in the world at once. I think that's God's Pin Art way of saying, "Stick to booze," but every time God spoke, I put my fingers in my ears and said, "La la la. I can't hear you. Doo dee dee. Not listening to you."

I was rattled by Marty's provocations for the rest of the night, but I had shaken the bad trip and was able to file his heavy vibes away under No Fucking Way Are We Ever Going There Again for as Long as We Shall Live.

The Kanata Golf and Country Club was in the upper-class section of Nowhere and we were well-known by the security staff. Tonight it was beautifully lit up by the moon and we all felt fearless. We were all such old hats at sneaking into stuff, we actually preferred it when they chased us. Steve would do karate moves and run in circles like he was training to be a Keystone Kop. We were bored brats who were desperate to get back to all the danger and excitement our immigrant parents had rescued us from. Adding acid to this game was like colorizing a black-and-white movie. We ran up and down hills and tossed flags like javelins. We threw garbage cans in the water and climbed trees as if they were made of stairs. We had the agility of Olympic monkeys and the whole thing was such a riot, we started laughing uncontrollably.

Then it happened.

Steve was bouncing along and saw a small circle of mud that was about two feet in diameter. Without a second thought he jumped on it, expecting a small "splatch" and maybe a slightly muddy toe. Instead his entire body vanished into the atmosphere and the only thing left was his disembodied head sitting there on top of the puddle.

Do you get what I'm telling you?

His body was gone. Disappeared.

If you were a Nobel Prize–winning physicist you would have been confused. We were stupid kids on fucking acid. Ergo, we *completely* lost our shit. After screaming "What the fuck!?" about seven hundred times, I calmed down a bit and started to get mad at society for having such technology. "Why is it okay to annihilate people's torsos and limbs using some kind of invisible death ray? I understand security can't tolerate trespassers and I wouldn't have complained if we were kicked out or arrested, but obliterated with a space gun? They shoot your body off if you walk on a golf course after hours? How long have they had this technology? Why isn't there more blood? The military are the only ones who should be able to use such guns—*not* that fat rent-a-cop with the woman's mustache! What if he gets drunk? He could end civilization! I'm going to fight for Body Gun–control legislation when I grow up."

My mind was racing.

Marty was bewildered and laughing but in control. Dogboy and I were gone and had begun howling with confusion. Steve had been murdered. We were both sitting on our haunches with our arms outstretched screaming, "Whaaaat!?" over and over.

Steve knew how important it was to laugh at a time like this—especially if you're not actually dead. He authoritatively said, "I'm all right. You can laugh," and while still having no idea what happened to his body, Dogboy and I both fell back and laughed our heads off with no holds barred. I felt like my teeth were cumming. As we both pounded the grass and continued roaring, Steve commanded Marty to get him out. Being the legal giant that he is, Marty had no problem reaching into the muck, grabbing Steve by the armpits, and hoisting his mud-dripping body from what now appeared to be a perfectly cylindrical hole designed for people to fall into.

Then Steve said, "It's shit," and the laughter went to a whole 'nother level. But Steve wasn't laughing. "I'm not high anymore," he said like a science teacher. The adrenaline had burned the lysergic acid diethylamide out of his system, and he was completely sober. As Steve washed all his clothes in a nearby creek, we calmed down enough to put the pieces together:

A golf course needs to have plenty of manure around to maintain perfect lawns, but you can't have a huge mountain of manure sitting there while people play. So, they had these cylindrical containers drilled into the ground. The holes are less of an eyesore and can still hold enough fertilizer for the groundskeepers.

We all walked back to Steve's house with him sopping wet but feces-free.

As Steve tried to explain to his mom what happened, we snuck downstairs to watch TV. He had a shower and came down later with new clothes on and a small joint we quietly and carefully smoked in the laundry room. As a particularly unfunny episode of *Who's the Boss?* droned in the background, Steve's buzz came back and I explained to him how I thought his entire body had gone flying off into the forest, leaving his head working but unattended.

As the laughter started up again, I considered drawing connections to cosmic exchanges and how Marty and I had the same hallucination earlier, but my mind snapped shut against it. Life's too short to risk getting serious.

around the back to another. "You're late so here's the deal," he said, leading me down a long hallway like I was about to go onstage. "She's already agreed to it, so all you have to do is take her to my room and get started. I put a condom on my dresser and you better hurry, because my parents are going to be home soon."

As the word "soon" came out of his mouth, we entered the living room. The whole entourage was there, and I realized we all still had our cherries intact except Jules. The boys were passing around a can of Pam cooking spray. In Canada, milk comes in thick white bags, and we would fill empty ones with what was mostly nitrous oxide from the Pam cans and then slowly inhale from the bag until nobody could talk. We called that state "the Stupids." Which is apropos considering how many kids die from it.

I was nervous as hell but knew this was going to be awesome. Then something occurred to me while standing in the middle of the living room amid everyone's juvenile glares and the smell of airborne canola oil. How the fuck was I going to initiate this? Jules was a slut, but we were all still middle-class suburban kids. "Slut" didn't mean "biker bitch with crabs who will fuck your dog while tongue-kissing him and juggling his balls with her toes." It meant, "Girl who doesn't say *no* quite as often as all the others." I couldn't just walk up to her and say, "Hey, Jules. Wanna *do* it?" I also couldn't grab her hand and walk to Cheese's room like a cult leader choosing tonight's child bride.

So, my dick took over and came up with this idea: There was a thin cane in a bucket by the fireplace. I took it out and tossed it about nonchalantly as I spoke. It was just a secondary prop to a bigger story. "You guys hear Jen has no vagina?" I asked the crowd with testosterone coursing through my veins like a pack of mad greyhounds. "Lawrence, why don't you tell everyone about your mutant girlfriend?" Lawrence got out from beneath the bus I had just thrown him under and tried to punch me, but I blocked it with a swat of the cane. He yelled, *"Hey!"* and fell back on the couch in a Pam stupor holding the red line I'd just planted on his arm. Jules laughed. I cocked an eyebrow up in a "What do we have here?" face. I was going for an Errol Flynn vibe, but my heart was almost pounding its way out of my rib cage. As Lawrence fended off candid questions from the others about his vaginaless girl-friend, I jokingly gave Jules some taunting spanks with the cane. She shrieked and ran off down the hallway toward Cheese's room. Thanks, penis. I'll take it from here.

After we were out of living room range, I abandoned the cane and gave chase. When we got to Cheese's room, everything became Vaseline-lens fuzzy and I was no longer at a buddy's house horsing around. I was on Unicorn Island with the mermaid fairy goddess responsible for rain-bows. The best word to describe it would be "phantasmagoric."

It wasn't Jules's first time, but she knew it was mine and she wanted it to be perfect. She had on a white sundress and looked like Doris Day or some kind of perfect fifties housewife. She pulled her dress over her head and revealed . . . OH MY FUCKING LORD JESUS IN HEAVEN ABOVE. She was wearing a corset and lingerie. That's right: a white silk corset laced up the front with white lace panties and white stockings held up with white garters. She was a Howard Johnson's vanilla milkshake layered in marshmallow and topped with whipped cream. I'll never forget the face she made. Kind of a sad smile, like a dog that peed on the carpet but was still happy you're home. "Is it all right?" she asked sheepishly. It was so all right I couldn't reply and made a spluttering choking sound that was meant to come out as, "You look so fucking beautiful, baby, wow." Jules pulled the bow at the top of her corset and her enormous breasts bobbled out to see what all the fuss was about. They stood there like the Grand Tetons, two majestic, magical mounds made of awesomeness that said, "Let's *do* this." Jules pushed me on the bed as I frantically grabbed for my dancing boner.

Before I could continue to be unable to say anything, she began one of these "blow job" things everybody had been talking about. Only it didn't feel like my dick was being sucked. It felt like it had been removed and replaced with the cosmos. I couldn't make out any par-ticular gestures, just extreme joy. It was like I was floating in space and every molecule of the universe was madly in love with bliss. If I'd seen a multicolored dolphin floating by me, I would have high-fived it.

With all due respect to everyone else who's blown me since, it never felt anything like this. My hands had pins and needles all over them, and the area on my face where a beard would be was tingling as if a billion ants in silk slippers were practicing ballet on it. When I touched this vibrating invisible beard with my pins-and-needles hands, it felt like I was pulling long cobwebs off and stretching them out across the room. I started wondering if she'd spit magic mushrooms into my urethra.

One of the few rational thoughts that entered my head during all this was the terrible realization that I was about to blow my load. This had been an amazing thirteen seconds, but I couldn't lose my virginity to a mouth. I sat up with a jolt and as Jules kept asking, "What's wrong? What's wrong?" I furiously tried to get a rolled-up rubber sheath around something that wasn't prepared to have anything on it but a cunt. Jules got on all fours and I got behind her in a red-cheeked panic like my hair was on fire. For a tenth of a second I paused and thought . . .

"Hey, there it is. The vagina! Live. Man, it really is basically in the asshole."

When I pushed it in, I was surprised at how much doggie style bends your dick down. It doesn't go in and out; it goes up and down. "Hmmm. That's interesting. I wonder if—" SPLOOJ! "Really, me? Three seconds?" Jules wasn't even sure if we had started yet. I took off the condom and held it by the window to make sure something had actually happened. Then, as several million abortions looked back at their deadbeat dad, headlights blinded my eyes. "Cheese's parents are home!" I yelled before taking a third of a second to get dressed. It wasn't a lie. They really were home. Jules tossed her panties and corset under the bed and threw her dress on at the speed of light.

Adults will read this and assume I felt bad about my split-second sexual endurance or that Jules was disappointed in how unsatisfying it was. But that isn't how kids fuck. The first few times the guy is happy if blood doesn't shoot everywhere, and the girl is happy if nothing weird happens, like an ear-splitting queef. Having a condom that actually did its job? Well, now that's basically a perfect lay.

By the time Cheese's parents made it through their labyrinth of a home into the living room, Jules and I were just two other teenagers sitting on the couch.

"Everything all right?" Cheese's father asked suspiciously in his strange Liverpudlian accent. Cheese said yes and I smiled at Jules. "If I find any of you have been into my liquor there will be hell to pay, understand?" We all nodded and kept flipping through magazines in an attempt to convince him teenagers are really geriatrics who enjoy staying in and reading on a Saturday night. Cheese's dad paused and stared a bit before walking out of the room. If he was worried about our ripping him off, he should have checked the cooking spray supply.

As his father was leaving the room, Cheese stood up and began fucking the air in huge comical pumps that made everyone else burst out laughing. Jules giggled and buried her face in the couch and I thought about how awesome it would be if I could stop time right then, put my dick in her mouth, and then stop time again forever. I had seen the light and things were different now.

Unfortunately, Jules got way dirtier. After getting married right out of high school she plopped out four younguns and abandoned them all to pursue a full-time position as a crack addict. I heard she was actually a sex addict who loved crack not because it was crack but because it made sex better. I recently found out she's better now and is slowly putting her life back together. This ruined my ongoing fantasy of going undercover in the crack community to rescue her. That would have been intense.

# The Stupidest Plan in the History
of Police Chases (1986)

In the mideighties, the moral panic du jour was drunk driving. Kids were shanghaied out of class and forced *Clockwork Orange*–style to watch gory videos of dismembered teenagers mangled by cars. Students' moms would hold hands and sing songs about the dangers of being tipsy behind the wheel. They were mostly right, but our gang thought the whole thing was "gay" and decided to take a pro-drunk-driving stance. We started a group called SAS (Students Against Students Against Drunk Driving) and competed to see who could drive the drunkest. If you couldn't find your parents' car the next day, you won.

The police would regularly come to our school to discuss the problem, throwing themselves to the wolves in the process. We would heckle and snicker and make fart sounds throughout, and we proudly took the resulting detentions.

During one Q & A with an officer, we were given an opportunity to address the movie we had just seen about a supermodel who was paralyzed from the neck down after being T-boned by a drunk driver.

"Yeah, I have a question," I said into the mic in front of the entire school. "Why do you consider being in a wheelchair so horrible? My mother is in a chair and has been her whole life and our family certainly doesn't see her as some kind of *tragedy.*" My friends blew this lie by laughing, and the teachers at either end of the stage burned holes in me with their eyes. The cop sighed and explained that there will always be people who want to joke around and not take this seriously, but it is *deathly* serious. Officer McClaren, if you're reading this right now, I apologize.

Two months earlier, I had turned sixteen and gotten my license. I was on a tear. On a cold Friday evening in December 1986, Dogboy called me to say his parents were finally leaving for the weekend. He lived in a huge, real house instead of the cookie-cutter McSuburbs the rest of us lived in. I immediately called our best partiers. Totti was an Italian punk with coarse broom hair and was so good at insults he was constantly making girls cry. His fat nerd friend Anthony always wore clothes that were too small for him so just looking at him was funny. I also made sure some farmers' kids named Szabo and Dick drove Skeeter and Cheese in from the sticks. Shit was about to get crucial.

First, we went to the "Beer Store." In Canada you can only buy beer from government-sanctioned sellers and that's the brand name they chose for each one. We waited in the parking lot until some derelict agreed to buy us some in exchange for a few out of the box. An hour after opening that first Pandora's beer, we were running up and down the stairs of Dogboy's house shotgunning beers and shouting along with the Beastie Boys' "(You Gotta) Fight for Your Right (to Party)." First it was just the two of us, but people started streaming in around nine P.M. By ten, we had a real party worth fighting for.

The problem with parties in high school is that you have such intense blue balls after being denied for so long that when you finally get a chance, it comes rocketing out like explosive diarrhea. We were out of control. There were piggyback fights and wedgie rumbles. We were acting exactly like the jocks we hated, and the girls were huddled by the kitchen in fear. Occasionally one would emerge to say something like, "Stop! He can't breathe," about the guy at the bottom of the dog pile, and we'd yell back, "Who cares?"

Just when we thought the party couldn't get any more fun, a "Hello, boys!" rang from the top of the stairs. It was Anthony, prancing around in Dogboy's mother's bra and panties. Seeing his lily-white fat folds protrude out of her expensive lingerie made us laugh so hard, we all died and came back to life.

"That's it!" I yelled after finally getting some air in my lungs. "We're going for a drive!"

Riding the momentum of Anthony's joke, everyone followed me outside into the freezing Canada cold. I had grabbed a set of keys that had a Chevrolet logo on them and jumped into a blue car that had the same logo on it. It was Dick's car. I was one of the drunkest people in the world.

As I rolled out of the driveway in my stolen vehicle, seven people crammed inside. Skeeter and Totti then climbed onto the hood. The snow was piled ten feet high on either side of the road, but we were laughing like hyenas. Our frontal lobes weren't developed enough to signal important emotions such as fear.

The car was old but in good condition and it puttered out onto the street with vigor. Skeeter and Totti were in clear and present danger as they held desperately on to the hood, and we had front-row seats to view the carnage. It was like we were watching an action movie on a huge flat-screen way before there were flat-screens. Skeeter looked like a rodeo clown in his skinny blond Mohawk and shredded jean jacket; Totti looked even funnier with giant black spikes coming out of his head and a long black trench coat.

When we started on our journey through the snowy 'burbs, the "boys on the hood" were laughing, but their smiles became inversely proportional to how hard I pushed on the gas. If I floored it, they'd look petrified. When I let off the gas, they cheered up again. I enjoyed playing with their facial expressions, but eventually I slammed down the pedal full throttle and gunned it.

"He's not slowing down," I heard Skeeter say to Totti through the windshield. Totti wasn't prepared to give up quite yet and kept crying at me to stop. I couldn't stop laughing, let alone use a brake pedal. Totti finally gave up and turned to Skeeter to say, "We're going to have to jump," which made the entire car cheer. Skeeter and Totti looked into each other's eyes with an expression that said, "We can do this." Skeeter jumped first. As the car swerved violently off of Katimavik Road and onto McGibbon Drive, Skeeter leapt with all his might and instantly disappeared into a snowbank like a gopher into a hole.

Totti was next. As he crouched on the hood and surveyed the safest place to jump, I sped up and everyone in the car yelled things like, "You can do it, Totti!" He's a much bigger guy than Skeeter, so when he finally summoned the courage to jump, he went smashing into the snowbank like a meteor and made a huge explosion of snow shoot up around him. Instead of stopping to make sure our friends were all right, we cheered louder and headed to the Kanata Town Center to do some donuts as our hapless friends disappeared into the background.

The grocery store at the back of this minimall was where many of us worked pushing shopping carts and stacking shelves. It was abandoned at this late hour, which made it the perfect place to crank the wheel to one side and force the car to spin in endless circles that jeopardized everyone's safety. The enormous parking lot's black ice had reduced the friction to about nothing. "Watch this," I yelled as I opened the driver's door, held on to the steering wheel, and leaned my entire body toward the pavement so my head was facing the tire. To this day, I can still clearly see the snowy front left tire spinning at twenty miles an hour mere inches from my face.

Donuts are a great way to make driving a car scary because you're not in control of where the car goes. The wheels are spinning in a direction you're not steering toward, and a huge lamppost is right around the corner. This circular dance with the devil went on for so long I was about to throw up. We had performed a half-dozen 360-degree turns by now, so I pulled myself up, straightened out the car, and went screeching out of the parking lot to rejoin Dogboy's house party.

*BWUP! BWUP!*

"What the fuck was that?" I yelled, praying to God I didn't just hear a police siren.

## The Stupidest Plan in the History of Police Chases (1986)

"COPS!" yelled everyone in the car. Of course it was the cops. What else were they going to be doing, arresting cows? I was shitting my pants but kept driving anyway.

"Quick, is anyone in the car not wasted?" I squawked like a crazy woman. Everyone looked at each other shaking their heads no. "Alan!" I yelled to a guy in the passenger's seat I barely knew. "Get in the driver's seat right now."

"Fuck you!" he replied. I needed another plan.

I clearly was in big trouble and I didn't want to make it worse by speeding or breaking any other laws so I came up with this unbelievably stupid idea: a perfectly legal police chase. I was going to drive at the speed limit, stop at stop signs, and even indicate before I turned, BUT I was going to do my turns at the very last second. That way they wouldn't be able to add any charges, but I'd still get away. This plan would have worked perfectly if the two police officers had been drinking all day and could barely drive. As luck would have it, they were both sober as the judge I was soon to be in front of.

After about one minute of this strange charade, they quietly pulled in front of me and forced me to park. We were now pretty close to the party and as I got out, farmer's-son Dick walked up and yelled, "That guy stole my fucking car!" to the cops. Thanks, Dick. As the cop pulled out the Breathalyzer, I came up with an even stupider plan than the "creeping escape" that had just failed. "I know," I thought while trying to not see two of everything, "I'll act like I'm inhaling while I exhale, and then I'll act like I'm exhaling when I inhale." The officer told me to take a deep breath and blow into the machine. As I surreptitiously blew air out of my nose, I puffed up my chest and pointed at it as if to say, "This guy is getting as much air in those lungs as he possibly can," even though I was doing the opposite. Then I put my lips on the machine and gestured with my arms like I was exhaling while I secretly inhaled. My reading was pretty good—negative 10, which means I was driving at two hundred times less than the legal limit. The cop told me to do it again and after two more pathetic attempts, he shouted, "Don't suck! Blow!"

I blew, and it sucked. I was twice the legal limit and on my way to jail.

The fifteenth stupid idea I had that night was to smile for the mug shot. I spent the rest of the night in jail, and my dad picked me up early the next morning, at which point he was treated to the said photograph. Seeing the black-and-white photo of his son in a studded leather jacket with a flippant smirk made him so fucking mad he didn't say one word to me for an entire year (seriously) and referred to me only in the third person as "that asshole."

During this time, I was expected to go to court and plead guilty to driving under the influence, so I did. What an eye-opener. Criminals are fucking losers. I wore a suit to the proceedings as any sane person would, but I turned out to be the only sane person in the courtroom. Ahead of me was a kid, charged with criminal negligence, who had no problem standing in front of the judge with his headphones on. When he was told this is unacceptable, he pulled them out of his ears and said to the judge, "OK, OK—*fu-u-u-uck*."

Just when I thought that couldn't be topped, a bum giggled his way up to the stand while looking back at his buddy and giving the thumbs-up. He had on a baseball hat with two foam tits on it that said I LOVE TITS in felt.

Both these guys got charged, but when I showed up looking like a model citizen, justice proved it was indeed blind and charged me, too. My license was revoked and I had a criminal record.

The good news is that I was made president of SAS. The better news is that I dismantled the organization immediately. Canadian law is pretty easy on minors, so the day I turned eighteen, the whole thing was flushed down the toilet and erased from the history books—which sort of sucked, because I really wanted that mug shot.

I'd like to say I never drove drunk again, but c'mon. The legal limit in New York is two beers, and if you can't command your vehicle after two beers you shouldn't be commanding a vehicle in the first place.

I can tell you that I never drove THAT drunk again.

# Desperately Saving Foreskin
# (1987)

EARL OF MARCH SEC. SCH.
Kanata, Ont.

87-88

Principal

S

My high school ID from this year is the only ID I own
where I don't have crossed eyes. (1987)

Prohibition taught society that banning alcohol makes drinkers tenacious. My crew, the Monks, fought the ageist laws of the 1980s by pouring a teeny bit from every bottle in our parents' liquor cabinets into a communal jar and calling the concoction "Jungle Juice."

This gasoline-flavored poison would get you so plastered so fast, the night quickly devolved into fistfights, puking, and tears. House parties were rare in Kanata, so we held "Bush Bashes" deep in the forest where cops and parents couldn't find us. The way home was very confusing and many of us got lost for hours. (A few years ago, some kid died making his way home, so Bush Bashes are now forbidden.)

After stumbling across the highway overpass with my friend's girl-friend Sarah, I told her to hang on a second then walked into a pile of bushes for a nap. She thought this was really romantic, so she pulled my flaccid schvanz out of my passed-out pants and started flopping it around. Wanking is a bit of an art form with us uncircumcised types. If you clutch the penis too low, the skin doesn't move up and down enough to feel good, but if you hold it too high, you can tear the frenulum on the downstroke. What the fuck's a frenulum? It's the penile version of that thing under your tongue that stops you from swallowing it. Here, grab the neck of your T-shirt and hold a tiny piece of the front collar between your teeth. That's how a foreskin is attached to a penis. It's a very small tag of skin and when it tears, it feels like someone ripped your tongue out.

I was so drunk and numb I kept saying, "Harder," as she beat me off and I remember something feeling really warm before falling asleep. I woke up alone at dawn in the bush and made my way over to Steve's house, where I broke into his room, stripped down to my underwear, and slept for another three hours.

"Hey, man," Steve said, waking me up at ten A.M., "what's with your underwear?" I looked down and was shocked to see I was getting my period. My tighty-whiteys were now crimson, and when I pulled out the waistband to peer inside, it looked like an old bowl of raspberry cornflakes.

Steve and I barked, "HOLY SHIT!" so loud, his immigrant mom banged on the door and asked if we were OK in Italian. "Sì, Mamma. We're fine," Steve yelled back. I calmed down enough to get into a hot shower with my underwear on. Thirty minutes later, I was able to slowly remove my undies and gently soap off the dried blood. I didn't have the courage to peel back my foreskin and check the damage, but I could tell it was severe.

## Desperately Saving Foreskin (1987)

I wanted whatever was in there to heal, so I didn't even touch my dick for two weeks. This led to overwhelming horniness, so while Steve was over one sunny Saturday afternoon a fortnight after the incident, I suggested we go over to Jules's house and fuck her brains out of her ears.

When we got to Jules's place, she didn't seem very into our plan. I went up to her room first and every time she protested, I'd put my hand on her crotch because she'd forget what she was saying and emit this ecstatic guttural moan. I've never seen another girl where you can shut her up just by touching her area. I call this rare phenomenon "Cunt Button." Five minutes after her first "no," I was fucking her from behind and enjoying the panoramic view of her breathtaking ass. She was wearing ankle socks with lace cuffs, and her big tits were swinging back and forth like bouncy balloons. I was the Chief Swine in Hog Heaven, but then I looked down and saw blood shooting out all over my pubes.

What?

I couldn't stop pumping her, but every time I pushed in, a ringed jet of furiously dark blood sprayed back into my crotch with showerhead force. After trying to ignore it for a few seconds, I pulled my dick out and was horrified to see a bucket's worth of blood on both of us and a puddle in the center of the mattress that was easily three liters. It was as if a shark had eaten her vagina while we were fucking.

I yelped, "WHAT THE SHIT!?" then pulled on my pants and ran the three blocks to my house, where I dashed straight to my room and hid under my bed. That's right, I hid under my bed like a fucking tiny dog during a thunderstorm. As I lay there shaking with fear and confusion, Jules and Steve took her mattress into the basement of her house, where they scrubbed the blood off with a small hose in silence. He said it was one of the weirdest moments of his life. I was confused by menstruation and didn't understand why her vagina did that to me. She was confused by my foreskin and didn't understand why my penis would do that to her. Her confusion was warranted; mine was not, or not for the right reason at least. Sarah had torn a hole in my frenulum, and getting an erection was now like opening a Transylvanian fire hydrant.

I tried to look at it but every time I pulled back my foreskin, I felt an electric shock of pain resonate through my entire body.

A week later, I was sitting with a Muslim urologist who told me I had to be circumcised. "It's like a hole in your jeans," he admonished me. "You can sew it up but it will just rip again." He made an appointment at the hospital for the next month, and I gulped.

I sat in the bath that night and thought very hard about what was going to be done. I was going to have a vastly different penis for the rest of my life, and there was nothing I could do about it.

Then I stomped my foot down like a Birkenstock-wearing feminist in a porn shop and said, "*No!* This is my body and I'll handle who does what to it. My body, my foreskin, myself." The next few weeks involved scalding-hot bath after scalding-hot bath and gently pulling back my submerged penis to allow soap to attend to the wound. Each bath was less painful than the previous one and soon I was ready to almost start masturbating again.

I let the operation date pass and, after a few very careful wanks, was ready to get back on the sex horse. Three months after Sarah's clumsy hands shredded my precious foreskin, my dick was sliding into a fifteen-year-old soccer star named Jen. I made sure the hole was sopping wet first, and it worked. I fucked her for the usual teenage minute and pulled out a blood-free dink at the end.

I had ignored the doctor's orders and successfully taken my foreskin back from the Man. Don't ever let anyone chop the end of your dick off.

# "He's Gone and Got a
# Bloody Tattoo!" (1988)

W hen my dad was growing up, Britain didn't really have a middle class. You were either a dockworker covered in shitty tattoos or an aristocrat who sipped tea and told someone to tell someone to tell someone what the dockworkers should be doing. My grandfather was a bookie who was determined to avoid this fate and changed our name from McGuinness to the much less Irish-sounding McInnes.

My father looks like a turtle with cancer. If he wore his hood up, he'd look like Darth Vader's boss. He's been in so many fights, his nose is flattened and his huge lips make him look like an albino KRS-One covered in gray stubble.

Though he seemed destined for blue-collar nothingness like his brothers, he got scholarships and a degree in physics and became a middle-class immigrant with middle-class kids. "The best thing about Glasgow," he once told me in an affected accent that sounded more like Sean Connery than a kid who grew up with ill-fitting shoes, "is you never get homesick." He has no intention of going back but it's still in him. When some carefree vandals were giggling their way through our backyard in Kanata one night, my dad leapt from his bed, jumped out the window, and kicked the living shit out of them—NUDE. My dad was charged with assault but the vision of his pendulous penis swinging back and forth while his bloody fists wrought endless carnage is an image those poor boys will likely never forget.

For the most part, however, his conversion to gentleman was complete and he projected his class ascendance onto my little brother, Kyle, and me. For one of us to do something trashy like get a tattoo would have erased his lifetime of hard work. To him tattoos were something you get in prison, and I'm pretty sure the only time he saw them was as a very young man when he briefly went to jail for trying to steal a car. (He's so arrogant, he and his friends opened the hood and assumed they could figure out hot-wiring from scratch. After about an hour of scratching their chins and staring at the electrical system, a neighbor called the cops.)

I was eighteen at the time and had recently got my first tattoo, a skull, on my right shoulder. I knew the shit was going to hit the fan if my parents ever saw it. They are both very dramatic and it's almost solely because they drink—a lot. I get why they drink. I have to be drunk to be around them sometimes, and they *are* them. Besides, my dad's roots are Irish, and as Richard Nixon once said, "Virtually every Irish I've known gets mean when he drinks. Particularly the real Irish."

Anyway, it was a brutally hot day in July and my parents were at the pub, so Kyle (who was five at the time) and I were playing soccer with no shirts on. I knew my brother was going to see my new tattoo, but I had a plan. I sat him down and very carefully explained what a secret was. "So, you can't tell anyone that I have a drawing on me. It's going to be there forever," I said, holding his shoulders and staring into his little-kid eyes. "Got it? It's very important that you understand this."

"Yeah, yeah, I got it," he said, and we went back to kicking the ball around. When my parents got back, Kyle and I were in the kitchen making chocolate milk and I had my shirt back on. My dad had just procured a six-pack and was heading toward the fridge when my brother sang out, "I-I-I-I have a se-e-e-ecret!"

My ears got red-hot and I rushed over to grab his arm. "No you don't," I said through my teeth while squeezing a bit too hard.

"Ow!" he said, pulling away and holding his sore arm. "That really hurt!"

At this point I knew I was fucked, so I just sat back and prepared for Parental Armageddon. "What secret?" my dad yelled angrily. My brother looked at me. "*What* secret?" my dad said louder. After sticking to his guns for all of ten seconds, my brother obediently whispered the secret into our dad's ear.

My dad then did one of the scariest and funniest things I've ever seen an adult do. He fell backward onto the floor flailing his arms like he was making a snow angel before bursting into fish-in-the-boat convulsions that looked like a robot dance mixed with a self-induced seizure.

As he jerked around on the floor, his beers left their plastic holder and shot around the kitchen in different directions like tear gas canisters. My mother then began jogging on the spot and pleading, "What is it? What is it? What is it?" Eventually my dad was able to control his spasms enough to eke out the words, "HE'S GONE AND GOT A BLOODY TATTOO!" He kept flapping around on the floor after he said it. He couldn't stop.

When my mom got the news she immediately started bawling and taking off her clothes. Apparently panic induces hot flashes. As I stood there in awe of their reactions, my mother plunged to her knees and stood at my feet like I was the messiah. "Please, son," she said, holding her hands in Scottish prayer and looking up at me, "tell me you regret it, son. Tell me you regret it." She was now wearing nothing but sweatpants and a bra. Women shouldn't pray in sweatpants and a bra.

After a good two minutes of doing the Alligator Death Dance, my father stood up and stared at me red-faced with his veins bulging and his eyes about to pop. I should have been scared, but I had been dealing with their insanity my whole life. "Go ahead," I said, putting up my dukes for the first time in my life, "*hit* me."

My dad would never hit his kids because that's what his dad did, so instead he screamed, "Aaaaaah!" at the top of his lungs and started running around the house. It was one long continuous scream as he ran out of the kitchen, through the living room, into his room, around his bed, back through the living room, back into the kitchen, then out again, step and repeat. He ran this hollering obstacle course at least three times. As this went on, my mother continued to sit at my feet in the prayer position, crying and repeating, "Tell me you regret it, son, TELL ME YOU REGRET IT." I couldn't help rolling my eyes. This was outrageous.

My dad's "Aaaah!" ended with his running back into the kitchen and strangling me—only he'd never do that, so he strangled the air around my neck like I had on an invisible neck brace. He was air-strangling me.

"What are you doing?" I asked as his hands floated around my throat.

"Get out," he hissed like a Scottish snake, "before I do something I regret."

I walked out the back door and the screen door slammed shut on my brother, who was trying to follow me. I turned back and he was standing behind the screen looking very sad and confused. "What did I do?" he asked.

I wanted to say, "Well, I hope you just learned what a secret is, dipshit," but I said, "Don't worry about it, buddy. They're just being crazy."

Since then the only tattoos I got were "What?" on the inside of my lip, "Approach with caution" logos on my legs, a Scottish battle anthem on my left arm with "Ain't No Nice Guy" and "Arm Your Desires" above that, and a sun with a dancing tree frog inside it above that. And on the other arm all I got was a poem about vices, "Aren't Thou Bored," and a gun, and an anarchy sign with the Crass logo, and then just "Destruction Creates" across the top of my back with a skull-head jellyfish eating Chiang Kai-shek and Fidel Castro that goes from my neck to my ass and around the sides of my ribs. I also have the word "Blobs" over my right tit. And my kids' names on my wrists. My brother doesn't have any tattoos.

# Anal Chinook: Revenge of the Punk Nerds (1988)

$B$y the time I was eighteen, punk had gone from a silly uniform for our gang to a religion I was ready to die for. On the weekends we'd take the bus into the city and I'd see the downtown punks walking with their friends and carrying beer to some awesome party I wasn't invited to. They had fluorescent-cone spiked hair, knee-high army boots, and studded leather jackets with leopard-print lapels. When I saw them walking in a pack like that, I was so awestruck, they appeared to be walking in slow motion. Fuck being chased around by security guards. I wanted to be chased by cops in riot gear. There were punk riots in Britain and entire squatted neighborhoods in Europe. My favorite band, Crass, was causing international incidents with their political pranks and even our own downtown scene was putting on Rock Against Racism gigs that British bands like Oi Polloi were flying down to play.

I started singing for a band called Anal Chinook (the latter word meaning "warm wind" in Inuit) run by a charming little hippie named Blake who still collected WWF toys and dressed like a roadie from *Fraggle Rock*. His parents were very laid-back and they let us play in the basement so loud, it once gave his dog a heart attack. We had to change the chorus of "Fuck You" to "God Bless You" but they gave us the freedom to practice whenever we wanted to so when we finally got a show in the city, we were more than ready.

First time onstage, ever. (1988)

On the night of our first show, the other bands we played with were nervous and stared at their frets, petrified of fucking up. The scene was really judgmental and violent back then and I was nervous too but as soon as I got on that stage, all my fear turned into adrenaline. I felt like a pit bull going into a dogfight. Our opening song was about acid rain so I grabbed the mic off its stand, stood on the monitor, and chanted, "It's raining, it's pouring, the old man is . . . DYING!" The song started with a bang and all one hundred punks in the audience exploded into a swirling circle of sweaty moshers. We sustained this level of energy throughout the show as kids jumped off the speakers into the pit and leapt around the stage like Super Mario. The show ended with me covered in my own blood and leaping into the crowd as Blake and the lead guitarist, Orca, played classic rock solos. From that night on, we vowed to make each show crazier than the last. Music historians call this evolution of the genre "Punk Pathetique." Seriously, they do.

We started gigging a lot downtown and were soon able to open up for every big punk band that came to town. We dressed in drag while opening for Millions of Dead Cops and fought the skinheads who tried to wreck the show. We dressed as Kiss and ate cow brains while opening for Dayglo Abortions and they loved it so much, they named a song after us. As far as Kanata punk was concerned, we were bigger than Jesus!

After we graduated high school, Steve and I left the rural suburbs behind and moved into a "punk house" downtown. He was now playing guitar for a Clash soundalike band called the Trapt. The tradition for houses back then was for one guy to dress real neat, get a two-bedroom, and then let another five punks move in when the landlord wasn't looking. We'd usually get evicted within the year and the punk house would just move to the next spot. The third time this happened we got an actual home on Percy Street and called it "Percy Street." It had several floors and a big living room that became party central for every teenage misfit within a hundred miles.

I was finally in the in crowd. Those punks I saw from the bus who were walking in slow motion? They were in my living room now. The guy carrying the beer was James Deziel, the drummer for the Trapt. The chick with the leopard print was a one-eyed beauty we all called Bumba Clut. The drummer for Honest Injun was drinking beer in the kitchen and Aidan Girt, a six-foot-tall, skinny, bald guy with huge glasses who had been in almost every punk band in the city, was living next to Steve's room. He was Anal Chinook's drummer now. I slept on a cot in the boiler room downstairs, which felt like the punkest place on earth. We drank together, stole groceries together, ran from skinheads together, and played music together. I was no longer a suburban kid reading about punk and hardcore in fanzines. I was living it. It was everything I had ever hoped for and it was kind of whatever.

You heard me. Being cool sucks. As Cormac McCarthy said, "There is no such joy in the tavern as upon the road thereto." I missed the road. Back in high school, my friendships were based on who was funny or who was just plain fun. At Percy Street, they were based on hair. You could be the biggest idiot in the world but if your jacket had the same bands painted on it that mine did, well then, I guess we're pals. I appreciated the camaraderie but let's be honest. It's not exactly a formula for a genuine existence.

The skinheads thing also got to be pretty tedious after a while. Everyone talked about them so much, I had to put up a sign that said NO MORE TALKING ABOUT SKINHEADS. We all pretended it was about fighting fascism but at the end of the day it was middle-class white kids (us) fighting working-class white kids (them) and they were way better fighters. The visible minorities and Jews we were supposedly defending didn't give a shit about our war, nor should they have. It wasn't about them. It was a bunch of class. It was just another version of political correctness and all that bullshit we were copying from our parents is about is the upper classes telling the lower classes how to think. "Hey, uneducated plebes," we were saying with our noses in the air, "it's not 'black' anymore. It's 'African-American.' Didn't you get the dictum? Let's fight." Somewhere along the road to the tavern, the hijinks had become pedantic. Besides, fighting hurts.

Aidan the drummer and I usually took the bus back to the suburbs to practice because the rest of the band was still there, but once in a blue moon they'd come visit us at Percy Street. When I'd open the door and see their uncool, suburban faces I'd almost smother them with kisses. Orca, our guitarist, dressed like a gym teacher, and Paul, the bassist, looked like a male feminist in his flowery vest and baggy cords. On this particular night, Blake was wearing a tea cozy on his head and bell-bottoms that said "Blake" on them in Magic Marker.

They had borrowed a car and made it down for a big summer party we were having because a bunch of punks were visiting from Montreal.

## Anal Chinook: Revenge of the Punk Nerds (1988)

After greeting Orca and Blake at the door, I dragged these hometown heroes past the cool kids into the kitchen, where we all started shotgunning beers. Within a mere four shotguns, Orca said, "I think I'm going to puke," and ran to the front of the house, where projectile vomit shot out of his face like a psychedelic dragon. Blake yelled, "Nice word balloon. What's it say?" at Orca's barfing, and that hilarious concept prompted me to stand on a chair and declare a Punk-Off. Without any notice, I ran up the wall and backflipped into the center of the living room, which shattered my kneecap with a large *snap*. Blake, Orca, and Aidan went outside to go streaking but my knee was filling up with blood and was beginning to look like a colossal bruised tumor. I spent the rest of the party incapacitated and slept in a chair that night.

The next day I tried to stand and felt a firecracker of pain shoot up my leg. This is the part of an injury where you start to panic and think about permanent damage. "Did I give myself knee AIDS?" I thought. I made a girl named Elise pick me up and drive me to the hospital, where an X-ray revealed I had shattered my kneecap. This was terrible news as we were booked to open for the Dead Milkmen in a couple of weeks. The doctor fixed me up with a removable cast made of Velcro straps and steel rods encased in canvas and told me there was no way it would be healed in two weeks. I hobbled back home determined to prove her wrong (yes "her," you sexist asshole).

I spent the next fourteen days limping around like a teenage war vet. I was trying not to lose my busboy job and practice for the biggest gig of our lives but I was walking like a hundred-year-old. Our stage shows had gone from wearing funny hats to epic sagas with gigantic props that belonged on Broadway. We did a song about my foreskin tragedy, for example, that included a huge foam penis Blake circumcised with his teeth while chanting, "He sold his cock to punk rock!" The Dead Milkmen show was going to incorporate my broken knee in a groundbreakingly brilliant way and the music had to be tight. The whole city was going to be there. Even my mom.

Two weeks later, I was on a dark stage in a wheelchair and dressed all in black like a death metal paraplegic. Behind me was a gigantic projection of a government movie about child safety we rented from the library for fifteen bucks. After a very quiet and eerie intro song, Blake stepped out of the darkness and summoned Ozzy Osbourne. Ominous guitar music filled the room as white fog did the same. Then a black kid from Blake's basketball team appeared through the smoke and said, "You summoned me?" in a normal voice. He blessed us all with magic devil powers and even healed my leg by removing the cast and commanding me to walk (which fucking killed). As we praised black Ozzy's satanic powers, Dead Milkmen vocalist Rodney Anonymous Mellencamp magically appeared with a pitchfork and killed him. We gasped in horror and were inconsolable until Blake pointed out that the show must go on.

Right before being "healed" by Ozzy. Note leg brace. (1990)

The rest of the set was all about bringing Ozzy back from the grave. We had written a song for the event with a chorus that went, "Oh-double-Zed-Y," again and again and we forced the audience to sing along in an attempt to revive the Sabbath singer. We encouraged people to stop slam-dancing and take a moment of silence to pray for our leader. I even climbed up to the rafters using a rope that took all the skin off my hands and hollered spooky-sounding pleas for him to return. Nothing worked until we all got together to shit in a bucket, which was then thrown into the crowd. That worked.

The shit wasn't shit. It was unwrapped chocolate bars but they were very convincing and got such good air, one of them flew by my mom, who was standing at the back with a girlfriend of mine. I was told later that my mom said, "Charming," after it flew past her head.

Ozzy was back and we reprised the Ozzy song with black Ozzy himself singing the chorus. We dragged this part out so long, Rodney showed up with his pitchfork again and chased us all off the stage. Then the Dead Milkmen went on. What an intro. As Crass did in 1984 after their Miner's Benefit, we packed it in after that show because it was obvious we had achieved perfection and there was no sense commencing our inevitable decline.

After the show, I caught up with my mom and asked her what she thought. She was angry about the poo but I managed to calm her down and explained it was four Oh Henry! bars and a Mars bar. "Oh," she said, finally convinced. "Well, good then, because throwing feces at people is illegal. You know that, right? It's assault." I was going to say, "Well, then monkeys in the zoo should be in jail," but I didn't because I realized monkeys in the zoo are in jail.

# Stomped by Very Stylish Nazis
## (1988)

T he Nazi skinheads in our quaint little government town were like exaggerations of Hollywood bad guys. Their leader, Geoff, regularly made trips down south to meet with militia groups and would come back with a trunk full of guns. He was a Coke-machine-shaped ogre who eventually blew his giant head off with an M16 while on the phone with his baby's mama. Just below him on the bully scale was Wolf, a stocky psychopath who carried a cane with a removable handle that doubled as a rapier, like he was some kind of British assassin from the 1800s. At the bottom of the top brass was the foppishly named Francois, a French-Canadian nationalist whose entire back was tattooed with three gigantic Klansmen riding their horses into battle— a battle that must have been happening somewhere down his ass crack.

We tried to fight these guys, but it was like fairies trying to wrestle Skeletor. Not only were we outmatched, we were outviolenced. It wasn't unusual to be sitting at a house party drinking beer and have a dozen of them swarm through the front door smashing everyone (women included) with baseball bats, only to disappear out the back as quickly as they came. Aidan was particularly damaged by one of these attacks and seemed weird afterward. They would come to our shows and beat us up in the pit, then they'd get onstage and attack the band. We occasionally won, but you sound like an asshole describing a fight you won so I'll leave those out. For the most part the "Boneheads" met little resistance stealing our beer, our girlfriends, and even our boots.

Back in the eighties, Dr. Martens were a coveted combat boot mostly used by British mailmen. They were orthopedic and very cool looking, so whenever skinheads saw a punk wearing them, the punk got "rolled for his Docs." Regular trips to Scotland to visit relatives meant I had special access to this Holy Grail of shoes, but I had to be careful about wearing them in downtown Ottawa.

In December of 1986, I got a call from my ex-girlfriend Christa. Despite being half-squaw, she was one of the girls the skinheads stole. "Wolf knows you have Docs," she whispered over the phone. "Don't wear them to the SNFU show." Then she hung up. I fart when I'm scared, and this warning turned my ass into a shit-powered leaf blower.

I didn't wear my boots to that particular show, but the word was out and it was only a matter of time before the Gestapo confiscated them. About a week later, I was walking downtown with Pukey Stallion, who was dressed head to toe in perfect mod clothing. I had all my best punk gear on, including my coveted ten-hole black Doc Martens. As we joked with each other across Rideau Street and through a beautiful shopping plaza where civil servants spent hundreds of dollars treating themselves, we came to a clearing and found ourselves smack-dab in the middle of about ten skinheads. They saw us before we saw them and had already spread out into a wide circle that blocked the most obvious escape routes. Pukey and I had been close friends since the first day of high school and I knew he would have my back because— Pukey? Pukey? *Hello?* Fucking cocksucker. He didn't go to get cops or friends or anyone. He went home. I now had to take on all these skinheads by myself.

These skins were definitely not locals. They looked like orphans and had weird zits and jeans that didn't fit right. One of them even wore running shoes, which is a choice so unfashionable for a skinhead, it's disturbing. A very tall skin in a tweed cap and cheap combat boots walked deep into my personal space and said, "Lemme try on your boots." Once again my overworked adrenaline glands were forced into action. I knew I had to get the hell out of there but the skinheads knew that too, so the more I scoped out holes in their human fence, the stronger it became. "I don't think that's going to happen," I said, trying to sound like Charles Bronson but coming across like Weird Al. Then he put his foot next to mine and called out to his friends, laughing: "Hey, I think we're the same size!"

A crowd of heartless spectators had assembled and this guy was now so close to me his head could have easily perched on my shoulder like a parakeet. "Take them off," he said in a tone that was borderline seductive. I knew it was time to fight but I was scared shitless. I overheard a young girl in the crowd say, "Holy shit, is that guy ever scared shitless." Out of nowhere, an even bigger skinhead marched up in a rage. "JOHN!" he yelled at my faltering assailant. "What the fuck is the matter with you?" Then he mimed how to beat me up like I was a foam dummy at a women's self-defense class. "You just go BANG," he said while miming a kick to my stomach, "and then BAM," miming a knee to my head.

"All right!" I yelled, breaking up the How to Kick My Ass seminar, "I'll give you the boots." Then I employed a dumb street-fighting trick my dad taught me that I never thought would work.

"At the count of three," I said with authority, "I'll take them off . . . One . . ." Then I swiveled around and shot out of there like a Jesus Lizard on Adderall. As my dad promised, the crowd stood there for exactly two seconds thinking, "Hey, wait a minute. He said he was going to give us the boots at the count of three. He only got to one. That ain't right." Two seconds is a lot of time.

"GET HIM!" John's instructor yelled.

I was a good ten feet ahead of these guys and I tore through the shoppers like Jason Bourne. I looked back to see if they were gaining and was stunned to see the gap was closing fast. I don't know if you've ever been chased by a gang of homeless Nazi skinheads before, but they look really awesome. Time goes very slowly when your brain is releasing its own amphetamines and I could see them jumping over people in slow motion with their perfect cuffs and their straightlaced leather boots. The bomber jackets seemed to be made for running and the neat white shirts with suspenders and short-cropped hair looked so badass, I wanted an oil painting of my imminent demise.

After knocking over an old lady and sending her Christmas presents sprawling all over the street, I made a sharp left and sprinted across the road. In Pac-Man, you gain a lot of traction by making turns, but in real life the ghosts catch up, and I soon realized the chase was over. As I approached the other side of the street, I looked to my left and saw a young bald racist running through the air like a ghost-white LeBron James in springy shoes. His flying scissors kick smashed into my solar plexus and sent me crashing against the curb like a bag of potatoes. Before I could react to that, the others showed up and started kicking me with the kind of relentless hatred you only get from growing up in juvenile detention.

I covered my head and managed to keep most of the beating to my ribs, but after a good twenty seconds (that's about a week in being-kicked time) I started to wonder if this was ever going to stop. It wasn't, so I came up with an idea. I'd scare them into thinking they'd paralyzed me for life. "My back!" I yelled while letting my whole body go limp, "I can't feel my legs!" These guys either didn't know or didn't care if I had a broken back and they kept whaling on my limp body like I was Rodney King. I gave up on playing dead and went back to protecting my head. When they finally decided to call it a day, I was a broken jar of jam dressed in punk clothes, and they dragged my bleeding body over to a park bench to exchange the boots.

As some chick untied my boots and handed them over to John, a huge Native guy walked up and said, "Is everything OK here?" I jumped up, yelled, "Hell no, kemosabe," and we put our backs together while kicking the living shit out of each skinhead using multidimensional space-age karate moves. Oh, wait—that's the fantasy I have every time I relive this story in my head. What really happened was I said, "Everything's fine," so the Indian shrugged and walked away.

I walked home in John's shitty boots and vowed to punch Pukey in the face the next time I saw him (which I did). The next morning I couldn't get out of bed and it was at least two months before I could laugh or cough without grabbing my aching ribs. Shortly after I was able to laugh without pain, Geoff returned from one of his southern sojourns and kicked the crap out of John. Apparently he had shamed the skinhead name by not fighting me one-on-one. A year after that, John threw himself in front of a train. Then Geoff blew his head off. After that, I was told Francois and Wolf went to prison, where they quickly became wiggers. The skinhead movement was dwindling when a punk gang from Toronto called Bunch of Fucking Goofs came through town and beat up every last one. That was the end of skinheads in our neck of the woods.

Everyone involved died or went to jail but that doesn't make me feel better, because I will never forgive myself for not high-fiving that Indian and dying with my boots on. That's the thing about being male: You quickly forget the times you were victorious. It's the times you pussied out that stick in your craw forever.

# Is Everybody on This Planet a Tree Planter? (1991)

I started university in 1988 and worked as a janitor at the school to pay my rent. Canada's system is British so tuition was only about $1,500 a year back then and part-time work was almost enough to live well without going into debt. Unfortunately, cleaning up the school before the students got there meant waking up when it was still dark out. That sucks. Before graduating several years later at a Montreal university where I transferred my credits, I worked on and off as a bike messenger, which made being a janitor feel like being a nude butler for sex-addicted supermodels. Not only did you have to get up at the butt-crack of dawn but you had to ride your bike through mountains of snow and piercing cold winds that made your dick vanish. Seriously. When I'd go pee, I'd look down and see nothing but foreskin and the meat part would slowly peek out as it was warmed by the traveling pee. It's really important to be hungry from your late teens to your early twenties and coming from a middle-class background, I never asked my parents for a dime. This meant doing jobs that were so hard, they make me appreciate the living shit out of everything I have today.

I pumped gas, cleaned pools, washed dishes, painted houses, bar backed, moved furniture, all that stuff, but the hardest job I ever had by a long shot was planting trees in Northern Canada every spring from 1989 to 1994. Despite sounding fresh, sunny, and green, this brutal vocation actually involves driving about twenty hours north of Montreal—oh, sorry, I meant two hours. Wait, no I didn't. I meant twen-ty hou-rs. How is there still land after twenty hours? If you were driving south, you'd be past Miami by then. When a logging company clear-cuts a huge piece of land, they have to pay the government a restocking fee. I'm not sure why the government has to get involved. It's in the logging companies' best interest to replant the trees. It's called "farming."

Anyway, we came in, replanted the whole place, and got the fee (after the government had taken out a healthy cut for themselves). Twenty years later, the whole thing would happen again. Logging sounds harsh, especially clear-cutting, but it's actually the best thing for the forest because it provides an incentive for making sure it remains a healthy place to grow. As the founder of Earth First! says, "If you want to help the trees, buy more lumber."

Northern Canada is a remarkably unforgiving place with a two-month spring that combines numbing cold with blistering heat and more bugs than a spider's wet dreams. The summers last two more months and focus on the blistering-heat part. Then it's back to snow.

To get there you drive and drive and drive until it looks exactly like the spot where the guy from *Into the Wild* died, then you set up a tent and wait for everyone else. Soon a camp forms with outhouses, a kitchen (made from a renovated school bus), and nothing to wash in. The focal point of the camp is the mess hall, a huge green army tent for eating and meeting that has about a dozen tables placed end-to-end in three long rows. The camaraderie is great and a bit of abuse does a body good, but spending May and June at the top of North America makes one thing very clear: Mother Nature does not like man.

A typical workday starts about three hours before you go to bed, as Monty Python would say. You get dropped off on your land when the sun comes up and it's so cold you have to dress like the Michelin Man to stay alive. The trees are frozen and you need to make gloves out of duct tape to be able to retain dexterity without getting frostbite. You're given a few trays of trees that look like tampons with a sprout of evergreen on top. You load these seedlings into three huge bags attached to a belt harness around your waist, and the bags push so hard against your ass cheeks, you can't not get hemorrhoids. By the end of a season you have an asshole that never really recovers. In fact, right this very second I have a wad of toilet paper on my anal lips to prevent leaking. I call it a manpon.

After loading up as fast as you can, you head out onto your land thrusting your heavy shovel into the dirt every six feet, sticking a tree in at the right height, and stamping it down, all in a five-second fluid motion. The mornings are so cold, you can't feel your fingers, but by noon it's so hot, a bolo tie seems like a wool coat. The bugs are so thick, it looks like the air is made of fishnet stockings. If you take a shit they cover your bag and eat it alive. Every time you bite a sandwich, it's 20 percent bugs. They get so intense that many planters forgo bug dope and just cover their bodies in Mazola oil so the bugs drown before they can bite you. I couldn't handle that level of sunburn so I just ducttaped long johns to my body until I was used to the bites.

Being left alone for ten hours a day is a mental enema. You start remembering scenes from grade school and getting songs you forgot you knew stuck in your head. You also talk to yourself quite a bit and anthropomorphize everything around you. If a branch whipped me, I would snap it to shreds in front of the other branches to put the fear of God in them. I'd also leave mosquito corpses all over my face to do the same.

Unlike hell, you eventually become numb to the pain and your body adapts. By the end of the season, you are so immune to the bugs some people even forget to put on bug dope. Your blood becomes so thin, you can actually watch a bite go from an itchy red dot to nothing at all within seconds.

The problem with having super-thin blood is that getting wasted becomes almost impossible. We'd front-load a six-pack and a flask of whiskey on the way into town during our days off, but it provided as much buzz as two shots would give a mortal.

Second-year tree planting, complete with
beard, dreadlocks, and blue balls. (1990)

In a strange way, I enjoyed all this shittiness and would even up the
ante by quitting everything cold turkey the day I got there. No drugs,
no booze, no coffee, and no masturbating. This last one was really hard
to pull off and dwarfed the other challenges tenfold. One sunny day
after three weeks of not beating my meat, I was tanned enough to use
the Mazola trick without getting sunburned. I broke out the oil and put
some on my hand. Now, I'm no fag but I hadn't been with a woman
in a long time and I kind of have pretty beautiful legs. They look like
Beyoncé's if she forgot to shave for a couple of weeks. As I smoothed
the warm oil on my more-muscular-than-usual frame, I realized I was
accidentally seducing myself. I filled the crevices under my taut breasts
and spread oil down my sinewy bronze arms. It was working. I had a
boner. "No," I said to myself with flushed cheeks, then, against my will,
I reached into my underwear (all I was wearing at the time) and began

to rape myself. I was no match for me and within thirty seconds, I was inseminating the cutover, a brief moment of pleasure in a world of hurt.

For all this suffering, most companies offer a whopping fifteen cents a tree. Somehow we were able to turn a two-month season of this into a good ten grand, but when I do the math, I get scared. There's something satanic about a gulag where it's only worth it if you do the same thing 66,666 times.

Though you hear a lot about tree hugging in college, the collegians who actually pull up their bootstraps and get up there are few and far between. The forty or so people who made up your average tree-planting camp were only about 5 percent hippies, and those were usually the four or five females who managed to defy their gender and live like homeless lumberjacks for two months. The rest of the crew were jocks, blue-collar students, French Canadians, Natives, hosers, and weird African exchange students, including one guy named Bumbum Boobah who was very lucky he didn't attend third grade in America. They were a motley crew whom you had trouble picturing in the real world, but none of them was more interplanetary than a professor from one of America's top universities who we called Dr. John.

John was a very tall, bearded scientist with curly hair and clothes from the garbage. Technically he was a professor on sabbatical enjoying the great outdoors, but he was really a mentally ill genius on his way out of society. When we started this particular season he was someone the university faculty was losing and someone who was losing his faculties. He was ten times smarter than any of us but was still kind of the village idiot due to his nonsensical rants. Oh yeah, he had multiple personality disorder.

Where John was on the decline, I seemed to be moving up in the world. It was only my third season of tree planting, but I was already a foreman. I think the quick promotion happened because I was like Roberto Benigni convincing his son they weren't at a Nazi death camp. Morale is king in this evergreen prison and I was happy to come up with stupid games for everyone. The previous year I started the Buddy Lemieux Hate Club. He was a fucking dick who owned the only store within a hundred miles and lorded it over our desperate heads like he was Gargamel and we were Smurfs. At the club we would all gather 'round and discuss what a shithead he was. Some locals from the village even ended up joining. I also hosted a talent night every day off (which was every ten days) and began Expert Night, where, every night after dinner, a different person would lecture everyone else on his or her area of expertise. Wrangling troops this disparate and getting them to move in unison was difficult. If being the clown at the death camp wasn't working, I was also happy to become a Nazi. I knew my boss put down $100K as a bid for the contract, and if we didn't plant the trees right, it was all over. A former rival called Paper Tree once had a motto: "Do your best—fuck the rest." They went bankrupt, nobody got paid, and the owner lost his house. As De La Soul once said, "Stakes is high."

Everything about this job is telling you to go home. Waking up for your first day is like waking up in a coffin. It's four A.M., snow is all over the tent, and leaving the womb of your sleeping bag feels like being born a trimester early. The silver lining is that you sleep fully dressed, including jacket and ski mask, so all you have to do is throw on your freezing-cold boots and head to the mess hall for coffee and eggs. Few people speak at breakfast. Babies born prematurely are like that. They just sit in their Plexiglas boxes waiting for the nurse to make more coffee.

"Good morning, everybody," I said as I walked into the tent. "I've got some great news. The first site is only an hour away and from what the assessors [the government workers who come by to inspect job quality] tell me, it's the most peanut-buttery land of the whole contract. Nice easy start. So let's plant some trees and make some money!" Peanut butter meant you didn't have to kick and scrape ("screef") to get to dirt. When you've been tree-planting for a long time you'll have dreams about planting a whole football field of peanut butter, which is kind of like dreaming the bats you're beaten with don't have nails in them. Everyone harrumphed a curt "yay" and slowly made their way to the bus.

I grabbed my walkie-talkie and joined them. When I got on the bus, I saw Dr. John had boarded early and was using his socks as puppets to play out a conversation with his other personalities. He was folded over in the seat with his face down on his lap and his hands way over his head and they were moving around like black eels doing a Punch & Judy show.

## Is Everybody on This Planet a Tree Planter? (1991)

"Hey, you're John, right?" I asked as the bus started up. He looked up and smiled. He had on a dirty ski jacket, even dirtier pants, a wool hat with holes in it, broken glasses, and bare feet with toenails made of old wood. "Are you all right?" I asked. John sheepishly put his puppets back on his feet and explained it was nothing. As I sat in the seat across from him and offered up some coffee, the bus steered out of camp and along the logging roads to our site.

After a bit of small talk and a lot of green scenery, I gently guided the conversation back to his socks. "So what was going on with the puppets?" I asked.

"It's for a thing I'm working on," he replied stoically, "a classical guitar opera." I asked who it was about, and he said Snuggles the Dog and the Super Man. Everyone knew he had other guests living in his mind, but I was now getting to meet them personally. Apparently, Snuggles is an adorable little guy with a heart of gold who looks like Rowlf the dog from *The Muppet Show*. "He'd never hurt a flea," John told me. He also told me Snuggles has a large poster of Moses in his doghouse.

I asked John why he called Superman "the" Superman, and he corrected me: "Oh, no, no, not the superhero—the Nietzschean 'Übermensch.' The über male. The Super Man wants Snuggles to die but Snuggles doesn't want to die . . . It sounds weird out of context." For the rest of the drive, I tried to conceive of a context wherein that wouldn't be weird. I thought about German fascism and Hebrew Bible scholars, but settled on "possibly a cartoon used to educate psychiatrists about mental disorders."

The first day went surprisingly smoothly. Tree planting is about working as a private contractor for the government, and like all things government, the people you answer to are not honest. For example, your first assessment is always two out of ten no matter what. "You had a lateral branch under the dirt," they'll comment, like trees were made of moth wings and couldn't survive in the wild. I didn't pay attention to most of what they said. All I knew is if we did our best and were nice, they'd give us enough perfects at the end to counteract all these early twos and we'd have a passing quality grade that allowed everyone to get paid.

My day consisted of walking and ATVing over several miles of scarified land and making sure everyone was alive and working. I'd also riff a little bit and occasionally scare the bejesus out of someone by jumping out from behind a bush. They were all an amicable, hardworking bunch. The Africans were always friendly and planted like cyborgs created to plant perfect trees. Jocks were similar. You had to watch the Indians and the hosers because they tended to stash trees and claim them as planted. And I'm sorry, but the girls were hopeless. It's man's—or maybe bulldyke's—work. Sometimes I thought the only reason women were there was to take advantage of the incredibly tilted female-to-male ratio. It wasn't unusual to see a girl with the head of a crow and the body of a tuna-filled garbage bag being followed around by a guy who was so handsome, *I'd* fuck him.

That night, we had spaghetti for dinner and the chef even put bread sticks on the table. Fancy. We consumed the meal like death-row inmates inhaling their last wish and I sauntered happily over to John, who was sitting by himself. "Hey, John, lemme ask you something," I said. "How would you feel about playing some music to the other inmates?" He told me he couldn't because the opera wasn't even close to done. "Fuck the opera," I said before adding, "No offense." I meant to say, "We'd like to hear whatever you got."

Without saying a word, John got up and left the tent. Soon after, his crazy face popped back into the tent holding a beautiful guitar in mint condition. Everyone clapped and slid down the bench to see the show.

After some brief tuning, John gently broke into Neil Young's "Heart of Gold." His fingers were filthy and covered with stray pieces of duct tape, but he played the song like it was his debut at Carnegie Hall. It was the most heart-wrenchingly sincere and perfectly in-key folk guitar I'd ever heard. He was a tramp who sounded like an angel and when we heard him say, "I've been in my mind / It's such a fine line . . . And I'm getting old," there wasn't a dry eye in the house. One of the girls, Jill McAlpine, was full-on bawling her eyes out. The song ends with the chorus, but instead of giving us that final strum, John kept the tempo and pulled us into some of the most evocative Spanish guitar this side of the Atlantic. His fingers were wandering all over the frets and it sounded like someone who had been playing guitar for so long, it was a part of his body.

I started to think about other mad genii: The guy who developed Morse code thought immigrants were out to kill him. Nikola Tesla, the true inventor of electricity, only stayed in a hotel room if its number was divisible by three. Einstein believed in Martians, Pythagoras had a cult, and Andrew Jackson regularly beat the shit out of people with his walking stick. "Wow," I thought, "Dr. John is so good at playing guitar he's making me philosophical about the entire world's sanity. Now, that's some sweet licks."

When he was finally done, he looked up and said, "That's it," with the most sane smile I'd ever seen him give. Everyone stood up, overalls at their sides, rubber boots covered in mud, and clapped their chafed hands like Oprah's studio audience.

John went to bed early that night. Maybe he tasted what it was like to be sane and it made him homesick for his old life. I left the mess hall soon after him and saw his boots sticking out the bottom of his tent. He'd bought a kid's tent to save money, so his enormous frame couldn't hope to fit in it and his two feet stuck out a good foot from the bottom like he was in a *Peanuts* cartoon. "Good night, John," I whispered as I walked by. He said nothing. He was already out.

The next day I got to John's land at around noon. We were spread out over a small city's worth of terrain, so even with an ATV to get me through the easy parts, I'd be lucky to check on a planter more than once a day. When I got to John, he smiled and said, "Hello," like he had never seen me before. He had on a wool hat and a sweater despite the fact that the temperature had risen to molten-lava levels. That's not good. I remembered that one of schizophrenia's primary characteristics is an inability to gauge temperature. "Who are you?" he asked like Data from *Star Trek*.

"I'm Gavin, remember?" I said like a cop trying to talk someone down off the edge. "I work here."

John found all this very intriguing and tilted his head to the side like a curious bird. "Oh, that's great," he said with a huge, dirty smile. "I had been hoping to meet someone soon and try to figure out what's going on here. What do you do?" he asked, now sounding more like C-3PO. I told him I manage tree planters and he asked one of the most disturbing questions I've ever heard: "Is everybody on this planet a tree planter?"

Holy shit. John was so far gone he had rebooted his hard drive and not only did he have no idea who he was, he had no idea what fucking *planet* he was on. Is there a farther gone than that?

I explained to John that an infinitesimally small percentage of the six billion people on our planet were tree planters and left him to his work. His trees were not looking great. Very few of them were the requisite six feet apart and about half the ones I tugged on came out of the ground like they had simply fallen out of his bag. This could be bad for all of us because it would hurt the average. I called the boss on the walkie-talkie and arranged to meet him nearby.

His red GMC truck pulled up a few minutes later and I got in. He was eating insects. The strange thing about blackflies (not really flies but small "buffalo gnats") is they bite the shit out of you in the field, but they won't bite you if they're somewhere they can't get out, like a truck. Though mosquitoes will devour a full-grown man in his tent, blackflies will spend the whole evening bouncing against the ceiling trying to figure out an escape route. This first led to our killing them in droves on tent ceilings for revenge, but then one guy ate one. Delicious. For some reason unbeknownst to science, one out of three blackflies tastes like raspberry bubble gum. The other two taste like potato. (Mosquitoes don't taste like anything.) As I stepped into the truck I began snacking too. The boss's name was Markus Saunders and he was of Nordic descent with a huge blond beard and long blond hair. He was tall with gorilla hands but he also had high cheekbones and that Northern European nose that looks like a chickadee.

"Something's up with John. I think he has to go," I said as I dabbed my forefinger on the windshield and procured two gnats to eat. "He's acting weird."

Markus stopped eating. "I've had too many of those," he said, undoing his top button. "I know John is incredibly weird, but firing people out here is all but impossible," he explained. "I need to make a long list of all their offenses or they drag my ass through worker's comp bullshit and all kinds of other bureaucratic nightmares. But I will have a talk with him and kind of feel him out." I was happy with that and walked off feeling satisfied. I had only eaten a few bugs, but I wasn't that hungry to begin with.

Markus spoke to John and said he seemed perfectly fine. A few days went by and John kept sailing along, so Markus asked him if he'd host that evening's Expert Night. "No problem," John said. After dinner, I went up to John and asked him if he was ready to start because, well, it's after dinner now. He had no idea what I was talking about. I explained. He looked puzzled but stood up.

"Hey, guys," he said.

"Hello, John," everyone said like we were in AA.

John looked around the tent and I could tell he was not prepared and had put zero thought into what his subject was going to be. Then he looked at the table below him and noticed some tiny white dots that were the result of the sun shining through minuscule holes in the top of the tent. "You see that?" he said, pointing to one of the bright dots. "That's the sun." He then looked up and calmly described the fundamentals of what we were seeing. "The holes act as lenses and actually project a full image of the entire flaming star—it's not a planet—onto the table," he said. "What a gift." Then he got closer to the one in front of him and started to describe the sun to us. "Look at it. That's a perfectly complete representation of a ball of fire a hundred times the size of our planet." We were spellbound. "Oh!" he added enthusiastically. "You see those dark dots just off the center? Those are sunspots. They're sort of cold patches caused by really strong magnetic activity. I mean, they're still hot enough to evaporate metal, but because they're so much cooler than the rest of the planet, they appear as dull, dark holes." Then he stood back up and addressed the crowd. "You know, studies have shown people are much happier when they surround themselves with people who are less successful. Those poor sunspots are in hell." Everyone laughed. The reclusive Dr. John had killed again.

Nobody drinks at the camp because you have to be up so fucking early. We save that for the day off. Socializing during the work week consists of the hour between finishing dinner at eight P.M. and going to bed at nine. Expert Night usually cuts that in half, so you've got thirty minutes to mingle, riff, and not flirt with any women because they were already snatched up instantly by guys seventy times better-looking than yourself.

After some hurried leisure, I passed John's silly boots on the way to my tent again and heard his guitar quietly strumming. The nights were getting warmer now and I didn't have to go to bed dressed like an arctic explorer, so I stripped down to my long johns and climbed into my sleeping bag. As I drifted off to sleep I heard, "YOU ARE A BEAR AND YOU EAT IN THE GARBAGE!" hollered at the top of John's lungs.

I leapt up and unzipped my tent. "John?" I asked his tent, which had pulled its boots inside. "You OK?"

Then I heard, "Prepare to die!" Before I could worry about my safety I saw his silhouette, which proved he was definitely still in there. Then came, "No, no, please, I don't want to die," followed by thunderous guitar chords. He was acting out his opera. I might have been safe, but Snuggles was fucked. I went to sleep that night worried about John and even more worried for our safety.

The next day, I avoided checking on John until the very end of the day. I knew his land was pretty peanut-buttery so it would be difficult for him to fuck it up. But when I got there, the mercurial John was nowhere to be seen. He had flagged off surprisingly large portions to show they were finished, which wasn't his style, so I walked in and began investigating. Something wasn't right. I'd see a tree here and then nothing for twenty feet and then tree, tree, tree, tree, tree. They were tight in the soil and the lateral branch was exposed but there appeared to be no rhyme or reason to where he stuck them. We weren't going to get paid unless the entire clear-cut was replaced with a grid of trees exactly six feet by six feet, and this wasn't even close. I marched over a few hills and saw John planting with unprecedented determination. "JOHN!" I yelled as I approached in case he was a Martian again. He could tell I was shocked, so he balanced his water jug on his head to cut the tension.

"Hello," he said, standing upright. His T-shirt was shredded and for some reason, he had covered himself in flagging tape (fluorescent ribbons we used to mark off segments of land). What really concerned me were his fucking eyes. They were swimming in pools of blood. The arms of his Coke-bottle glasses were long gone and had been replaced with strips of flagging tape. He had sort of mummified the top of his head by wrapping the colorful tape around his lenses and back around his head again and again until his glasses were pulled tightly against his eye sockets. He looked like an album cover. It gets worse. This bizarre design left small holes at the edge of each eye where blackflies could get in—and they did. Several dozen blackflies had snuck into the space between the glass and his eyes and they bit with impunity because they knew they could just come out the same way they came in. They bit the skin around his eyes so much, tiny pools of blood had formed at the bottom of the glasses where they were tightest against his skin. This collection of blood moved around when he talked the same way water does in your mask when you've been snorkeling for too long.

Dr. John the morning of the collapse. Note glasses made of flagging tape. (1991)

"Um, John," I asked, "what's going on with your trees?"

He didn't know what I meant. "I'm not done yet," he said, "and you had better let me finish or it's all a waste." I asked him if he was going to go back and fill in the spaces, and he snapped "NO!" at me, which was the first time I'd seen him act aggressive outside of the insufferable carnage Snuggles was forced to endure. "It's a message to God," he said angrily.

"What do you mean?" I asked. "What's a message to God?"

He looked at me like I was an idiot. "Didn't you see? It says 'John.'" I still didn't get it. "The trees!" he yelled with gnats swarming around his eyes and blood splashing onto his eyeballs like a monster in a Japanese cartoon. "They spell J-O-H-N! In twenty years I might be dead, but God will look down upon us and he'll see my name. His name. It's all his." I was kind of starting to grasp what was happening and trying to decide between being angry and petrified. Then he got closer to me and said into my face, "Read John One. It says, 'In the beginning was the Word, and the Word was with God.'"

His breath stank and his face was so filthy there was no real demarcation between his curly hair and his beard. He was a hairy caveman with a plastic rainbow headband and blood goggles. He also had a shovel in his hand. Tree-planting equipment is tough. The shovels weigh about twenty pounds with a steel handle, blade, shoulder, and cutting edge. To be brained with one of these would take a tenth of a second and even if you weren't knocked unconscious, you would definitely bleed to death on the way to the hospital, which was at least seven hours away. As I stared at his death blade in my peripheral vision, I realized this motherfucker had lost it a long time ago and what I was seeing was some mentally ill zombie shit. He was in a blackout of madness.

I have spoken to some guys who have been to prison and they tell me the best way to deal with a psycho is to shrug him off. If you're playing cards with the other inmates and someone comes up to you with a broken pen while shouting, "You want me to stab this in your fucking face!?" you have three choices: You can get tough and threaten him (stabbed); you can whimper and beg for mercy (stabbed); or you can shrug your shoulders like he's asking you if you want another Jujube and casually say, "Nah" (not stabbed).

I looked John right in his unbelievably gory face, shrugged my shoulders, and said, "You're not getting new land until you go back and fill in those spots." Then I turned around and walked away thinking, "Please don't kill me. Please don't kill me." I had no idea if my fake coolness had calmed him down or if I sealed my fate as a blasphemer who must be executed in the name of the Lord. As I pondered this ultimatum, I heard the *fwum, fwum* of the Reaper's scythe hurtling through the air. I whipped around to see the last *fwum* miss me by two inches and the shovel smash against a tree stump, taking off a fist-sized chunk of wood that was meant to be my cerebellum. I had escaped death by a mere two inches. I knew I had to stand my ground, but fear poured over me like that bucket of pig's blood in *Carrie*. "You just fucked up big-time," I said like he was about to get three weeks of detention. "BIG-time!" I stormed off but it wasn't easy to walk because adrenaline had my knees jiggling like a pair of tits.

I avoided the school bus and went back to camp in Markus's truck. I explained exactly what had happened and he told me he'd handle it, like I was complaining that the Porta-Potty was full. His apathy infuriated me. "Dude," I yelled, "*handle* it? Who do you think you are, Harry Houdini? You can't 'handle' this. He doesn't need a talking-to. He doesn't even need to be fired. He needs his family to come here with the men in the white coats and have him taken away. He's GONE." Markus agreed. We stopped at the refers (large eighteen-wheelers full of baby trees) to check when they'd be ready to unload and spent a few hours refueling the ATVs. When we finally got back to camp, we agreed we were going to take John into town and see about medical help. We made our way over to his tent only to see a small rectangle on the ground where it used to be. "He went into town with an assessor," Bumbum said in his weird Nigerian accent. "John said he had to get his medications and was leaving on the five o'clock bus. He'll be back tomorrow." We gave chase but stopped at the nearest phone realizing that's what we'd do when we got to town anyway. After about twenty quarters and several dozen wrong numbers, we reached John's brother, who was surprisingly unimpressed.

"This is how it always goes," his brother told us. "John forgets his pills once and then starts thinking he's better than a pill-needer. Soon enough he's off the deep end again and can't be convinced he needs help." We learned his family had tried to get John into a home many times, and it had only occasionally worked. He told us John would be long gone by now and it would be impossible to find him.

We drove back to camp stupefied and helpless. When something like this happens, you wonder if your input made things worse. I was sad I hadn't handled it better, but I was also kind of relieved I no longer had to work with the shovel-swinging alien astrophysicist who spoke to God and made atheist classical guitar operas about a German nihilist who kills a puppy that has a poster of Moses in his doghouse.

# Hey, Dude, Where's My Nose?
# (1992)

I was twenty-two in 1992 and my look was mostly composed of dirt. I was living in Montreal but went back to Kanata regularly to visit my family. I had also started a new band called Leatherassbuttfuk with a fat guy called Bullshitter Shane.

After an evening of visiting our respective folks, we went for a beer in downtown Ottawa. I had on rubber boots, a few homeless-man dreads that were just clumps of tangled hair, and a jacket with a hole in the back that was bigger than the jacket. Shane wore a soiled baseball hat, an old leather jacket he stole from a dead skinhead (yes, Geoff), and boots with holes in the toes. People called him Bullshitter Shane because he could talk his way into any job or woman's pants, or in this case, band. He was playing "not guitar," which meant he'd furiously shake the strings back and forth to play or just drag the guitar along the stage. Whenever Shane needed money he'd shave his beard and lie his way into a waiter job that paid hundreds of dollars a night. Then he'd spend it all on his friends, get laid, and go back to a life of poverty.

On this particular evening we were with a preppy contrarian named

Jeff who rebelled against our rebellion by shunning our filthy ways just to spite us. While we were in rags, he wore suits and ties and even occasionally tried to pull off an ascot, which isn't really possible. It's like wearing a monocle. He'd recently had his entire mouth wired shut after playing devil's advocate to the wrong guy in the wrong bar and receiving a series of skull-shattering knuckle sandwiches that left him speechless.

Ottawa is on Quebec's border, which is like Salt Lake City playing footsie with Las Vegas. Where our town shut down around midnight, the French province over the bridge had bars that never shut and girls' legs that did the same. You didn't go out drinking in Ottawa without ending the night in the town of Hull half a mile away. I had borrowed my parents' car and on our way into a parking lot to make the trip over the bridge, a stocky jock wearing his school's sweater yelled, "Ottawa trash!" He was standing next to a customized pickup truck filled with other sports enthusiasts in finely marbled shape like a bunch of testosterone-fueled dunce statues. I laughed it off. I don't think Shane even heard it. But Jeff decided it would be prudent to respond. "Ooooh, I'm s-o-o-o scared," Jeff said through his wired jaw, so it sounded more like, "Vvvvh, I'm sch-o-o-o schared." Back at the bar, Jeff had used that same strange accent to tell us how lucky he was to have a jaw at all. He said it took the surgeons thirteen hours to rebuild, and if it suffered any kind of trauma again he would basically have no face. Then again, if he had had no face, he wouldn't have had a mouth, and we wouldn't have been in this situation.

As his blockheaded football friends climbed out of the truck, the buffed-out heckler stormed us. Shane and I put Jeff behind us and prepared for what was sure to be a pretty serious beating. It was.

"YOU CHALLENGING ME!?" the jock yelled up into Shane's face before adding, "YOU CHALLENGING ME!?" Shane exhaled a tired sigh, turned his hat backward, and began to roll up his sleeves. Apparently beating up jocks is tedious work. Before I could blink, the jock extinguished Shane with a cobra-fast punch that sent him crumpling to the ground like a deflated balloon. All the other frat boys were starting to surround us, and I started farting uncontrollably. Shane regained consciousness fairly quickly but was only able to make it up to doggy-style position before his assailant yanked Shane's head back by the hair and started pounding him in the face so fucking hard and fast, it was like watching a pile driver crush a soda can. The punches were unyielding and each one shot blood out of Shane's face and sprayed it across the parking lot. I hurled myself at the guy. It was meant to be a tackle, but the effect was more like a lemur throwing itself on a station wagon. Without even slowing down, the angry pugilist yelled, "Get this fucking guy offa me!" and kept pounding.

Then everything went completely black.

When I woke up I was about six feet away lying on the pavement. Bart Simpson was there, running around me in circles (seriously). I was also literally seeing stars. Blood was everywhere and when I put my hand on my face to touch my nose, it was gone. I was only partly conscious but it was very clear I had been hit with a two-by-four that had lopped off my nose. I remembered reading about farmers who brought their dismembered arms to the hospital and realized I had better find my nose if I didn't want to look like Michael Jackson for the rest of my life. As I slowly drifted back into consciousness, I realized it wasn't a big piece of wood but a big piece of fist that had accomplished this feat. Then I saw two very athletic college students staring at me in horror. One of them yelled, "Holy shit!" and the other yelled, "Let's go!" and they scurried back to the truck. This is how E.T. must have felt. When the guy assigned to disfiguring Shane looked up and saw my face, he dropped what he was doing and they all jumped into their vehicle before peeling out like murderers.

I touched my face again and realized the nose was still there after all. It just wasn't in its original spot. Instead of the bridge part pointing straight down, it was now tucked under my right eye, perpendicular to its original position. I didn't know a nose could immigrate to such a faraway part of your face. I also didn't know I was bleeding to death. I tried plugging my nose with my fingers, but that made the blood gush down my throat like I was chugging an endless beer, so I just let it spray.

I walked over to Shane, who was trying to see where he was despite having a huge pile of baby cunts for a face. He couldn't see and it was anyone's guess which mounds held his eyeballs. "Let's go to Hull," he suggested with a blind, insane smile. This would be a great idea if there was a bar full of nymphomaniac necrophiliacs in Hull, but we were not getting into any establishment that didn't say HOSPITAL on the front and even then, there'd be trouble.

With blood still gushing out of my sideways nose, I got in the car and drove us all to the hospital. Jeff, who started the fight and didn't get hit, said he was in no condition to drive. When we got to the ER, it was obvious the nurses thought we were a bunch of homeless drunks who were out picking fights. I tried to convince her she was only 33.3 percent right but she still made us sit for five hours in the waiting room and another three on a gurney in the hallway. Shane and I were bored to bloody tears so we started using our faces as comedy props. The entire front of my face was caked shut with blood and every time I opened my mouth, it broke a seal that leaked a beer bottle's worth of fluid. "Check this out," I croaked from the gurney. "Raaar!" When I made this monster sound, my Halloween mask of a face spewed blood. Shane had a trick, too. His face was now so turgid with blood, his eyeballs were a good two inches in there, but when he pried open one of the cracks, you saw this bloody eyeball deep in the cave. "Raaaah," he groaned as real bloody tears poured out of the crack. This hilarious game went on until our bedding and clothes were completely drenched and the doctor was ready to finally take a look.

When I got settled into the doctor's office I complained to him that my bones had probably already set, but he informed me that that actually takes weeks, which makes sense. Then he sat me up and climbed on top of the bed like he was about to fuck my mouth. I'm not kidding. He was standing with his crotch right next to me. "Hello?" I asked. Then he put one hand on my head and another on my nose and with all his body weight and strength went, "Rrrngh!" which brought the cartilage from under my eye back over to its old spot in the middle of my face. It took everything he had and the sound was so disgusting, I dry-heaved. I had just heard an ear-splitting squelch from INSIDE my head and as he stood there enjoying the fruits of his hard labor, the dry heave became a puke. "That's normal," he said, fetching me a pan. "It's a very nauseating experience. Just lie here for a while. You'll be all right."

When he came back fifteen minutes later, he told me I'd have to have plastic surgery. "If you don't," he warned me, "you'll always have this weird C-shape to your nose." I told him plastic surgery is for women, and today I have this weird C-shape to my nose.

# Unlaid in Taiwan (1992)

W hen the previous generation graduated with a BA in English they'd accept some job like head of the National Poetry Commission or maybe they'd "sell out" and take a job checking the copy on corporate brochures for twice the average person's salary. When I showed the Quebec job market my English BA in 1992 they told me to *va chier*, which is French for "fuck off" but translates literally as "go shit" because frogs suck at swearing.

My generation had some valid complaints about our lack of options—"No future," as the Sex Pistols called it—but it often felt like I was the only one of my friends who tried. We were the Slacker Generation and after one no, most threw in the towel.

I wasn't satisfied with hitting the bong and watching TV all day. I wanted adventure. So, Steve and I scraped together just enough money for return tickets to Europe, where we hitchhiked around the continent staying at punk squats and earning our keep by doing random chores. Punks considered each other family members back then and none of them hesitated giving us the shredded T-shirt off their back. We stayed in a squatted neighborhood in East Berlin at a place called Meinza Squat where punks had held back police in a three-day siege the punks eventually won. We hitched a ride with a band and ended up in an Italian squat called Forte Prenestino, which used to be soldiers' barracks and was sunk into a hill. They got their power from exercise bikes in the basement people took turns using, including guests like us. In Germany we went to a riot where punks were shooting skinheads with fireworks and police were forced to escort the skinheads to safety. It was a fucking blast and it was all free but meeting all these creative people making stuff made me realize I was now ready to start my own thing. At the risk of sounding like an ingrate, I was also getting tired of punk. The whole movement was about never stagnating but after a decade of religious devotion, it was starting to feel more like a cult. It was time to move on and start something new.

After six months of squatting and one serious case of body lice, we were back in Montreal and flat broke. Steve returned to his job as a bike messenger where we both used to work, but I wanted to do better than check-to-check. I wanted a nest egg to start something big, like maybe my own comic book or a band that would change the world. I met a girl who had just returned from Taiwan, where she'd made a ton of money teaching English. "Trust me," she said. "EVERYONE there wants to learn English." I told her I had no idea how to teach and she said, "Doesn't matter. All you have to do is speak English. There are plenty of schools that will pay for your ticket if you commit to a certain number of hours a week."

A week later, I was on my way to Taipei thanks to the generosity of a private school for young girls, and I only had to teach there one day a week.

Being white in Taiwan is like being famous. Actually, they get mad if you say "white" because that's politically incorrect. The term is "Western." Everyone waves and tries to talk to you and if you have a problem, it's their problem. There's no crime so if you see a bike you like, pick it up and ride away. If you get stopped by a cop, start yelling and he will be so embarrassed by his poor English, he'll let you go. The place is a bully's paradise. I quickly got in on a communal apartment with a bunch of Australians who were sharing bunk beds to offset the rent. We'd teach English in the day and drink beers at "Western bars" in the evening.

None of the Australian guys wanted to teach kids. I don't know why. I taught some businesswomen and their feet reeked. Also, adults belch in your face in China. So, I scooped up all the kid jobs and soon my occupation was teaching English to fourth graders all over the city. A translator had to be with me at all times because I don't speak Chinese but nor does anyone else in the world. The language is so inexplicably complicated that the Chinese TV shows have subtitles so people who are sixty can still practice all the bizarre little idiosyncrasies. I know maybe three phrases in Mandarin and I break a sweat every time I try to say them correctly.

My only responsibility was to be cool. The school administration didn't expect the kids to learn anything at such a young age. They just wanted them to think happy thoughts whenever anyone said "English" later on. I let them pull on my mustache and I showed them what earwax is (theirs is powdery like American Indians'). We'd also draw each other a lot. They always drew me with big hairs sticking out all over my body. They weren't used to body hair. I drew racist caricatures of them that made them laugh.

The classes at the private girls' school were particularly easy. I decided my only goal there was to teach them the theme song to the *Transformers* cartoon. Unfortunately, these kids were so scared of sticking out, they didn't really try, and that made for some frustrating sing-alongs. No matter how often I told them the correct pronunciation, they'd all mush the words together into a robotic, "Dee Transforma. Mo dan mee da ah." They knew how to say, "More than meets the eye"; they just didn't want to show off.

This trait is one of the thousands of strange quirks the Chinese have but I am most annoyed by their crippling fear of dust. It's a country of 1.3 billion dustophobes. They don't wear those face masks because of germs. It's dirt particles. Hey, Taiwan, there's no such thing as a dusty tongue. You, too, mainland China.

During every break, the girls would put their chairs on their desks and start washing both with a bucket of soapy water. They'd mop the floors and Windex the windows. They were like Stepford daughters. The girl who was assigned the hideous task of cleaning my dusty chalkboard erasers wore protective glasses, gloves that went up past her elbows, and a special mask with a breathing filter on it. She then went outside and banged them together like she was holding two nuclear weapons.

I took the brushes off her when she got back and got some dust on my pants. God forbid. When the class started again the kids were pointing at me and making these guttural sounds like they were watching a beheading. I asked the translator what was going on and she pointed to my pants. "Oh, this," I said, pointing to the white handprint on my leg. "You mean THIS?" I asked, hitting two erasers together so a white cloud appeared in front of me. The girls were caterwauling now and I decided it was time for the entire nation to get over this stupid phobia once and for all. "La la la," I said, rubbing chalk all over my clothes and face like Pee-wee Herman in a trance, "I love dust. It's the best. I'm getting it all over me because dust is the best. La la la. Dust-dust-dust . . ." By the time I finished my ceremonial dust dance, I looked like a hardworking baker, and when I faced the class I saw terrified kids standing on their chairs completely spasmodic. It was like I had eviscerated myself and was about to throw my entrails in their hair. I was getting even angrier, which is the opposite of what I was being paid to do. At the peak of this earsplitting mania, I bit into a piece of chalk, yelled, "IT'S JUST CHALK!" and chewed it really loud with my mouth open. The girls shrieked so hysterically the principal stormed in and dismissed the class. That's when I realized I had totally lost my temper.

They don't like confrontation in China so the principal shook my hand with a huge smile, saying, "Thank you very much." He patted me on the back and told me I was a very good teacher. That's how they say "You're fired" in China.

Outside of the chalk incident, I did pretty well over there. One problem that was starting to hurt my feelings was how totally repulsive I was to Chinese women. Facial hair was unheard-of and the fact that I combined it with dirty sweatshirts and old sneakers made the idea of sleeping with me tantamount to rubbing shit on your cunt. There were some upsides. All the clean-shaven handsome dudes were busy fucking rice balls, so I had my pick of the white-girl litter. I found an Australian who thought my dick was "gorgeous" and I boned a Jewish girl whose whole body broke out into goose pimples every time she climaxed. I still rub one out occasionally to those two.

After four months it was time to head back. Unfortunately, I was going to leave without having banged the epicanthic folds off a local, and that's one souvenir short of a complete trip.

A few nights before I left, a stunning Chinese (Taiwan is technically still Chinese; the word "Taiwanese" is usually reserved for the natives) woman who had given herself the English name Uma asked me if I wanted to go see a metal band at a bar called Man Dog Ant. She looked kind of punky and I knew her through my roommate Alan, who was also her teacher. He was a boyish-looking British guy who wasn't interested in her for some (possibly gay) reason. When we got to the club, she introduced me to the band and after an Engrish introduction they got onstage and started doing a parody of heavy metal. The guitar solos were over-the-top hilarious and the way they were pretending to be scary was so funny I spent half the time with my head on my knees dying laughing. It was comic genius until the very end, when I realized they weren't kidding.

I realize now that she was furious and humiliated, but because she was also Asian, she didn't end the date there. To them losing face is like going into debt, so before she could kick me to the curb, she needed to redeem herself. I thought things were going swimmingly. She borrowed a motorbike from one of the guys and asked me if I could ride. I lied and said yes.

Uma helping get the bike started. I kept stalling
it. (1992)

Changing gears was clunky at first and we almost died on the highway a few times but I eventually got the hang of it and we followed
a mountain road that wound up and up and ended at a beautiful restaurant overlooking a nearby bay and most of Taipei. We sat down on
an outdoor patio and she ordered some vegetarian food. Real Chinese
food is dogs and worms and all the horrible shit that feels xenophobic
to simply list, but with vegetables there's a ceiling of disgustingness
you can't go past. I was a vegetarian at the time, thank God. As the sun
set behind the mountains, I could see strings of lights on fishing boats
bobbing up and down in the bay. Taipei is a dirty city down below, but
the rolling hills of forests and rock that surround it are magnificent.

She had regained face and was talking and laughing and saying
things like, "I hate when I eat at a place in Taipei and a stray dog shows
up. I lose my appetite."

"Yeah," I said back, "especially when you're already eating a dog!"

This was a make-or-break joke that could have ruined the night, but
she chortled. "Well," she said, "I wasn't eating dog the last time I saw a
stray, but I did have some dog the other day."

Just when I thought this date couldn't get more perfect, the sky filled with fucking BATS! They came out of nowhere and were furiously eating insects and darting all over the place just a few feet from our table. "They'll be gone really soon," she said, smiling. The wall of flying mammals vanished minutes later.

When we got back to my communal shithole, I apologized for the mess. She was going to have to climb up into my bunk and we couldn't horse around because it would shake Alan in the bunk below. Neither of us cared, however. Just holding each other was enough. She went to the bathroom and I looked at Alan and gave him the thumbs-up. He returned the gesture.

"Hi, Alan," Uma said after she returned.

"How are you?" Alan asked in his gross English accent with his pale white skin and his wet fish lips. Uma sat down on his bed and they had a quiet chat I had trouble hearing, which was weird because I was right above them.

Some time passed and I heard her getting under the covers—*his* covers. WHAT? I lay on my back and stared at the ceiling with my eyes open so wide, they almost slipped out of their sockets. "HOW IS THIS HAPPENING?" I scream-thought. I was beyond confused. Was he a hypnotist? Was this her revenge for my laughing at that shitty band? Was I just a Trojan horse to get to Alan the loser? Then I felt the bunk start to move. It became impossible to ignore I was being jostled around in my own bed by their humping. "Unbelievable," I said aloud while climbing down the ladder. I slept on the couch in the living room and went back to Canada that Monday because that's when my ticket was for.

Uma and Alan got a place together just before I left. I considered kicking his ass but if I started punishing men for being more attractive than me I'd have no fists left.

I came back with three thousand bucks in my pocket, which is a lot less than I'd hoped for but a lot more than anyone I knew had. I was ready to start my own business and chose drug pusher because it sounded the easiest. Pot wasn't cheap back then so I only got three ounces for $1,000 but the customers started to pour in and soon I had enough to buy a lot more. It was by far the easiest job I've ever had in my life.

# The Time I Gave Myself an STD
# (1993)

Times were good in Montreal then. I had money in the bank and nowhere to spend it. In an apartment with three art-school girls my rent was only $100 a month and the beer at Le Biftek across the street was only $5 a pitcher. There was nothing to do but fuck lazy sluts so I carpet-bombed the city with my dick. By the end of the attack, every pussy in the city looked like Dresden and I had every STD known to man.

If you're "sexually active," as they say at the clinic, you are going to get diseases. You can wear a condom if you want, but venereal warts and herpes will still wriggle their way around the rubber and you're shitfaced anyway, so who cares? Fuck safe sex. I'm not going to get a girl pregnant because I know how my genitals work. I will never understand guys who cum inside of women and are surprised to see it took. Were you not paying attention in grade school when they brought this up?

Some even dumber people believe the myth of heterosexual AIDS but anyone with any kind of real sexual experience knows you're only risking warts, herpes, gonorrhea, chlamydia, and maybe crabs. They all sound a lot worse than they are. I've had every one but crabs and none of them were more than a minor inconvenience. And this was back then. Today it's almost fun to get an STD.

Venereal warts used to need a blast of liquid nitrogen (which burns like an icicle knife but only for a tenth of a second) but now you can take pills beforehand to make yourself immune. They say herpes is permanent but I had one outbreak, then another two months later, then another two years later, then—I don't know. That was almost ten years ago now. It seems to be done. I think your immune system eventually just figures it out. When I first got chlamydia at the age of eighteen you had to take one gigantic pill a day for five days. Today the doctor gives you five little pills right there at his desk and that's it. You're cured. (Here's a trick: To avoid that hideously painful swab where they put a wooden Q-tip down your dick, lie and say you definitely gave it to a virgin, which means you definitely have it. The pills are harmless, so if you don't have it, you don't do yourself any harm.) Same with gonorrhea. Take the pills and all you have to do is not fuck for twenty-four hours. Also, don't let a chick blow you. Simple, right?

The first time I got gonorrhea, I almost had a heart attack. Seeing your dick in trouble always gives a guy a soul-shaking scare. I had a strange burn in my urethra that begged me to sort of milk it out, which I did. As my thumb and forefinger traveled from the base of my gigantic shaft to my glistening, magenta, male-model-like head, a large, thick droplet of fluorescent yellow pus appeared out the top. SHIT!

I ran to the local clinic and waited the thirty minutes it took to get an unscheduled appointment (the upside of free health care). I got the pills and was told very clearly not to have any kind of intercourse for twenty-four hours—"not even da blow job," the doctor said in his French-Canadian accent. As a young man living amongst *les filles de roi*, this sounded like an eternity.

I didn't go out that night and by midnight, I was ready for a good old-fashioned wank. Roommates be damned. About twenty seconds after making love out of nothing at all, I was done. I soon realized I was sitting on a couch miles from any paper towels or even discarded socks.

## The Time I Gave Myself an STD (1993)

I contemplated using the handful of cum as hair gel, but I had a shaved head at the time so it would have been more like a yarmulke made of Elmer's Glue. Getting up with my pants down was a possibility, but if the girls caught me shuffling around the house with a handful of cum I would never hear the end of it. That left one option: eating it. I did that occasionally as a young man. I think it started as a feminist thing. I make women eat it, so I oughtta be able to eat it myself. So down goes the watery oyster and I continue watching *Murder, She Wrote* because it's on the only channel you get on a TV you found.

The next morning I wake up excited to be back in the singles scene. Only there's one problem. My throat hurts. Like, it really hurts. Each swallow burns like I'm eating fire ants. I called the doctor and left a message saying "we" had an emergency on our hands. When he called back, I asked if it was possible the infection could have crawled up the back of my dick and into my body, infecting everything all the way up to the throat. He said that's impossible and the only way to get gonorrhea of the throat is to ingest semen. I hung up the phone. Oh my Lord. I had given MYSELF gonorrhea of the throat.

Who the fuck am I to make fun of guys who get girls pregnant? I have a third of their IQ. I will literally bet you $100 I am the only person on Earth who ever gave himself an STD. This shame was magnified tenfold when I walked back into the clinic and saw the same doctor who had just treated me the day before. His face looked like someone took a shit in it. This guy went to medical school for twelve years and stayed up all night memorizing Latin terms and now his job is treating people who literally go fuck themselves.

# Shitstorm (1994)

Selling pot was fruitful but every time I saw a cop car near my house I'd start farting so bad, it made me feel sorry for my underwear, so I gave it up. I also stopped living with the art chicks because one of them lost her mind on herbal E and the others became annoying lesbians who were always boring me to death with angry rants about the patriarchy. Montreal is like France when it comes to comics and though it sounds geeky everywhere else, it's kind of an artsy-fartsy thing there. I had begun hanging out with French cartoonists and self-publishing an autobiographical mini-comic called *Pervert,* which made a tiny bit of scratch but not much. I've always said whatever you do should be at least a little profitable, otherwise you're basically paying people to read your poetry. Shit was selling, but it was far from selling out, maybe a little too far. but it wasn't exactly paying the bills. I was living in a tiny apartment off a hipster area called Le Plateau and hungry for more. My bed took up about a third of the room, so I built a loft six feet off the ground and fit my drawing board and a small bookshelf in the space beneath it.

Shooting a giant teddy bear on said
bed while friends visit. (1994)

The only problem was that the space above the bed was now only about three feet. If I was fucking a girl, there was no way she could ride me without wearing a helmet, and doggie style was replaced with "froggy style," where I'd lie facedown on her back and wiggle up and down like a horny toad.

Another unfortunate side effect of this extremely tall bed was being able to hear the old man upstairs in stereophonic clarity. "Hello?" I'd hear through the ceiling like he was sitting on my chest. "Oh, I'm fine," he'd add in his geriatric voice. I wasn't convinced. "No, I don't have the heat on. I can't afford it. You know that." I concluded that he was talking to his estranged daughter. Then I heard, "I sleep with my god-damned jacket on!" and the bang of an old-fashioned phone slamming down on the receiver.

I'd seen this old man in the building a few times. He was English (not "British" but "Anglophone"), wore a long green army coat that almost touched the ground, and had some sad-looking medals surrounding a plastic poppy. He also had a green beret and cheap boots and was obviously a World War II vet with nothing left but apocalyptic memories of a war that left seventy-two million people dead. That's twelve million more than the second-biggest war ever, the Mongol conquests.

I had just started a new magazine with a sullen ex-junkie named Suroosh Alvi, and we'll get to that shortly. I had no money but was living a pretty good life. I'd work at the magazine in the day and then work on my comic at night. I was still getting pretty laid too, though I tried to avoid cramming girls into my bed space because it was like squeezing two people into a midget's coffin. I also didn't like the idea of an old man in winter clothes beating his soft gray hard-on to the rhythm of my pumps. So I'd usually fuck girls on a chair by the fridge and shush them if the whimpering got too loud.

It was winter in Montreal, which is like saying it was hot in hell. "Montreal" comes from "Mount Royal," as in "Royal Mountain," as in the snow reaches thirteen feet high after the roads are plowed. If you can make it through the ubiquitous fortresses of packed white powder, the freezing wind gets so severe, it seals your nostrils shut. Being old in those conditions must feel like being an anorexic in a mosh pit. I have no idea how the old man survived as long as he did.

"Hello?" I heard on a chilly February night as I lay in my bed reading a graphic novel by a guy named Henriette Valium. "Yes, ahem, well, I was in the theater today . . . ," he added, beginning a long explanation. He was obviously calling a stranger who had no idea why he was calling. "No . . . I know you sell the tickets. That's why I'm calling." More pauses and stuttering. "Hello?" he said, undaunted. "Yes, no . . . I know. I realize that. I was there today at the three o'clock?" He seemed to be talking to the right person. "Exactly, yes. I had the dark green coat on. Older gentleman." I exhaled a sigh of relief. Now we could get down to business. "At any rate. All I wanted to say is that I think you're very attractive and well, that's it. I don't expect anything to come of it. I just have to get that off my chest. That's the kind of person I am. I say what I feel and I get on with it."

"What the hell is he doing?" I thought. "Of course she's attractive. She's probably nineteen and they stuck her in the window because it's good for business. Dude, the war ended half a century ago. You must be at least eighty."

"Well, I'm sorry if I made you uncomfortable," he said. "That was not what I wanted to do."

He seemed frantic, but how did he expect it to go? Was she going to say, "Ooh, Gramps! Eighty-year-old veterans make me wet. Come by my place and put your weird, old face all over my body"?

"Look," he said, trying to stem the tension. "I just wanted to say, you're a very attractive young man. You have a very beautiful face and I'm sorry if I made you uncomfortable . . . No. Yes. And for that I'm sorry. Good day and again, I apologize."

My face now resembled an owl that just snorted an eight ball of cocaine.

Did I just hear "young *man*"? They had homosexuality back then? There were homos in World War II? I thought the Village People invented fags and then they all died in the eighties.

I sat up and hit my head on the ceiling. I needed a drink. I slid off the bed, landed on the floor, and walked over to the fridge. "What is it with gays?" I thought. "Don't they have mirrors? He's a little kid and you're at death's door. Ever heard of 'one's league'?"

I didn't hear from my neighbor for about a week after that. I think he was sick because I'd hear coughing from the bed and when the phone rang he wouldn't answer it. There were endless trips to the bathroom with lots of hopeless cursing. He was obviously alone in the world. Who was going to check in on him if he died? Did this fall under my jurisdiction?

Then I heard some creaking of the floorboards and a very angry "GODDAMNIT!" It sounded like he had spilled something and I could hear him waddling over to the sink to prepare a washcloth. Then I heard creaking so near the wall it sounded like that was what he was washing. Who spills stuff on the walls after the age of one? For the next three days I heard a lot more swearing and a lot more scrubbing. Why was he skating around the room on Brillo pads and cursing like a sailor? Had senility eaten his brain alive?

Then came the worst phone call since Hitler said, "Sure, go ahead, invade Poland. You think I give a shit?"

"English! Hello? Is this Emergency?" He seemed calm but had obviously dialed 911 because you have to choose your language first in Quebec when you call those guys. I silently crawled up to my bed and put my ear to the ceiling. "Yes, well, I'm not sure who to call but I'm at the end of my rope," he said. "I give up. I'm throwing in the towel." There was a pause. He gave them his name and address. Another pause. "I simply cannot hold it any longer. I don't know what you do. You come over here and put a cork in it? You put me in a hospital? I don't know. I can't deal with it anymore. It's out of my control."

I thought he'd never beat the ticket-booth call. I was wrong. It kept going. "Up until last week I could hold it in. It wasn't easy but I could do it. Then these past three days it's just been getting worse and worse. It's all over the walls and the floor. I cannot hold it in no matter what I do. The bathroom is just, well . . . it's a mess." Despite the fact that my bed was six feet off the ground, my jaw hit the floor with a plonk. "My EXCREMENT!" he yelled angrily before hanging up the phone.

I was in shock. He had an exploding rectum? Is that what happens to gays when they get old—their fucking *assholes* give out? A million questions were racing through my head. Why the fuck didn't he just wear a diaper? I thought he wore his winter clothes in the house. Now he was dressed like Piglet and spraying feces around the room like a dying gay wood chipper who hates his landlord? "That's it," I decided. "I am never letting anyone fuck me in the ass."

Three minutes later my buzzer rang. I pushed the talk button. "Hello?"

*"Salut là, avez-vous appellé une ambulance?"* I buzzed them in and they banged on my door. When I opened it, I saw four adrenaline-pumped guys my age panting and wondering why I looked so healthy. Two were holding huge oxygen tanks with masks swinging off them on rubber straps, and the other two had a stretcher. "Upstairs!" I yelled, pointing straight up. They nodded and ran upstairs, but I saw one of them pause for a split second wondering how the hell I knew the problem was upstairs. Was I the murderer? He made a mental note to both remember my face and avoid me on the way back down.

I stood in the hallway waiting and ten minutes later, I saw the old man with the broken asshole get slowly lowered down the stairs. He had an oxygen mask on his face and was strapped in the stretcher with a blanket on him. I watched them stagger across the lobby, through the front doors, and out into the merciless cold. I never saw him again.

A few weeks later, I could hear sawing and banging and drilling upstairs. When the landlord came by to collect the rent, I invited him in for a coffee. "How you doing?" I asked cautiously.

"Oh, man," he said in his half-immigrant/half-Quebecois accent, "I been workin' upstairs on dat apartment, la. 'Ard work. It smell so bad we 'ad to replace da drywall and everyting." I asked him what happened and the landlord seemed reluctant to soil my virgin ears with the unimaginable.

"Did his ass explode?" I asked, breaking the ice.

The landlord was taken aback. "Ow did you know 'bout dat?" he asked.

"Because I fucking heard it, dude," I told him. "Every word."

land but I'm not sure. They were very secretive. Looking back, I think they had received money to start an English version of their paper and had chosen Suroosh to head the operation. Possibly because Allah told them to. It was meant to cover multiculturalism in Montreal. Suroosh named it *Voice of Montreal*, ignored his instructions, and made it into a music zine so he could write about bands he liked.

As he was putting together the first issue, a slacker friend named Rufus told me I should meet up with Suroosh and do cartoons for him. I was on the tenth issue of my comic *Pervert* at the time and had won some irrelevant awards. The comic was evolving from simple graphic novel to more written content, including CD reviews and a long letters page where I'd make fun of other people's shitty art. I was DJing at Le Biftek with my buddy Derrick Beckles, AKA Pinky Carnage, whom I used to deal pot with. He had also quit due to massive farting. Pinky was a lanky grunge Negro who looked like Buckwheat if Buckwheat played for the NBA, shopped at the army surplus, and was in a band. Pinky was a tree planter too and we had just returned from a brutal season up north. I bought myself an enormous Suzuki GS850 motorbike with some of the money and was looking forward to another carpet-bombing. I walked into the *Interculturelles* office wearing a pompadour, leather jacket, creepers, and my motorcycle helmet. Suroosh thought I was rich and very tough, though I was neither. After showing him some cartoons, we talked about writing. He was basically the only employee and was meant to write the entire first issue and sell all the ads. I told him I was only tangentially interested in journalism and then went on a tirade about how people should write the way they talk and just say whatever came to their minds instead of being so careful about everything. He offered me the job as editor and I said, "No thanks."

A few days later, I was smoking a joint on my roof and talking about the future with Dogboy, who had recently moved to Montreal to focus on partying. He seemed happy living life in cruise control, which pissed me off. "Don't you want to really sink your teeth into something?" I asked. After I heard myself ask that I remembered the frustration of coming back from Europe to nothing. That's what I went to Taiwan for, to get a nest egg. Selling pot was supposed to make the nest egg big enough to get something going but all I was doing was this stupid comic book.

"The only thing I want to sink my teeth into is a fucking smoked-meat sandwich at Schwartz's," he replied. "You in?"

"No," I said, looking out over a city devoted to not working hard. Then it hit me like a skinhead bat to the forehead: I'd just had the future handed to me on a silver platter and said, "No thanks."

The next morning I jumped on my motorbike and almost crashed it into the *Interculturelles* building. I ran upstairs and begged Suroosh for the job I'd turned down. He seemed surprised and then explained it wasn't possible. "I asked about it after you left and learned this whole company is entangled in all kinds of government bureaucracy," he said. "I can only hire people on welfare because the pay is in welfare."

"No problem," I said, shaking his hand excitedly. "I'll be right back."

I'd been boning French chicks for a while now and was always shocked to see how many able-bodied young white women had no qualms about being on welfare. They'd give me protips such as "Act crazy and retarded," and I'd huff and tell them I'd never consider such a thing in a million years. But an hour after shaking Suroosh's hand I was sitting in front of a social worker with my eyes crossed pretending I didn't speak any languages sufficiently. When she handed me some forms to fill out, I used my left hand and not one letter was between the lines. By the time I walked out of that office I had the best-paying welfare available and an envelope with $100 tucked in it to tide me over.

I got straight to work writing record reviews such as, "The first song is all 'dfffh dffh dffh' but after that it's nothing but guitars going 'neer neer n'neer.'" Suroosh grew up listening to punk, too, and our naïve arrogance and fuck-off attitudes quickly separated us from the pack. In a city with only a handful of Anglophones to entertain, we were getting noticed.

Our bosses gave us government pamphlets on upcoming ethnic parades and we threw them in the garbage while writing about prostitutes and rap. Suroosh's heroin withdrawals had put his mind in a dark place, and we both got into what was called "hate literature" back then, which was more about death and suffering than anything racial. A Danish magazine called *Sewer Cunt* seared our eyeballs with its graphic depictions of murder, and an American zine called *FUCK* was so harsh it gave our brains third-degree burns, but nothing charbroiled our souls like Jim Goad's *ANSWER Me!* He didn't give a shit what anyone thought and wrote about the upside of rape as if he was contributing to *Reader's Digest*.

My Scottish roots were also taking over. When the Scots settled upstate New York they gave places names like Cunt Creek and Fuck Mountain because the Scots are funny dicks. They weren't trying to be edgy. They were just a bunch of fucking assholes. The core of my humor was this same old Scottish "fuck off, you cunt." Scotland also has this obsession with justice where they grab people for butting in line and get annoyed when people are weak. I was walking through Glasgow with my ninety-year-old grandmother one afternoon and there was a couple in front of us dressed the same. They both had denim overalls and cable-knit turtleneck sweaters and my gran was incensed. "Look at that wee jesse," she said, because "jesse" means "wimp." "She's laid that out on the bed for him this morning and he's gone and put it all on without a second thought." After she said that I thought, "Oh, so *that's* where I get the [*Vice* street fashion satire column] 'DOs and DON'Ts' from."

Despite the shocking content, we felt there was a future in this—mostly because we had no intention of giving up, ever. Our bosses didn't seem to share this enthusiasm and wanted us to stay their tiny golden goose. Every time we talked about getting serious with the business and making a real go of it, they'd come up with a reason why it couldn't be done. We were their welfare-state cash cow, and the last thing they wanted was to let the real world fuck it up.

We had a black saleswoman who I suspect was mentally ill. After a year of not really making money, I decided I would take over and start selling ads. I asked crazy lady what I should do to help, and she suggested selling a page of florists' business cards since it was almost Valentine's Day. I don't know if you've ever cold-called fags and tried to bullshit them into giving you money for nothing, but after the thirty-first hang up punctuated by "Whatever!" I was ready to go to jail for manslaughter. I couldn't handle it. So, I wrote a plea to my Leatherass-buttfuk bandmate Bullshitter Shane. We needed him to take over sales.

Shane had fucked off to Europe too and had talked his way into an opulent lifestyle teaching English in Budapest. I'd been sending him every issue as it came out and he'd defend it to the other expats over there who called it trite. Luckily, the trip had run its course and he was ready to come back. A few days after landing in Montreal, he pulled the same cross-eyed welfare scam at my behest and started as our head of sales right after our first-year anniversary. Our saleswoman realized this made her obsolete. She handled it by running out onto the street and shrieking at cars. Shane wasn't a good salesman—he was a *great* salesman, and he did it beautifully every day until taking over the magazine's editorial content when I abdicated the throne thirteen years later.

Shane's work ethic was inspiring too and his marketing talents were peerless. He'd call me from a pay phone late at night and say, "We are going to be rich," into the receiver again and again like a financial pervert with OCD. We were publishing one issue a month and we based the print run on how much income we had, so we never went into debt. It was the perfect business model but the bosses didn't seem happy with it, and they didn't like the new direction, either. When Shane tried to send the magazine to potential clients, our bosses told him the stamps were too expensive.

In the summer of 1996 my old tree-planting boss Markus was making the two-hour drive from Montreal to Ottawa, so I hitched a ride to go visit the folks. On the trip I explained to him how we were prepared to give *Interculturelles* an ultimatum: Get serious or we're doing it ourselves. Markus is an entrepreneur and didn't understand why we'd even bother with an ultimatum. "Just leave," he said. He was right. What were we waiting for? I called Shane and Suroosh the second I got to my parents' house. "Let's start it from scratch and change the name from *Voice* to *Vice*! They won't have a case."

*Interculturelles* threatened to sue us for leaving so we paid them off via a payment plan that took forever. Two months after the drive with

Markus we were on our own, working and sleeping in a loft together and loving it. We were finally free and the new direction was even better than the old one. *Voice* was an okay name because we let people speak for themselves and would often allow a prostitute to write an article instead of interviewing her, but *Vice* implies offensiveness and that made more sense. We liked to push buttons until our fingers bled.

We went national in 1996 by offering radio stations and record stores free ads if they stuck us in cafés and record shops. Soon we were using the same technique across the border to get *Vice* into New York and L.A. This was exactly the kind of project I was talking about on the roof with Dogboy, not fake welfare scams. I get really annoyed when people say *Vice* was started by a government program. It started *despite* a government program. The only way we could get a business going in Quebec was to sneak in the bureaucracy's asshole and then bust out of their stomach like aliens. The rest was by dint of hard work. If the bureaucrats had their way, we'd still be noodling away in their rectum distributing ten thousand copies of ethnic parade information around office lobbies.

Leaving *Interculturelles* was like being unchained. Things started to get exciting. I worked my ass off every waking moment and cut costs to the point where we were doing the whole thing for free. Paying a designer was expensive so I learned desktop publishing and took over that job. I shot the pictures myself, wrote the articles, edited them, and laid them out. When people said we needed more women or minorities, I made up ethnic-sounding or female aliases for myself. Suroosh helped with editorial and focused on music. He had this incredible ear and could foresee the future of bands. He was almost never wrong and later predicted the indie success of Chromeo, Death from Above 1979, the Streets, Bloc Party, the Stills, Fucked Up, and the Black Lips, to name a few. Shane always had a better work ethic than us but being independent really put things into overdrive. He traveled by bus to other cities and had meetings with corporate heads who had no idea how he got in there. We couldn't afford lawyers so deals were done with handshakes and if someone fucked us over, they were dead. We were banned and sued and threatened and ripped off, but the only thing that could have stopped us was murder. We sent drugs to clients in the mail and got violent with competition and regularly fucked the gross old cougars in charge of buying ad space. Rival magazines often accused us of "eating our way to the top." My old lesbian roommates liked to bitch about the patriarchy but the matriarchy's a bitch too.

While Suroosh remained clean, the rest of us sank ourselves into drugs. We regularly OD'd on mescaline (which in Montreal was probably just horse tranquilizers). I don't have many stories from this time because life outside of work was just sitting on couches in club basements and listening to dance music that was so shitty, you had to be off your head to enjoy it. I spent every weekend high on ecstasy or GHB, Frenching with my friend Mireille all night, and returning home in the early morning to fuck my lesbo girlfriend Alex in the ass.

We had our difficulties, too. Our computers were refurbished pieces of shit we were hustled into buying and they contained so many defects, it wasn't unusual for me to lose a ten-page layout I'd spent all night assembling. Every time something like that happened, I'd get up off the floor, sweep away all the pieces of the chair I just smashed to bits, and focus on the fact that most people would have quit at this point, and that I wouldn't. I was also happy not to be planting trees anymore.

For the most part, our lives became a mirror image of the Sex Pistols movie *The Great Rock 'n' Roll Swindle*. We wrote about our drug trips, got in fights, and documented every moment. We hired an ex-con loan shark as our editor and he wrote about murder. In a city where everyone was polite and shy, our fearless gonzo journalism stuck out like a thumb covered in shit. When we were fingered for being "sexist" after featuring nude porn stars in the magazine, Shane, Suroosh, and I posed buck naked for a photo and slapped it in the front of the magazine. We started a record label and put out all our friends' bands. We were making the most money we'd ever made in our lives doing what we loved, and it kept going because every time we got some extra cash, we put it right back in the company.

As the buzz snowballed, we started getting interviewed by the same uptight, starchy old-person media we'd been lampooning. We sabotaged every interview with bullshit. When asked about *Vice*'s future,

Shane told the reporter we had just been bought by local dot-com billionaire Richard Szalwinski.

We didn't think anything of this stupid lie as it was just one of many, but a few hours after the article was published, we got a call from the man himself. Szalwinski appreciated our bravado and wanted to meet. The next day we were sitting in his gigantic office and telling him about our company. Richard was an ex-nerd in designer glasses, a St. Barts tan, and a floral Gucci suit. He had made $500 million by getting in early with the CGI guys who did *Jurassic Park*. We saw a really loud Letterman-looking guy with a very nasal voice who kept saying, "The most important thing is we have fun. That's number one." I liked him. At the end of the meeting, he said, "Come back tomorrow with a one-page business plan and if you don't try to fuck my ass, I'll invest." We ran home and spent the next twenty-four hours trying to fit three hundred pounds of bullshit onto one piece of paper.

The second time we were in Richard's office he had the sheet in his hand and was impressed. He brought in a greasy, corpulent Frenchman who was his bus-dev guy and they read it aloud together. The bottom line was about a million dollars for 25 percent of the company, and after a few easy questions he said, "Let's do it!" We shook his hand and the fat guy's hand and I respectfully said, "You won't regret it, Mr. Szalwinski."

"Call me Richard, you fuck!" he yelled back in his nasal voice. "And only assholes shake hands."

We calmly walked out of the building, across the front lawn, and when we were out of sight, we went from mild-mannered businessmen to frantic teenagers who'd just won the lottery. We ran in circles shouting, "AAAAAAHHH!" and occasionally stopped to hug the living shit out of each other. By the time we were done, we had grass stains all over our pants and were speechless. After getting our checks, Richard said the first order of business was moving the whole operation to New York. "That is, if you have the balls," he said. We did.

# The Cuban Penis Crisis (2000)

Shortly after I moved to Brooklyn, my parents invited me to join them on a trip to Cuba. It seemed like a good idea at the time because I tend not to think about things the way a smart person does. Besides, I had just become rich.

Canadians love going to Cuba because it's difficult for Americans to do and Canadians love anything un-American. My parents love Cuba because they're Scottish and all Scots care about is saving money and drinking alcohol. Cuba combines the two in a generic resort setting surrounded by razor wire, beyond which is an environment that goes way past cookie-cutter and into wrist-slitter.

I flew up to Ottawa and met my mom, dad, and then-thirteen-year-old brother at the airport a couple of hours before we were booked to leave. Within about five minutes of meeting my folks, I remembered how deranged they are. My father is cursed with an abnormally high IQ. He's a certified genius—a physicist and engineer whose ground-breaking work with sonar called Russia's nuclear submarine bluff and eventually led to the fall of communism. He's responsible for the world's fastest tank and once got out of a drunk driving charge by doing math problems so complex, the officer needed a calculator to keep up (he barely remembers this as he was black-out drunk at the time). People with these kinds of minds either go mad like Dr. John, become workaholics, or lobotomize themselves with alcohol. My dad chose all three. He has a sense of humor about it though. I once accused him of a drinking problem and he said, "The only *problem* I have is that I'm addicted to it and I let it affect my life detrimentally."

My mother, on the other hand, was not meant to be a boozer. She's a retired teacher who loves gardening, painting, and antagonizing civil servants. She terrorizes the local museum for not having enough Scots and would probably be the next Braveheart if she wasn't stuck in a house with assholes. Living with an alcoholic is like swimming with an anvil. Eventually you sink. Poor woman. Loving a drunk genius ain't easy and she's always on the verge of a nervous breakdown.

For example, he gets these lyrics from songs or commercials in his head and repeats them like Rain Man for days on end. When I met them at the airport, his broken-record mantra was from a car commercial and went, "I don't wanna work. I just wanna bang on the drum all day." Todd Rundgren fans will be familiar, as will anyone who has driven home listening to rush-hour classic rock radio. When a Glaswegian sings it, however, the line becomes even more grating. "Ah don wonnee wurk," he unknowingly mumbled to himself again as we waited to board, "ah jus wonnee bang on da drum all dee day." My exhausted mother cried, "Oh for fuck's sake, Jimmy," and I noticed his Chinese water torture had made her cry. How many times would you have to hear that song before it made you shed tears of sheer desperation? If you guessed once every ten minutes for three weeks straight, you just won an all-expenses-paid trip to Cuba!

The plane was filled with Canadian parents and their kids but there were a few hosers who were under the impression this family resort would be filled with horny sluts. When we arrived in Santiago de Cuba, the airline put us on an airline shuttle bus that took us through a Mad Max movie and dropped us at a sequestered resort, also owned by the airline. We checked in past the armed guards and went to our corny, pastel rooms to get depressed. The resort was on a beach and was composed of an outdoor entertainment area next to a restaurant with a large swimming pool flanked by two medium-sized hotels. There were cement paths that weaved in and out of everywhere and they were decorated with bushes, plants, and sickly palm trees. It was exactly like every resort I've ever been to, but shittier. My brother and I were on the outskirts of the first hotel, closer to the main road. We had our own beds and on each one was an eight-by-ten piece of paper listing our itinerary. Every guest was given a schedule for breakfast, lunch, and dinner. Beer was free and it tasted like it too. Other events were announced at dinner and fun was mandatory.

Socialism sounds cool in a classroom and nobody can deny the sexiness Che Guevara emanates from each rotting pore but in reality, it sucks. Every adult knows it's just communism lite, and that means bureaucrats with "Godlike power," as Milton Friedman put it, and a citizenry of "childlike dependents," as he also put it. Nobody wears Che T-shirts in Cuba and the fat man in a beard who runs the place is just a reverse Santa who takes every gift God gives and hands it to someone less deserving. Without the invisible hand of capitalism slapping overachievers on the back and spanking lazy bottoms, waiters mope around like the whole thing is below them.

My parents added an extra layer of weirdness to this already bizarre trip. When they drink, they can go from cheery-as-can-be to scary person at the drop of a drop. My mother loses her mind and behaves like someone is channel surfing her personality, whipping through moods like ecstatic, furious, Papua New Guinean, and just TV static. My father, on the other hand, goes from witty bon vivant, to slightly more cynical bon vivant, to a kind of schadenfreude grumpy, to dark satanist, to the most horrible things you've ever heard about Africa personified. Then he passes out.

It was our first dinner at the resort and both parents were in their final stages of drunk. Dad was sitting deflated with no lights on and Mum was chastising him for refusing to eat. "You're not a bloody thirteen-year-old girl, Jimmy," she yelled, referring to his alcohol-induced anorexia. Then, before she could really tear him a new ass, some mariachis showed up singing Mexican music. My mother instantly changed the channel and was now smiling ear to ear and enthusiastically dancing in her chair. This was particularly disturbing as she still had tears streaming down her face. I looked at my adolescent brother and as soon as our eyes met, this horror movie became a comedy. "This isn't sad. It's funny," we both said with our eyes. It was an epiphany I was having a little too late in life and my brother was having a little too early.

Kyle and I burst into that silent, bouncy laugh you do in class when your teacher tells you to stop laughing or else. (Remember those laughs? Talk about putting out the fire with gasoline.) As gravity slowly pulled slightly chewed food from my brother's incapacitated lips, I was forced to put both hands on the table to help me inhale. It was the most intense laugh session I've ever had because it was pure catharsis. Why were we trying to decipher this insanity and make it work? Insanity is insane. He's not anorexic. He's just not hungry because he drank beer all day. She's not sad. She's just crying. As Charlton Heston said in *Planet of the Apes,* "This is a madhouse, A MADHOUSE!"

My brother and I got up to get refreshments and silently agreed to stop trying to translate our parents' drunken gibberish into some kind of English. "You know what's great about hanging out with Dad?" I asked my brother as we walked toward the buffet. "We get to see what we'd look like if we had AIDS." As we laughed, we passed a table of scowling hosers and they gave our chortles an extra boost. They were beginning to come to terms with the notion that family resorts are not known for their abundance of poon tang and this whole vacation was a huge mistake. I was coming to terms with the notion that a little brother can also be a little friend and this vacation was going to be fun. Just then, a motherfucking Indian goddess walked by and smiled.

I'm not talking about one of those stupid Hindu gods where an elephant with eighty arms is dragging a panda man through the ocean on a flying carpet made of sousaphone-playing cobras. I mean an incredibly pretty East Indian twentysomething with perfect tits and a face so cute, it made Bambi look like an abortion who got thrown in the garbage during a heat wave. You see, I'm not into "handsome" when it comes to beauty. Michelle Pfeiffer can keep her enormous cow-catcher chin. She looks like Dick Tracy to me. I like cute chicks who look like cartoons. This girl was a brown Sandra Bullock without the man chin. She had eyelashes drawn by Disney, a ski-jump nose, blow-job lips, and a big, huge smile that looked like its sole purpose was to baffle Alice during her stay in Wonderland.

Being the suave motherfucker that I am, I responded to her furtive glance by dashing my eyes to the floor and not looking up until she was gone. I had just disowned my parents and "switching my mind back into freak mode," as Nate Dogg put it, was too difficult. My brother and I brought our drinks back to our estranged family members and I sat there furiously trying to think of a way to get out of the wimp hole I'd dug for myself. As my brother stared at my now-sleeping father, my disgusted mother threw down her napkin and went back to her room. A curiously enthusiastic voice came over the loudspeakers and told us to adjourn to the Fiesta Club, which was a huge parking lot made of paving stones and filled with lawn furniture and a fake stream. It was actually kind of nice and the gentle breeze on the tiki torches was making this seem like a classy resort. I was also drunk.

Kyle and I dragged our *Weekend at Bernie's* dad over to a table at the Fiesta Club and watched with bated breath as the camp counselors assembled on a makeshift bamboo stage to begin what turned out to be a cruel, racist pantomime. Hard-hitting house music was pounding in the background and it became very clear, very fast that these entertainers were about half a century out of date. The counselors went into the audience and began dragging up volunteers for a competition. They managed to get half a dozen Canadians up onstage and began blindfolding them. Then they said it was a banana-eating competition. But wait, there's a twist. While they brought a banana to the first guy, they unblindfolded the others and quietly walked them off the stage. He had no idea he was now all alone. At the shout of "Go!" our hero devoured the banana in a few embarrassing bites. When the blindfold came off, I couldn't help but notice he was Asian. "You win, China!" exclaimed the host. Then he turned to the uncomfortable audience and said, "But he also loses." He was expecting a huge round of applause but Canadians are way too polite to enjoy public humiliations so they chose to writhe in their seats instead. My dad's sense of justice startled him awake and he yelled, "Oh for fucksakes. At least give him a bottle of rum or some'ing!" before falling back asleep. I noticed the huge can of beer he was holding was full of warm vodka, and so did my brother. Then I realized something even more bizarre. The dance music they were playing was a very family-unfriendly song called "Fuck U in the Ass" by the aptly named Outhere Brothers. My brother and I had already gone into our heads and flicked the switch from "terrible" to "awesome" so all the trash being flung into our faces was just more grist for the mill and we were ecstatic. Could this night get any better?

Just then I looked over and saw my Paki was still smiling. She too had a brother who was about thirteen and she was sitting with him, alone. I came up with a plan that only a drunk man could come up with and headed over, brother in tow.

"Can we sit here?" I asked like a good buddy not trying to get laid.

"Sure," she responded with that Cheshire smile. "I'm Sonya," she said.

"I wanna fuck you in the ass," I said, realizing how risky an intro it was. She seemed concerned but I pointed out the background music and she burst out laughing. So did her brother, Rajiv. I was in.

Onstage, our oriental countryman was still being abused. "Where are you from?" asked the host. The victim replied, "Toronto," and the host came back with, "I donnnn't thiiiiink soooooo," to the crowd. He was making his Cuban eyes all Chinesey by pulling them sideways with his forefingers. We were in awe.

Sonya didn't care that I had avoided her gaze earlier but I was consumed with it and needed redemption. While Kyle and Rajiv considered trying cigarettes, I took Sonya aside. "I have to tell you something," I said with a face so serious I couldn't believe it. "You know earlier when I walked by you?" She didn't really know what I was talking about. "Well, I ignored you over by the buffet table," I said. She did one of those drawn-out "OKs" that means, "Where are you going with this?" and then I said, "My mother's dead."

"What?" Sonya and my brain said in unison.

"Yeah," I began like a blind man in a drag race, "that woman you saw with my dad is not my mother. It's his new girlfriend. She's real overbearing and wants to replace our mother even though it's barely been a year. It's driving me crazy. She even invents stories and tries to write herself into our family history. When I saw you earlier she had just insisted I call her 'Mom' and I was so fucking mad. Besides, it's 'Mum' in Canada." Sonya put a consoling hand on my leg as I told her about my mother's abrupt passing and what a wonderful woman she was. We later went for a walk along the beach to talk about it. Our cockblocking brothers followed us into the dark.

As we walked along the white sand, the moon lit up my bullshit like a giant lie detector in the sky. Sonya pointed out that my brother was surprisingly carefree for someone who recently lost his mother. I came up with this . . .

"He didn't react at all when the doctors told us there was nothing more they could do," I told her while blinking slowly. "At the funeral he was the same way—stoic, stone-faced, emotionless. This went on for weeks. He barely spoke. Never got angry. Never complained but more importantly never cried." Dramatic pause. Glance at the moon.

"A big part of mourning is going through the pain," I told her knowingly, despite not knowing what I was talking about. "And I knew he could never move forward unless he confronted his pain." Sonya gave an understanding nod. "Then, one day, we went bowling. He asked me if I wanted a drink because he was getting one and I told him to get me a Coke. When he came back, he had two Diet Cokes in his hand and he gave me one." Yet another dramatic pause. "I looked at him and I said, 'Kyle, what are you doing? I don't drink Diet Coke. I've never had a Diet Coke in my life.' Well, you know what he did? He collapsed and began crying his eyes out. He cried and he cried and he didn't stop—for three days." At this point, Sonya was also about to cry despite the fact that, to this day, I've never gone bowling with my brother. I like bowling about as much as I like Coke, which is not much.

Sonya stopped and let our brothers catch up. She kissed Kyle on his forehead and he gave her a "What the fuck?" look. "Come on, Rajiv," she said to her brother before turning to me and saying, "We'll see you guys tomorrow. I had a really great time tonight. Thank you." As they

*At this point, you might be thinking, "This guy is obviously a liar, so who's to say this whole book isn't full of lies?" This accusation is very serious because the whole book is based on the idea of the stories being true.*

*Therefore: I hereby swear that every story told by me in this book happened. I am offering a $1,000 reward to anyone who proves otherwise. That obviously doesn't include "Oh, there were five guys there, not four" or "It was a redhead named Lola, not a blonde named Lisa." You get $1,000 if a story told by me in this book is made up, not if I get an irrelevant detail wrong.* *

*I never lie. I may pull the occasional prank but I always make it clear it was a prank within the week. Otherwise it's a lie and as I said, I don't lie.*

*So, enjoy my dead mother while she's gone because she will rise again in a few days.*

---

* I should make clear that this offer comes from me alone and not my publishers or anyone else involved in bringing you this book. Also, this offer is subject to the terms and conditions I've put on my website at howtopissinpublic.com.

The next day our newly formed foursome snuck around the compound making fun of people. The horny hosers had bombed with Sonya and we spied on them as they tried to figure out a way to actually meet someone who was going to fuck them. Later, we ran into my parents by the pool. It was early afternoon but they were already pretty gone. I was worried my mum was going to blow the whole part where she's not alive anymore but her attorney Mr. Booze had advised her to speak gibberish. After being introduced to Sonya and her brother, Mum went off on a bizarre tirade that involved me, "or was it Kyle," smearing shit all over my crib and saying, "Look at me, Mommy." I've never heard that story before or since and not knowing which kid it was really sealed Mum's fate as someone only pretending to be my mother. I looked at Sonya and she looked back at me consolingly.

Later on, in our room, my brother begged me to stop the charade. "I can't take it anymore," he said. "Today Mum asked me to do something and I caught myself thinking, 'Who the fuck are you to talk to me like that? You're not my mother.'" I assured him the cat would be out of the bag as soon as it started to get boring, which it showed no signs of becoming, so he should hang in there.

We spent the better part of the trip hanging out with the Pakis but no matter how well I played my cards, I could not get in her pants. I don't know if it was because her father kept checking in on us or our brothers kept botching the deal, but I didn't even get a kiss on the lips. Talk about bros before hos. Then my brother really blew any chances of my getting a blow job. He told us about a rape that was happening right then.

We were all lounging in the pool, riffing and shooting the shit as I stole glances at Sonya's unbelievable body. We joked about how stupid the word "restroom" is. Someone is so ashamed of going to the bathroom they pretend they're just going there for a break. "What a spot for a time out," I said. Then Sonya told us about a reality show where some junkie said, "And when I awoke, I saw I had gone to the restroom all over myself." We all died laughing. This inspired a recurring joke that I continue to deploy, using the word "restroom" in a stupid context, like, "No matter how well you shake your dick, a little drop always goes to the restroom in your underwear."

Kyle's confidence was up after all our bonding and he was starting to talk about his life back home. He told us about his girlfriend Tammy and how hot she was. It's weird hearing this kind of stuff from a sibling fourteen years younger than you because as much as he's your brother, you're also kind of his dad. Even today I carefully enjoy his drinking stories only after I'm sure nobody in the story was driving.

"Has she got big tits?" Rajiv asked.

Sonya and I said, "Ew," and my brother proudly said, "Oh yeah. Huge ones. She's really developed for her age." We heard about what it's like to be a kid, which I had totally forgotten about, and then he accidentally dropped a Hiroshima-sized bomb on the whole pool. "Her stepfather's a total dick though," he said.

"Aren't they all?" I added, referring to our fake mom.

"Yeah," he said. "He's always telling her what to do and bossing her around." I rolled my eyes but didn't really care because that's adolescence, right? "Yeah," he said before adding, "then at night he'll come into her room and grab her tits and shit. He's an asshole." I nodded knowingly until I realized what I'd just heard. I leapt off my inflatable chaise lounge and stood in the shallow end dripping with incredulity. "WHAT!?" I said at him so loud he immediately regretted saying anything. It was too late. The cat was out of the bag. Kyle's girlfriend was getting molested. That's called rape. She had a live-in rapist. That's a felony. We had to do something. We told Kyle he had better handle it the second we got back or we would. He was bummed.

The trip back was relatively uneventful until the hosers, who were rumored to have been taking cabs back and forth to the city to fuck prostitutes, started drinking heavily on the plane. "Who hates Cuba?" hollered the drunkest one, expecting a huge chorus of "Hell yeahs" from the Canadian families around him. He was forced to settle for his friend halfheartedly yelling, "Cuba sucks," and that was that.

A few days after getting back, I gave up on Kyle handling his girl-friend's situation and told my mum the story. She immediately ran to the phone and dialed 911 while staring at me like I was a pedophile. I immediately felt like a shitty idiot. After a very quick transfer of lines,

Mum put me on the phone to Detective Weiss. "Start at the beginning," he said.

"I live in New York City," I said, "but my parents are still here in Canada . . ."

I don't know if you've called the cops on a child molester but holy shit do the police ever move with the quickness. Within a few hours of the detective hearing my story, the police were at the place where this dude worked and escorting him to the station. This makes sense. When a criminal lives with his victim, there's plenty of room for coercion. Without a chance to test out his lies, he came up with some bullshit about Tammy and Kyle making the whole thing up because the night before he told Tammy she couldn't go to a party. According to him, the accusation was their revenge.

Do you see what just happened there? The story Kyle told in Cuba went from a depressing anecdote to a crucial piece of evidence that blew the rapist's defense out of the North Atlantic Ocean. How could the accusation be revenge for something the stepfather had done the day before if it was being discussed in Cuba a week before? The detective called me up and we went over the Cuba conversation several times. It wasn't the kind of evidence that would land someone in prison but it would definitely rattle things up and maybe lead to a confession.

The police took Tammy and Kyle out of school the next day and interviewed them both for hours. Obviously everyone in his school went into a gossip frenzy but my fourteen-year-old brother never gave up the ghost. I'm still proud of him for that. The truth would have ruined Tammy's junior high life so he bit his tongue and made up something about the two of them skipping school and almost getting expelled.

The detective was adamant about getting everyone who was in Cuba involved in the case and that meant I had to call up Sonya. I still hadn't come clean about my mother's life and realized it would be prudent to combine that confession with the news because she was now an integral part of a criminal investigation.

I called, and, after some niceties, she asked me what was going on with the stepfather. I told her what had happened and she agreed to talk to the detective as soon as possible.

In high school we used to make up words. You know when you almost have a car accident and the adrenaline makes you feel itchy across your shoulders like a shawl? That's called a Mink Prickly. You know when you get butterflies in your stomach so intense it feels like there's an inner tube around your stomach and the air valve is poking through your belly button? That's called a Tube. In a sick way I think I like giving myself them. I had both when these words came out of my mouth: "There's one more thing, Sonya," I said with a Mink Prickly and a Tube, in a roller coaster, at the very top of a huge hill, about to plummet downward into the darkness . . .

"My mother's not dead."

Silence.

"It was a silly prank that kind of spiraled out of control. I was going to tell you but I wanted to do it in person so we could laugh about it." Silence. "And yeah, I regret it. But the molestation shit is true. And yes, our conversations in Cuba have become part of the case." She hung up. I called her back and she didn't pick up so I gave it a day. I felt terrible but I also felt good and that made me feel like a dick, which also felt pretty good.

The next day, after the detective told me he had spoken with Sonya, I called her up and spent a good three hours convincing her the whole thing was a wild ride and it made the trip a lot more interesting. I got the feeling she was embarrassed by how easily she was duped and was actually turned on by my ability to fuck with her mind. I'm serious. She even told me she'd be in New York the next week and we should "meet for some drinks." "Yeah," I thought, "you drink vodka and I'll drink your pussy."

I went back to New York to wait for my Indian bride and the trial went forward with the momentum of a tornado. As is often the case with these instances, the mother went from accusing Tammy of lying to resenting her for being such a little tart to dropping to her knees, bawling her eyes out, and begging for forgiveness. This part kind of makes me sick but it came out that the mother ultimately sensed something was up because Tammy was going to bed wearing multiple pairs of pajamas and a bathrobe tied extra tight around her waist. The mother admitted she had repressed this vision because she wanted the relationship to work so bad. Now, I ask you, ladies and gentlemen of the jury. What happens when you try to molest a bear's daughter? The bear rips your head off and hurls it into the woods like a softball, right? What about a duck's daughter? A seal's? I'm not positive but I'm willing to wager you'd have to stoop down to the insect world to find a mother who doesn't have a problem with your raping her offspring. Nice peers, lady.

While the worst adults alive were being punished for their perversions, Sonya and I were united in New York and ready to celebrate. I had a boner the size of Mars the second she called me from the airport. I saw drinks and dinner as an annoying obstacle in the way of what really needed to be done. Fucking. Unfortunately, women are not as horny as men and after forty thousand years of post-Neanderthal evolution, they've learned the importance of drawing out a courtship. I managed to keep the date down to beers and maybe a slice of pizza by saying, "Let's meet at a bar and then we can go out for Italian." I was a ticking cum bomb.

This was not going to be a quickie on the couch. This was going to be an ordeal, a punishment if you will. I asked her if she brought high heels and she said she did so I emptied her suitcase all over the floor. I settled on turquoise socks, the heels (which were a little too strappy-sandal for me but the socks took care of that), and a white wife beater. She obliged and got into the costume. I then tied her wrists behind her back with a long-sleeved shirt and used a pair of scissors to cut tit holes out of her undershirt. I surveyed my creation for a while and the alchemy turned my dick from wood into diamond. When she was ready, I walked her over to my bed, lay her on her stomach, and prepared the leg-binding. This involved bringing her ankles up to her ass and keeping them there by fastening belts where her thighs met her calves. Then I put a fucking ball gag in her mouth. That's right, a ball gag. Here's a tip if you have stuff like butt plugs and dildos lying around your house: Always wash the shit out of them after every encounter and always keep them in the same box they came in. No woman is going to go near a used sex toy so you always have to pretend this is its first time out of the box.

Sonya was lying on her stomach literally bound and gagged. The belts were forcing her high heels to poke her ass cheeks and her pussy was sopping. This is what you get when you make a guy wait this long for sex. You get a ritual sacrifice. I took out my video camera and filmed her from the top of her head to the bottom of her knees then back up her calves to her feet. I ate her ass for so long I almost got E. coli and after a few slurps of her beaver juice, I pounded that bitch all the way back to Cuba. After fucking her for so long she was about to get a UTI, I pulled out and turned her face into a spilled milkshake.

Sonya stayed for three days. She'd go shopping while I was at work and then she'd model for me when I got home. I don't think I ever saw her without high-heeled shoes on. That's the great thing about visits like these. Just when you're getting bored, she leaves and your life is back to normal. It's somewhere between a girlfriend and a person you jerk off into, and it's pretty much the best possible scenario for a single man.

Back in Ottawa, Tammy was freed from her perverted stepfather and the family became obsessed with my brother. Mum said Tammy's mother was even pushing for the kids to become a couple and eventually marry. The sex offender didn't do any jail time but was sentenced to community service and sexual rehab and all the governmental programs with which Canada loves to reward its criminals. I ran into Sonya a few times after that and it was always an instant three-day relationship that never went anywhere.

Ten years later I called my brother for updates on Tammy, and being the B-29 bomber that he is, he dropped another Hiroshima on my ass. Ready? <u>The mother got back with that dude and now they were living together.</u> I couldn't wrap my head around it. What kind of person does that? Lady, you are officially no longer a member of the mammal kingdom. Welcome to the ephemera that is a bug's life. Your existence is irrelevant and your time on this planet has been a complete waste. Thankfully, Tammy is a fairly normal human being who told her mother to fuck off when she said, "Trust me, he's changed."

# THE DEATH OF COOL

Tammy's living in Ottawa now and getting on with her life, somehow able to cope with the fact that her mother's actions pretty clearly said, "I don't care about you." Sometimes it takes the worst parents alive to make you realize how lucky you are to have yours. While Tammy has a mother who deserves to die, my brother and I are blessed with a mother who, despite her love of boxed wine and occasional bouts of dementia, would die for us.

# The Story of Vice:
# Part Two (1999–2001)

After we got our checks from Richard Szalwinski, Shane and I bought a solar-powered hippie house on a Costa Rican mountain where we spent most of our summers. Suroosh put his check in the bank. Szalwinski moved us into a gigantic office on Twenty-seventh Street and Sixth Avenue near the Fashion Institute of Technology in Manhattan. We were well paid and the magazine finally had a budget where I didn't have to do the whole thing myself, but something wasn't right. We were hemorrhaging cash and were encouraged to do so. Ironically, it was like life back at *Images Interculturelles*.

Every budget was ten times what it needed to be. For example, Richard and his people, who called the shots, wanted us to start selling things online. Fine. I said I could photograph some stuff with my digital camera and put up an ad, but instead they shelled out $350,000 for a camera that takes a picture at 360 degrees. We used it once. They liked that we had a record label and were very interested in Vice being more than a magazine—that's why I stopped italicizing it. "Let's do stores!" Richard yelled, and we rolled out some of the most embarrassing retail spaces I'd ever seen. Our clothing line was even worse and I couldn't stay on top of the sprawl. Every day there were new people in the office whom I didn't recognize. This wasn't our company anymore.

The turning point for me was during a meeting about some French homo who had begun choosing products for us to buy en masse and sell on the site. He was a chubby man with corny streetwear, but I liked him enough. "Now, Gavin," the stranger leading the board meeting said, "you're going to be working with him so we want to make sure you guys get along."

"Sure," I said, shrugging. "I love faggots."

The conference room was full of faces I didn't recognize, and those were the faces that didn't laugh. The next day I got pulled aside by some office-manager type who told me I was going to have to do sensitivity training. I thought he was kidding.

The training consisted of my sitting with a lawyer uptown who thought the whole thing was as stupid as I did. "I know," she said, "it doesn't make any sense. You said you love them. I'm just telling you what the law is." She went on to tell me that saying anything personal about a coworker is grounds for a lawsuit.

"What if I give someone shit for being late?" I asked.

"That's fine because it's work related," she said, "but if you asked if someone was single or even what sign they are, that's a no-no." We both laughed at this joke of a law, but I went back to work grumpy.

Suroosh and I had a long talk about the way things were going. It didn't feel good to bleed money. Our office rent was $17,000 a month but deep down we were still the same *Vice* magazine that was selling ads from a Montreal loft and calling bullshit on liars.

Companies that made tens of thousands were being valued in the hundreds of millions during the dot-com boom. It wasn't real. Richard wasn't interested in reality, however, and during the peak of this hubris, he said we should take the money he gave us and put it back in the company. "I'll give you good bang for your buck," he promised, "book value." Shane realized the magnitude of what Richard had just said so he grabbed a pen and made him put it in writing. Richard signed it without a second thought. That was the dot-com mentality: "We may be rich now but this is only the beginning."

A year later, in 2000, I noticed the Con Ed guy coming around a lot. He'd ask for the office manager, who would then try to find Richard, but nobody had seen him in weeks. Then our Internet went down. We tried to get a straight answer out of people, but nobody would talk to us. So we rented a car and drove to Richard's house.

We arrived in Nantucket and banged on his door. "Hey, guys!" he yelled in his unusually effusive way. His girlfriend looked like a kidnap victim dying to get out. He asked if we wanted steaks and she happily wrenched them out of the freezer to thaw. You could tell they didn't get a lot of guests. We told him we weren't there for pleasure and he looked disheartened. "You want to talk about *work*?" he said, like we'd said "homework."

"Yes," Suroosh said.

Richard brought us out back and we sat on huge lawn chairs. We wanted to know how much money the company had and how long it was going to last. "Hard to say," Richard said playfully.

"All right," Shane said, "a year?" Richard shook his head.

"Six months?" I asked. Richard shook his head.

"A day?" Suroosh asked, almost kidding. When we finally realized Richard was completely out of money and the lease was already way past eviction, we went, "Whoooooaaaaa," the way they did in *Animal House* after they killed that horse, and we continued howling with fear all the way back to New York. We'd have to begin all over again.

# Dinner with the Clash (1999)

Wait, before the bubble burst with Szalwinski and we had to start again from scratch, a few things happened that I still gotta stick in.

I've known a lot of celebrities over the years but it's not because we all met in Monaco during Brigitte Bardot's birthday party. I know them because I published a magazine for a long time and we needed each other to survive. I know celebrities the way a hairdresser knows supermodels or a sound engineer knows rock stars. It's work. The two things I've learned about fame are (1) it sucks, and (2) anyone who ever uses the words "my fans" is a douche.

Outside of that, they're all pretty much what you'd expect. Zach Galifianakis is weird, Curtis Mayfield is (was) a sweetheart, Chloë Sevigny is quiet and horny, Rufus Wainwright is a baby megalomaniac, Rip Taylor is high-maintenance, Jimmy Kimmel is hilarious and mean, Jennifer Aniston is kind and normal, Patton Oswalt is smart, Debbie Harry is a cunt, Lou Reed's an asshole, Cameron Diaz is dumb, Selma Blair is insecure, Kristen Schaal is quick, Jason Bateman is a douche, Fred Armisen is shy, David Duke is a health nut, Louis C.K. is concerned about your kids, Paul Stanley thinks he can paint, Steven Seagal is grumpy, Aziz Ansari is all over the place, America Ferrera is small, Janeane Garofalo

115

is smaller, Sarah Silverman is as funny as you think she is but gets pissy when there's no pot, and Ghostface Killah is exactly like your best friend.

Johnny Knoxville and I were pitching a TV version of *Vice* magazine we called *Jackass 60 Minutes* for a few years. While staying at his house I got so high on speed, I crashed his daughter's birthday party and invented a game where anyone who doesn't catch the ball is going to die of AIDS. He chased me out of his house with a Taser gun and we haven't really spoken since. I believe "Even Steve-O knows kids are off-limits" were the last words he said to me, and they were via text.

I was flown to Cleveland to interview the Strokes for an *NME* (British music magazine) cover story but they kept delaying it, so by the time we got started, I was blind drunk from sitting in a bar all day. Hearing the tape of this interview is like listening to a different person and the only thing I remember clearly is watching the show from the edge of the stage, then sitting on the stage next to the bassist, then sprawling out and falling asleep on the stage in front of four thousand people. They were not jazzed.

All in all I'd say, outside of the cash, being famous looks like a real pain in the ass. Famous people are not constantly getting accolades from well-informed peers who love their work. They're getting harassed by twenty-one-year-olds who say stuff like, "Aren't you the guy from that thing?" If you're really famous, you make everyone so awkward when you walk in the room, you might as well be the Elephant Man. Bill Murray calls fame a "twenty-four-hour-a-day job" and tells people who want to be famous, "Try being rich first. See if that doesn't cover most of it."

Anyway, the best famous person I ever met was Clash front man Joe Strummer. His band was heavily influenced by glam legends Mott the Hoople, whose whole thing was being at one with the fans. They'd let anyone come backstage or into the recording studio. In a way, they invented the whole punk ethos of "kill rock stars." The Clash continued this tradition and treated everyone like their best pal.

Shortly after moving to New York, I met Joe at a hotel in SoHo to discuss his 1999 album with the Mescaleros, *Rock Art and the X-Ray Style*—only, I hate talking to musicians about music. I want to hear about their process about as much as I want to watch a woman douching before I go down on her. Just give me the good stuff and leave the rest behind the curtain.

I brought Joe a pile of DOs & DON'Ts and asked him to comment. He cared about fashion exactly the same way I did, with exaggerated passion.

"He looks like a bloody juggler," Joe said, looking at a woman in orange overalls. I told him it was a girl and he looked up blinking. "Uh-oh," he said, "looks like I'm going to have to spend my lunch break at LensCrafters!" The guy's jokes reminded me of my gran's in that they were awesome.

We got along smashingly and after the interview, we went out for lunch together. It took forever to get there because every time he saw a pile of garbage he had to root through it. "Why are you so fascinated by everything?" I asked him. "You act like you just got out of jail." He said it was a genetic trait he couldn't do anything about. "Ask Bo Diddley," he hollered while pulling a broken lamp out of the garbage to see what was beneath. "He's the same way. There's something about guitarists where we can't go by a skip without checking it out."

I had the Clash's first album in my bag because I wanted to ask him some questions about the early history of the band. "This is Mick Jones's favorite album," I told him.

"I know," he said. Then he grabbed it out of my hand and said, "You see that picture? That's in Camden Market in the alleyway outside our rehearsal space." I was interested because I think I know exactly where it is. "See? You care. I was there with the missus and the kids recently and when I realized how close we were, I dragged them over. It was a bit farther than I thought and the kids were whining because they wanted Pokémon or something like that and I kept saying, 'Trust me. It's going to be worth it!' So we make our way there and I tell everyone to close their eyes. I stood in the exact same spot I'm standing on the album and made the same expression and everything and I said, 'All right, open your eyes!' Guess what happened. Dead air. Nothing. The kids said, 'All right, can we go now?' and the missus says, 'All right, Joe, that's enough, let's leave, please.'" I laughed and Joe signed the album with the words "Open your eyes! I said to the crowd but NO!"

at the top. I think autographs are queer but this is still one of my most prized possessions.

After lunch we went to drink pints at a bar on Seventh and A called Niagara where a mural of him now sits. About one minute after ordering our drinks, a geeky NYU student came up and said, "I'm really sorry, but are you Joe Strummer?" Joe said, "Yup!" and after agreeing to pose for a picture, he suggested they switch shirts and do it again. "I'll be you and you be me." Joe then put on the kid's polo shirt while the kid put on Joe's leather jacket and sunglasses. Their photo shoot went on for another twenty minutes and I told him I had to go. It was cool Joe was willing to indulge the kid but it also blew our hang. I told you fame was a pain in the ass. We agreed to meet for dinner later on that night.

I was dating an artist named Rose at the time. She was a tall Jew with jet-black hair who only did blow jobs. I told her about the dinner and she said she already knew Joe and had dated a friend of his, a seminal photographer who had often shot the Clash. Great. We all met at Three of Cups on First Avenue and when I walked into the room Joe yelled, "Here he is!" like we were old pals.

The table was a who's-who of local musicians, including Chris Robinson, the singer of the Black Crowes, whom I sat across from. I was introduced to everyone at the table, including, by chance, the photographer Rose had dated. He stared at her like she was his dead mother. "Hello," she said victoriously.

Joe dominated the table with funny stories and effusive flattery directed at every guest, but Chris started feeling courageous as the night wore on and turned into a very loud Southern gentleman who was unlike the guy I sat down with. "I love me some bah-bee-kyew," he yelled, unprovoked. "Pig foot, pig toe!" he added, like I was going to say, "Wait, 'toe.' Is you crazy? You eat a muthafuckin' toe?" I didn't say anything because I don't give a shit if someone likes food. "Shit," he said, cocking his head back, "I'll eat a PIG'S ASS if they cook it right!" I thought this sounded a lot like the Chris Rock bit where he goes, "I'll eat a PIG'S ASS if they cook it right!" and I said as much. Chris was oblivious but his girlfriend leaned over to me and said, "He gets progressively more black and Southern the drunker he gets." I was impressed she could be so blunt about her boyfriend while he was sitting right there (to really see Chris black it up, I highly recommend checking out his "Kinky Reggae" tribute to Bob Marley on YouTube). I looked over at Rose and she was chewing her food while staring at her ex and not saying a word. "You all right?" I asked.

"Mmm hmm," she responded without looking at me.

While Joe held court, I looked over at his photographer friend and couldn't help but notice how cripplingly uncomfortable he was. He barely spoke all night and when he did talk it was quietly into the ear next to him. When Rose got up to go to the bathroom, he waited until the door closed behind her. After it clicked shut he looked at me and said, "Mate, what are you doing? Do you know who that is?"

"Um, Rose?" I answered, confused. Then the woman sitting next to him came over and explained that Rose was a fucking lunatic who had been stalking this guy for years and I really had to get her out of there. Apparently, she had been sending him endless letters and showing up at his studio unannounced. He hadn't called the cops but he was thinking seriously about it now. Great. Thanks, Rose.

After our meal, we went upstairs and I dillydallied with Joe for a bit before telling him I had to leave. Joe demanded I stay, which is what he did to absolutely everyone who had to go, including strangers. The end result was this hulking pile of humans surrounding him like an army wherever he went. I shook his hand and took Rose home, where she sucked me off and went to sleep.

I had a *Fight Club* moment where I went back over our short relationship and realized, yes, she is completely out of her fucking mind. I quit answering her calls, and she eventually stopped leaving messages. When I saw her two years later, we gave each other awkward smiles that hurt my cheeks.

A year after that, Joe Strummer returned from walking his dog and collapsed dead on the living room floor. He didn't know he had a congenital heart defect, nor did anyone else. He was fifty years old.

# I Said, "Jesus Is Gay," on National Television (2000)

Almost right after setting up our New York office, I was booked on Bill Maher's show *Politically Incorrect*. The taping was in March, right in the middle of a bender I was on in Texas with Pinky. We were attending Austin's South by Southwest music conference and had to leap on a plane at noon to make it to L.A. in time for the show. Guests on the show usually researched all the questions in advance and had all their answers prepared, but we just saw it as another page in the party book. I listened to the questions they gave me to research about as closely as you listened to economics lectures in high school.

When we got to L.A., our buddy David Choe met us at the airport. He's a painter who started as a graffiti vandal and petty thief and he single-handedly made it cool to be Asian again. He's handsome but he also looks like a racist cartoon of a Chinaman because he's always smiling. Choe dresses like a cholo and was driving a beat-up Chevy Nova at the time. "We should go straight there from the airport," he said after we threw our bags in his shitbox. "It could take forever to get there because of the traffic."

"I fucking hate L.A.," Pinky said as we pulled out of the parking lot. "It's like *Waterworld* but with cars instead of Jet Skis. I mean, are there even any houses in this city, or do people just pull over and sleep in their cars when they get tired?" He was already dipping into the scotch I didn't know we had and I asked for some of the same. The stewardesses were pretty stingy and the lack of service had delivered a crippling blow to our mutual buzzes. The beauty of benders, however, is it's very easy to get them back on track.

After Choe pulled into HBO Studios, I stuffed the scotch bottle down the front of my pants and double-checked our cocaine supply. We weren't about to risk a no-booze policy at this thing. The staff at the entrance were unable to detect any of our contraband so Choe, Pinky, and I stumbled down the hall and into the greenroom with ease. There are two ways to approach a situation like this: You can be nervous and hope everyone likes you or you can just throw up your hands and treat everyone around you like puppets someone hired to amuse you.

We exploded into the greenroom like a triumvirate of bullies looking for a nerd to wedgie. It was a pretty big room with two long couches and a small kitchen partially separated by a frosted glass partition. It looked like a teachers' lounge for the most expensive private school in the world. We had cut it a little close timewise, so all the guests were already present and accounted for. None of them seemed to care that the Three Musketeers had arrived. Quietly sitting on the couch was Bishop John Shelby Spong, an incredibly smart but dull religious man who looked like a very tall Montgomery Burns. I've never really understood the whole Christian scholar thing. Congratulations, you read one book. Next to him was Robert Conrad, a sexy tough-guy actor from the sixties best known to later generations for his "I dare you to knock this Duracell battery off my shoulder" ads. He looked like Ned Flanders–meets–Steve McQueen and was there with a new bride who looked like a child. Over by the window, where cell phone reception was apparently better, we had Lisa Ann Walter, a pretty redhead with perfect tits who looked like a young Joy Behar dipped in babe sauce. She was discussing some deal with her agent, which is always weird to see because you're watching someone discuss a company they work at and the company is themselves.

A nebbishy homosexual with a headset and a clipboard immediately swooped in and introduced me to the other guests. Pinky and David hung back on a couch closer to the door as Pinky plotted how to drink scotch and do coke without getting caught. David's race lacks the enzymes to do the same, so he just looked at magazines. Everyone gave me a friendly but brief wave and I made a mental note to do everything in my power to get into Lisa Ann's pants—which I never did.

We still had an hour to kill and everyone seemed preoccupied with the spouse or manager they'd brought along for the ride, so Pinky and I oozed toward the kitchen part of the waiting area, where the partition provided a semblance of privacy. HBO was being broadcast on a giant screen in the middle of the room, which was a great distraction for everyone else's eyes and ears. I moved over to the fridge, which was completely out of view, and pretended to care about it. "Fancy a swig?" I whispered to Pinky, and he said, "Yes, but I wish we had ice. Warm scotch tastes like gasoline." Nobody was looking so I took the small coke bag out of my pocket, dipped my key in, and snorted a bump the size of a mouse's eyeball. It burned like a motherfucker and made the back of my throat taste like nail polish remover. Pinky took my keys and did twice as much as me and then bent over in pain like someone had just stabbed him in the nose. How glamorous. We did this a few times and it was less pleasant each time. Sometimes I think the only thing coke does is make you want more coke. I turned to Pinky and said, "I'm not sure I should be doing this. Cocaine often brings out the worst in me."

"Me too," he added, and presented a coke booger so huge and disgusting, it made me dry-heave.

The buzz from Austin was back with a vengeance and we were ready to rock. I zinged Pinky with, "I don't know what all these Muslim women are complaining about. I love getting stoned," and he zinged me back with, "Give a man a bump, you have a friend for the night. Teach a man to shoot up, you have a friend for life." We were *on*.

Just as we were indulging in our unprecedented wit, the Neb arrived with his clipboard and asked us if we were all right. "Shit!" I thought. "How are we going to explain standing here by a (probably) empty fridge?" Neb smiled and asked us if we wanted a beer. Then he opened the fridge we had been ignoring and made the four shelves of beer evident to our bloodshot eyes. "There's Beck's and Budweiser," he said cheerily with his clipboard to one side. "There's some weird pumpkin beer in there too if you're into that. What else? There's Heineken . . . drink up!" Each word felt better than when you take off a wet bathing suit and replace it with underwear from the dryer. I almost Frenched him for telling us what lay right beneath our powdered noses.

Lisa Ann was still on the phone, and religious people are boring, so we both gravitated to the handsomely gray-haired Robert Conrad. Pinky is a TV junkie and has been all his life.

Feeling his oats, Pinky strutted up to Conrad and sang the chorus of "Wild Wild West," a terrible Will Smith title theme song to a terrible Will Smith movie, which was based on the Western TV show that made Conrad famous. Conrad smiled politely and Pinky's shitfaced face lit up. "Have you heard that song?" he asked way too quickly.

"No," Conrad replied, unamused.

Then Pinky sniffed the coke snot off his lip and brought his A-game by pulling an old episode of Conrad's show out of his ass. "Man," Pinky said, leaning into Conrad with a weird grin, "'Night of the Vicious Valentine' . . . when that crossbow was rigged into the piano and that pompous prick gets shot right as he's patronizing you? Golden."

Robert Conrad immediately came to life and leapt up out of his chair to talk about the old days. "You wouldn't see that today," he lamented enthusiastically, which was weird because I didn't know you could do those two things at the same time. "People don't put the same kind of thought into scripts," Conrad said. We agreed, though I personally had no idea what anyone was talking about. Conrad led us over to the other end of the room to get down to some real talk. We were now back near the fridge where the cocaining took place. I wondered if he was going to ask us for a bump. Isn't that how all old movie stars die? Robert didn't want to take any drugs, but he did take a shine to us and seemed determined to pass on some words of wisdom before he left this earth. David remained on the couch, lost in a magazine, and couldn't have cared less what he was missing out on.

"Look, guys," Conrad said while peering back to make sure his child bride couldn't hear him. "When I was your age I screwed everything that moved. I didn't care what they looked like."

I love conversations like this and had a million questions for our new mentor. "But if hot chicks see you fucking dogs you're done, right?"

Robert Conrad looked at me like I had just pulled my dick out and asked him to count the veins. "What?" he said. Then he came back in, unfazed, with, "Heck no. You have to get every single girl you can. If a woman's not interested, that's not your problem. Wait for the next bus." This was some of the soundest advice I've ever received and today, as a much older man, I can only begin to wrap my head around its wisdom. You see, when you're married, you have nothing to beat off to but your memories. If you've only fucked, say, ten women, you have to keep recycling those same memories again and again like a dog-eared porn mag with the staples falling out. However, if you fill up that wank Rolodex with as many business cards as it can hold, Old You will go back in time and kiss Young You on the mouth.

"But you aren't like that anymore?" I asked.

"Absolutely not," he responded. "I found Jesus Christ and I'm madly in love with my wife. Look at her." He looked back at the stunning young lady before adding, "She's perfection. Eventually, you have to settle down."

"When?" I asked.

"How old are you?" he replied. I told him I was thirty and he laughed and slapped me on the back. "You have another good ten years, buddy. Enjoy." Then he walked off smiling. Three years later he careened into another car while wasted out of his mind and has been fucked-up ever since. Three years after that, I proposed.

By the time we were called out to the show, I couldn't help but notice I had become completely fucking shithoused. I was too high and felt more out of place than a Japanese break-dancer. Cocaine is a difficult thing to regulate when you're sneaking it up your nose behind appliances and the odds of your accidentally inhaling a huge chunk are even higher than you. Couple this with the realization I was going to be on national television and I started to panic. My parents were going to be watching this. What the fuck was I doing? You see, people think they're better when they're high but they're actually way worse. You're High You for about 0.000000001 percent of your life. You're You You for the other 99.9999999999 percent. Which You do you think you're going to be more comfortable being?

The people with the headsets shuffled all of us to the right of a big curtain that was just out of the audience's line of vision. When I heard Bill Maher say, "and the editor of *Vice* magazine and Viceland.com, Mr. Gavin MuhGuinness, everybody," I ran out to the stage and proudly showed the crowd how underdressed I was. I had on a V-neck T-shirt covered in beer stains, ratty cords, and my dad's old Wallabees. I thrust my hands into the air like a champion, which made the crowd cheer even louder, and I could see the inversely proportional enthusiasm on Maher's face. He could instantly tell I wasn't there to have a serious discussion. The surprisingly diminutive Bill came over and shook our hands as we sat down on chairs that were positioned in a circle. Video cameras on big cranes swooped around the stage and stared at us like curious robots. There were maybe two thousand people surrounding us in a semicircle but they were least fifty feet away so the cameras could swivel with ease. As Bill led into the first question I started to feel my teeth grind back and forth. Too much cocaine has a way of making your hands turn cold and clammy, giving you Mink Pricklies. Bill looked at his cue cards and then looked up at us and said, "So JonBenét Ramsey's parents are writing a book about everything they've been through. Do we think this is acceptable, for someone to be profiting off of this story when they're still a suspect? Gavin, let's start with you."

Oh yeah, I seem to remember being warned about this topic. I had some loose ideas about American justice and how ridiculous it is to judge a person's facial expressions in the aftermath of some horrible event. They'll say, "The suspect didn't flinch during the trial and looked at the victim's parents with a blank stare." Who cares? It's a weird situation. Why do you care how they behave? How would you behave? Shit, if I was the bus driver who went off the road and killed all those kids like in that Atom Egoyan movie I'd probably be a catatonic robot during the trial. You can't imagine what it's like to be in that situation, so why are you treating him like a kid who chopped down a cherry tree?

That's what I wanted to say. Unfortunately, I wasn't in control and what came out of my mouth was, "I don't know. People talking. Always talking. You know. Who cares? I mean, if I had the bus and killed all the kids I'd be like . . ." Then I started feigning a seizure on my chair. Bill tapped his card on his knee and quickly moved over to the next question. I resigned to keep my mouth shut until shit cooled down a bit.

During the commercial break one of the clipboard people ran over and crouched next to my chair. "Are you OK?" he asked.

"Yeah, I'm fine," I said with my eyes bugged out.

He sounded like a guidance counselor and said, "You need to talk more. It doesn't matter what you say, just talk." I told him I needed booze. He was thrilled my problem was so easy to solve and ran off to fill my coffee mug with Guinness. I inhaled it and asked for more and he was happy to oblige. By the time we came back, my cocaine buzz was finally under control and I was ready to fuck with this smug little dwarf.

Bill brought up his favorite topic, religion, and everyone had something to say. I sat back and bided my time because I wanted the second thing to come out of my mouth to be perfect. When asked if he believed in God, Robert Conrad jumped out of his chair and held his hands up to the sky. "Praise Jesus," he said. "Praise the Lord!" He wasn't kidding. The bishop pointed out that the number of people who identify themselves as Christian has been steadily on the rise and, despite Hollywood's disdain for it, America is still 75 percent Christian. Lisa Ann tried to get a word in edgewise about her mother but Bill wanted to get to his next question. "Good," I thought. "I'm ready to redeem myself—through Christ."

"All right," Bill said to the group, "we've got George Bush saying he follows the words of Jesus and even asks him for advice. Bill Clinton often said the same thing. All of a sudden, presidents are telling us they have a close relationship with Jesus—and even ask him for advice! Is this right? Should a country that promises to separate church and state have presidents that talk to Jesus?" The guests all looked at each other wondering who was going to take this on first. This is where Bill usually chooses someone. "I think what's really important to note here is that we finally have a GAY JEW in the White House," I said straight-faced. A stunned silence swept over the show as they all looked at each other. "He's gay," I added. "You saw him. Come on. Everybody knows this. It's a fact," I said.

After several seconds of awkward silence Bill let out a stupefied "What?" Lisa Ann Walter turned to me and said incredulously, "He wasn't gay." The bishop was smiling and shaking his head. "Well he seemed pretty gay to me," I said. "Long hair and a dress." Bill Maher finally came up with, "Just because he had long hair doesn't mean he's gay. I mean, I used to have long hair." Nobody knew what to do with this theory so I took the edge off by saying, "All I'm saying is it's a well-accepted theory," and Bill then zinged me back with, "So now it's a theory? A second ago you said it was a fact," and the crowd cheered. I stood up on my chair and chastised the crowd for cheering. "STOP ENCOURAGING HIM!" I yelled, waving my arms in the air like a lunatic. Audiences seem to like it when you acknowledge them so after this fake temper tantrum they cheered and hollered every time I did something in the hopes I'd make them part of the show again.

The crowd was delirious and Bill Maher was bumming out. When Lisa Ann Walter finally got to mention her mother, I hollered, "She never liked me!" This threw her off a bit so I grabbed her arm and yelled, "I always loved you," and tried to kiss her. Bill Maher suggested Robert Conrad kick my ass but he didn't know Conrad was my nigga from backstage and Conrad said, "No. I like this guy."

Eventually the show was over and we said our good-byes to a screaming audience that sounded like they were getting paid per clap. The clipboard people were patting me on the back and telling me I was

DEFINITELY going to be on the show again, which is basically what the principal in Taiwan said when I was fired.

That night, back at the stunning hotel suite HBO had set us up with, Pinky and I finished off the cocaine, the scotch, and later, the minibar. As I lay on my back drifting out of consciousness I remember Pinky saying, "Remember in Montreal when we'd show up at a party and just evacuate it by doing one of our gay dance routines or just hogging the spotlight until nobody could take it anymore?" I mumbled a response that sounded like "continue" and he said, "I feel like we're on the verge of doing that with all of television. Let's get inside television and just fuck with it." I drifted into the blackness at this point but his last words, "fuck with it," stuck and I remember thinking, "Yeah."

# Lying to the Press (1999–)

W hen hiring writers I noticed the least interesting ones were those with journalism degrees. Their incompetence really hit me when the more experienced ones started interviewing us for features in other publications. They had no idea who we were and why they were writing about us, so fucking with them was irresistible.

Quebec's answer to *The New York Times* is *Le Devoir* and they wanted to interview us because someone else did. That's how it works in media. One writer has the balls to dig up a new story and the others cling to it like lampreys on a shark. The original story that got us into this print assembly line was based on a prank. The truth was, we changed the name from *Voice of Montreal* to *Vice* so the old owners couldn't sue us, but that's boring, so we changed the narrative to "The big, ugly, American corporate newspaper *Village Voice* threatened to shut us down so we had to change the name." Once this caught on, it was in every newspaper in the country and not one person fact-checked it or even called *The Village Voice*. Canadians love David-and-Goliath stories about American bullying, and they weren't about to let facts ruin the fun.

The woman from *Le Devoir* showed up late wearing a fur coat and had notebooks and pens flopping all over the place like a drunk aristo-

131

crat. It seemed to me that she didn't care about her job and was in it for the galas and luncheons, so when she pulled out the same old, "How did you guys meet?" I decided to intercept that football and run with it. I don't suffer fools gladly, but I will gladly make fools suffer.

"It's actually a pretty amazing story," I told her with a shit-eating grin. "Shane and I were best friends from a very young age but as we got older, we noticed some changes. We couldn't quite place it, but there seemed to be some kind of urge growing within us." She nodded her head very thoughtfully and jotted down my prevarications. "Anyway," I added as if it was *An Evening at the Improv*, "we were about eighteen and I was tickling him . . . just messing around and being crazy. I ended up on top of him and our faces were about an inch from each other when, whoops, we just started kissing." She was scribbling away like her pen was on fire. "The second our lips touched," I told her, "a million questions were answered. You know what I mean?" She said she knew exactly what I meant, which I thought was weird because I didn't. I added another twenty tons of perjury to my name and she devoured every morsel. When the photographer came in an hour later, Shane and I posed locked in an embrace and that's how the feature ran: TWO LOVERS FIND THEIR VOICE IN PRINT. From that point on, almost every interview I did was a stream-of-consciousness, free-association swirling turd ribbon that was mainly a test of the writer's incompetence.

Pranking the media went from a lark to a lifelong commitment. If the reporters had done their homework and asked us something that wasn't easily answered with a tiny bit of research (like reading the previous article about us), I'd give them honest answers, but it almost never worked out like that. I told journalists we all met in rehab. I said I was an ex–gang member who had been scared straight by my homie's death. The less research they were willing to do, the crazier the story I was willing to concoct.

Then we moved to America, where journalists are even less interested in truth.

Where French v. English was the big deal in Montreal, America was all about race. So when the *New York Press* came to interview us, I dressed up as a Nazi skinhead and had Shane dress as a British soccer hooligan. Suroosh wore a suit and we put a bandage on his head covered in fake blood. He was our hate-crime victim. We played our roles to a T, and when the reporter asked us if we get annoyed by all the hipsters in Brooklyn I said, "Well, at least they're not fucking niggers or Puerto Ricans." This caused a minor earthquake in the local media because you're not supposed to use that horrible, horrible word but I'm sorry. Whenever people say "African-American," all I hear is "Black people freak me out." Eventually all this niggermarole brought *The New York Times* to our door. When they prodded me for a similar quote, my self-destructive instincts kicked in and I told them, "I love being white and I think it's something to be very proud of. I don't want our culture diluted. We need to close the borders now and let everyone assimilate to a Western, white, English-speaking way of life." In a culture where "racist" includes anything but white self-flagellation, this quote ballooned into a gigantic Super Ghost that has haunted me ever since—and maybe it should. It definitely wasn't complete bullshit like the other pranks. I don't think being white is anything to be ashamed of. Hell, we didn't start slavery, we ended it. I was well aware the poobahs at the *Times* would turn my Western chauvinism into "Nazi hipster wants to kill Mexicans," and I threw gas on the fire anyway. I'll always be one Google search away from being fired from a normal job but I'd rather it be like that than have to search for the proper words every time I open my big mouth.

My most involved prank was prompted in late 2009 after I had left Vice, and the media website Gawker encouraged readers to send in votes to decide who was the Hipster of the Decade. The finalists were myself, a woman who went to jail for fraud and was known as the Hipster Grifter, a group of promoters called Misshapes, American Apparel founder Dov Charney, and the anonymous creator of the website and radio show Hipster Runoff. I had some footage lying around of myself eating cornflakes soaked in piss to see if the expression "Who pissed in your cornflakes?" has any basis in fact. It was for a sketch comedy DVD I did called *Gavin McInnes Is a Fucking Asshole* but we couldn't use it because it was so fucking gross, it dominated the whole movie and ruined all the jokes that followed it (kind of like when Sinéad

O'Connor ripped up that picture of the pope on *SNL*). I decided to pretend it hadn't been shot yet and used it as evidence of a prank where I had been tricked into eating it after losing a bet.

While posing as my buddy Arvind Dilawar, I invented this whole complicated challenge to the Gawker readers that said I'd convinced Gavin to eat a bowl of piss-soaked cornflakes if he won the competition. This brought in a ton of extra votes but not enough to win. When "Gavin" didn't win, "Arvind" tricked "Gavin" into thinking he DID win by Photoshopping the results. As far as the public was concerned, Gavin foolishly believed the lie and thought he was the Hipster of the Decade. Meanwhile, I was both guys and knew full well I hadn't won. Posing as Arvind, I posted the footage of Gavin eating the bowl of cornflakes. Are you with "me"? I know. It's involved. Basically I duped Gawker into thinking someone had duped me into eating a bowl of piss. They ate it up like untainted breakfast cereal and reveled in my humiliation.

The headline read HIPSTER OF THE DECADE LOSER GAVIN MCINNES ACCEPTS "AWARD" BY EATING BOWL OF PISSED-IN CEREAL and the article went on to say, "Dying. No, seriously. Okay: Street Carnage impresario Gavin McInnes told his blogger he'd piss in Corn Flakes and eat them if he won our Hipster of the Decade contest. He lost. So . . . why's he pissing in Corn Flakes and eating them? Well, the answer: he was *pranked.*"

There's something really satisfying about reading someone who is pranked say, "he was pranked." It felt great but nothing will ever top the one I played on our hometown's leading paper, the *Ottawa Citizen*, ten years earlier in 1999. Besides being useless at their jobs, journalists are also sycophants looking to mingle with the "tastemakers." After talking to the kid who was flying down from Ottawa to interview us, it seemed abundantly clear he was just looking to have fun in New York. I explained I was trying to get a show on TV with the help of Tom Green's old producer and the reporter suggested he come to the pitch. "Fuck no," I thought to myself. "Of course," I said aloud.

I decided we were going to create an entire universe for this reporter à la *The Truman Show*. I wasn't only pitching shows to MTV—we were *merging* with them (a concoction that ironically ended up becoming somewhat true a decade later). I enlisted my friend Matt Sweeney to be the network exec and he brought in his cousin Spencer as their Next Big Thing. Matt suggested we all meet at an incredibly expensive restaurant in SoHo called Canteen.

When we got there, the reporter nervously pulled out his tape recorder and repeatedly thanked everyone for the privilege of being there. Matt is a tall, skinny musician with a funny mustache and his cousin Spencer is a stoned-looking young artist who was squatting in Tompkins Square Park at the time. They were both acting very serious and self-important, the way their characters should be. As my bill mounted, I realized Matt had stuffed a scam within a scam and was actually hustling a pricey lunch out of me in the process. After a bit of small talk, Matt got down to brass tacks. "Spencer is my eyes and ears," he told the table before looking at Shane, Suroosh, and me and adding, "He says you guys are *it*." Before we could interject he added, "I think it's time to merge." Someone at the table suggested we change the name from MTV to ViceTV, but Matt was good at his job and called the guy a cretin.

The reporter was blown away. This was a real-deal New York meeting with the city's biggest players and he was in the thick of it. By the end of the meeting, we were all millionaires and I was stuck with the biggest lunch bill I'd ever had, $350.

Over the next few days, we stuffed that reporter so full of horseshit he smelled like an ass. We were buying a building in midtown for ViceCo. We set up franchises across Europe, China, and the Middle East. I collected antique cars. The list was endless. When the feature finally came out, it took up three entire newspaper pages carrying the headline TOM GREEN WANNABES WANT THEIR MTV. (My father still keeps this article in his office and regularly brings it out to show guests. "They usually cringe when I read it," he once told me proudly, "until they find out the whole thing's fake. Then they love it.")

I showed the piece to the Tom Green producer and was surprised to see her go beet-red with rage. "You can't do this!" she screeched, apparently having never heard of hijinks before. "It's unethical." Then she called the *Ottawa Citizen* and ratted us out. Thanks, lady. When he realized what happened, the reporter completely lost his shit and spent the next few days calling everyone in the feature and babbling about ethics and honesty and yadda yadda yadda. I think he was drinking. He was especially mad at Matt Sweeney, a person he hadn't noticed was phenomenally easy to look up.

In response to the first few calls, Matt told him to calm down, but Matt eventually became annoyed and gave a line that I have used maybe ten thousand times since. "Relax, guy," he said flatly. "It's New York City. You got hustled."

# New Wave Hookers (2000)

P asserby was an art gallery in the West Village with a fun bar and a dance floor that lit up like *Saturday Night Fever*. A hilariously eccentric group of designers called As Four would often be there dressed in mummy rags and stilettos with their circular purses and pointy beards and tits hanging out, but it was also kind of scuzzy. You'd see junkies among the artists and it wasn't unusual to see a drag queen beating the shit out of someone who was trying to steal his handbag.

Pinky had come to visit New York from Montreal and he was dressed like a grunge B-boy in basketball shoes and dirty jeans. Vice was still in the throes of the dot-com boom at this point and I was not spending my money wisely. I was rocking a Eurotrash velour tracksuit with no pockets and spotless $200 kicks. I was also buying way too much gold and had a huge ring on every finger. One said "Love," another said, "Hate," and there was also "Brooklyn Lager," "NYPD," and, of course, "Vice." I had gold teeth and had blown almost $1,000 on a huge gold rope chain around my neck.

Pinky was smoking a cigarette outside Passerby and I was with him. Then a cab pulled up and three of the hottest women I'd ever seen climbed out. I also remember a dry-ice haze all around, but that's probably just in my head. They were all dressed like those girls in the ZZ Top videos they call "the Eliminator Girls." They had fingerless gloves on and huge hair with tutus and weird plastic jewelry. They looked like slutty versions of early Madonna but the last one to get out made my whole body ache with lust. Her name was Blobs and she stepped out of the cab with skintight yellow jeans and white ankle socks with kiss marks all over them stuffed into stilettos. When she stood outside the cab she was tall with Chinky raccoon eyes and lips bigger than an inner tube (turns out she wasn't a Chink—they were American Indian eyes). Pinky and I turned into Lenny and Squiggy and bit our fists. They looked back at us like the snobby cunts they were and marched into the club with their noses in the air.

"I have to have her," I said to Pinky.

"Who?" he asked.

"The last one."

Inside, the girls danced and made fun of people, and I chugged beer trying to summon the courage to talk to the last one but it took way too long. About three hours later, when my buzz was sufficiently strong, I headed toward her but just before I got there, she started screaming like snakes were shooting out of the floor. She was holding her hand in the air like it had been badly burned and her friend Annabel was screaming, too. Both ran to the bathroom and Blobs left her purse on the floor as everyone stared at it. I assumed she pricked her finger with a syringe but it was much worse. It was poo. Someone had taken a shit in her purse.

"Are you serious?" I said to a guy who called himself A-Ron the Downtown Don.

"Yes!" he said, smiling and shaking his head. "Old New York is back." I was told later that some junkie fashion designer from As Four was having his monthly shit and the bathrooms were full of people doing blow so he squatted on a handbag and pushed out the constipated loaf into the only place he could hide. That was the end of Blobs going to Passerby and I didn't see her again until months later.

I didn't want to stay there after Blobs left so Pinky and I wandered out onto the street. Pinky said, "Let's go get veggie burgers," because we were vegetarians. Pinky's pockets were bulging with all our shit because I had nowhere to put it and together we looked like a British coke dealer and his grunge enforcer. It was a warm spring night and as we walked from the relatively empty Twenty-sixth Street and onto a busy Eighth Avenue, I felt mad at the world. I had just lost the One.

I had my best buddy in town, however, and that meant the riffs were a limitless barrage of lightning bolts destroying everything in their wake and I very quickly cheered up. People hated when we got together because they couldn't handle how fantastic we were. No matter how hard you tried to step to us we would Celebrity Roast you to a crisp before you could finish your last sentence. Back in Montreal, a big-titted slut named Sarah and her snarky friend Rebecca said, "You know, you guys are great alone but when you're together, you're total assholes and it bums people out." Pinky put his finger on his mouth in a pensive way and then said, "Um, yeah, but didn't we fuck you?" Snap! Because we had. The first time we met them.

Tonight felt like every conversation would be exactly like that. Women would try to tell us to fuck off, but we wouldn't be able to hear them because they'd have our dicks in their mouths. We were strutting like teenage roosters and if there was a soundtrack playing it would have included songs like "I Get Money" and "I Run New York." At the crest of this ego tsunami, a car full of incredibly hot black chicks pulled up next to us and crawled along at a walking pace. The car was a beat-up Honda Civic but the girls were pimped out. The women we saw at Passerby were fashionable and well aware of the cultural references we were referencing. This was on some other shit. These girls were so intense it wasn't so much sexy as it was scary. They were dressed in thigh-high leather boots and had the kind of colored contacts you didn't see until ten years later on Halloween. They had long, crazy nails with diamonds in them and fluorescent pink miniskirts. They were what I now know to be "freaks" but all my naïve Canadian eyes saw were three New Wave hookers looking for a friend.

"Where you goin', baby?" the dark-skinned driver said to me out her window with Farrah Fawcett blond hair blowing in the wind.

"We're goin' to get veggie burgers," I said in a Canadian accent that sounded like a prepubescent farmer.

She said, "What?" and I said, "Vegetarian burgers." I could tell she had no fucking clue what I was talking about but was so eager to hook up, she was willing to pretend she did. "You want a lift?" she asked, smiling and revealing even more gold teeth than I had.

"Fuck yeah," I said.

I pushed Pinky to the other side of the car and we both got in either back door. Now I could really see what we were in for. The driver was still the freakiest, but the girl in the passenger seat and the one squeezed between Pinky and me were definitely top-flight fly booty bitches. They looked like black ghetto versions of Lady Gaga. They all shared the driver's *Charlie's Angels* hair in various colors but the one in the passenger seat had on a fucking catsuit with a leather string lacing up the area below her love melons so tightly, it made her cleavage heave up to her throat. The one between us was wearing white hot pants, a shredded neon yellow tank top, and my Achilles' heel: heels with ankle socks. Seeing her short pink socks peek out of five-inch patent-leather white pumps made my heart flutter and I shot a thankful glance up to God that said, "Mah nigga."

The Honda took an immediate right and the insanely hot slut driver looked at me through the rearview mirror and asked, "Where we goin'?" I told her about the burger joint in the East Village we always go to and Pinky piped in with, "It's just by Saint Mark's Place—in the vicinity at least." When this black man opened his white mouth, every girl in the car turned around like he just said, "I'm a bomb," and blew up. Though Pinky looks like every other black dude in Bed-Stuy, he is from Canada and talks like a white news anchor with a pickle up his ass. He's about as African-American as Nelson Mandela. After staring at him for a second they looked at each other and giggled.

"OK, we go there then," my ho added. I had already chosen the driver as my mate but there were three of them and I figured the best way to do this would be to switch it up regularly for the duration of this long-term relationship. I thought of the Beastie Boys song where they say, "And we all switch places when I ring the bell." Maybe we'd get a bell. We'd go up to the Bronx twice a week for sex parties with our new steady girlfriends. We'd bring dildos and double dongs and watch them fuck each other before whipping out our real dicks and showing them why man is better than machine. Then I started getting mad at all my cynical friends. "*Penthouse Forum* is a lie," they'd scoff. "Shit like that doesn't happen in real life."

"Oh yeah," I thought, having a silent argument with people who weren't even there, "then what's this? Huh? I'll tell you what this is. This is sexual people with big libidos who aren't chained down by societal norms. We are post–sexual revolution, post-AIDS, post-fear. We seize life by the sex organs and mash them together until they explode into a sea of secretions. We are the New Millennium Lovers!" I was so far gone, I already had a name for our sex cult. Then I caught my girl staring at me with her green eyes. I was sitting directly behind her and she couldn't take the sexual tension.

"Oooh, you fucking fine, you know that?" she said.

"They both making my pussy wet," passenger-seat ho said. Pinky started to seem uncomfortable and I remember getting pissed at him. Was he just another one of these naysayers who hate the exciting and spontaneous world we live in? Then the girl with the ankle socks grabbed my fucking package and said, "I bet this one got a big ol' dick." Even though I wasn't remotely hard, I pulled down my track pants and underwear to my ankles and she ran her hands up and down my hairy inner thigh. I felt like I was cheating on my driver girlfriend, but this was an orgy, so fuck it. Then my girl said, "Where you live? I need to get that fucking dick." I'm still ashamed of how nerdily I said this, but I gots ta keep it real. I said, "Well, I'm down on Ludlow Street but it appears you ladies are a little too horny to wait that long so maybe we should just—"

Before I could say "pull over," she had screeched into an empty space next to a fire hydrant. We were barely three blocks from Passerby and it was on. In one fluid motion, she yanked up the parking brake, turned completely around, and shot her chair back so the top of it was pinning me to my seat. Then she got right in my face and said with those alien eyes, "Oooh yeaaaah. I'm gonna suck your dick and you gonna fuck me in my ass. You know that?" As she put her arms around me, she stuck out her tongue and flicked it up and down like a horny cobra. It had a diamond in the center and I was hypnotized.

As she continued to rub her hands and tongue all over my neck and ears, I looked over to my right and saw the girl in the middle was opening a box of wet wipes. "Wait a minute," I thought, finally gaining some sanity, "why would she have a box of wet wipes? She didn't know we were going to meet tonight. She didn't even know the New Millennium Lovers existed. Shit! Has she done this before?"

I looked over at Pinky. We were in a car full of crazy-looking prostitutes slithering like snakes and moaning like alley cats in estrus. And they brought wet wipes! Pinky was as bug-eyed as I was and out of nowhere I started an involuntary panicked chant: "Too weird. Too weird. Too weird. Too weird. Too weird. Too weird." Then Pinky chimed in, "Too weird. Too weird. Too weird." We were not trying to be funny. The New Millennium Lovers were fucking scared. We kept our necks straight like Beaker in *The Muppet Show* and started swerving our torsos back and forth doing a petrified robot dance and repeating, "Too weird. Too weird. Too weird. Too weird." Like the whole system was shutting down and it did not compute.

With my pants still at my ankles I began scrabbling for the door handle. Pinky did the same and our mantra was getting louder: "Too weird! Too weird! Too weird!" Our hostess looked equally sketched out as I finally jiggled the door open around the same time Pinky did. I stumbled out of the car and fell on my ass in the middle of the road, and Pinky rolled onto the sidewalk. As I frantically scurried backward to get out of the way, the car SCREECHED out of its spot and laid rubber all the way down the block, almost swerving into the parked cars on the other side of the street. By the time I pulled my pants up and walked over to Pinky, they were gone.

"Did we just blow the greatest opportunity of our lives or did we just save our lives?" I asked him.

"I don't think they were horny," he replied.

"But how did they know we weren't criminals?" I asked. "How did they know we didn't have guns? They must have had their own gun in the glove compartment. Holy shit, we almost died!" I grabbed Pinky freaking out. "Pinky!" I pleaded. "Please tell me my wallet is still in your pocket."

He hit his hand against his hip. "It is," he said, relieved. Then he looked up at my face and asked, "But where's your gold chain?" I touched my neck and felt nothing but neck. That hypnosis had cost me $1,000.

It's New York. I got hustled.

# Asian Cocaine Orgy (2000)

I always did pretty well with poon tang and it's because I just keep going for it. I'm always down and girls can tell. They know I want to smell their ass. They can smell it on me. Nothing is out of bounds. If a woman was menstruating I'd just say, "Well paint my dick white and call it a tampon because I'm horny." Shit, to this day my only problem with women breast-feeding in public is they don't wink back.

For a while I didn't even care what her personality was like. If she wasn't funny, I'd take her back to my place early. "Fuck 'em if they can't take a joke." Some, like Stéphanie, Nancy, and Jasmine, were potential wives. Others were just colostomy bags for my cum. I couldn't imagine life without pussy. When I think of a guy buying a blow-up doll not as a joke, it makes me want to cry.

When I was in a band, my currency was up and I could fuck almost anyone I wanted to. When the bands were done and Vice was broke I marked myself down to 50 percent off and fucked fatties, AKA "slumpbusters." I managed to lay a good three hundred women over the course of twenty years and they were usually in the 7 range. That sounds like a lot of bitches but over seventeen years of fucking, it's just over one a month.

I was never into buxom blondes because that's what my mother is and I have a reverse Oedipal complex. They had to be brunettes, and that left mostly Jews, Chinks, Negroes, and Pakis. If you ever get the opportunity to fuck a Jewish broad, grab it by the short and curlies and hang on for dear life. Their dirty talk is so raunchy it will straighten out your dick. "Kill me" replaces the usual "Fuck me" and it's not unusual to get an e-mail from them the next day that says, "Thank you for raping me last night." I can't talk about it anymore, or I'm going to get a boner.

After seeing Blobs for the first time I could feel I was getting toward the end of my single days. I was starting to get bored. I'd give myself handicaps to make it interesting. I'd try to fuck two Jennifers in a row. It took a mountain of planning but I once fucked five different Asians in five consecutive days. Another way to keep it fun was threesomes. I preferred two girls and me but I often spit-roasted chicks with a buddy (dick in the cunt while she sucks him off). I've had people say to me, "Isn't that queer? Being with another guy?" Anyone who says that hasn't tried it. You're way too busy taking care of business to care about a nude dude over there. It's like two mobsters digging a hole for a dead body. Your focus is on the hole and if your shovels happen to clink, big whup. Shit, I once tried so hard to double-stuff a woman I didn't realize I had actually pushed my dick past her asshole and into her vagina, where it was snuggled next to the other guy's dick. It was weird for about a third of a second, then I beat off into her hair.

Vice retained a Montreal office after moving to New York and we'd occasionally go back there to do boring stuff like check on the books or see how a new employee was doing. This time it was my turn and I was looking forward to it. For the first time ever, I had some money in my pocket and could afford a nice hotel and some serious partying. Ideally I would get a few grams of Gary Glitter and have a threesome with some drunk French sluts. Then I'd go get drunk with my buddies.

Threesomes are a cinch if you're good-looking and famous. I'm ugly and hated so I had to work hard to set them up. I was also lucky enough to come across an insatiable whore named Sally Woo who was a reporter and was quite possibly the solar system's naughtiest girl. She also had a pussy so tight, I wouldn't have been shocked if her pee came out as mist. I met her doing a feature on *Vice* and after flirting with her for about two minutes, I noticed she had no panties on and she had moisture dripping down her leg like a horny teardrop. I'm not kidding. That's how much of a filthy whore she was.

Her voice sounded like a frog was being strangled but she was hot and like many Chinks, her body was perfect.

The night we met and many nights after, I abused the shit out of her with my dick. There were no limits with Sally: anal beads up her butt, a ball gag in her mouth, I could tie her up with rope or duct tape . . . Shit, I could sit on her face if I wanted to. I once fucked her butt with so much relentless gusto, her anus looked like a baby yawning. Her name was written in stone in my little black book and it stayed there the entire time I was single.

Sally lived in Quebec City, which is a few hours' drive from the Montreal office I was visiting, but she was such a horndog she agreed to make the trip and meet me. "But here's the deal," I said on the phone from New York. "There's going to be another girl there, my ex-girlfriend. Her name's Genevieve and I can't guarantee she'll be into this so we're going to get sneaky."

She was "totes 'trigued," as she liked to say because abbreviations are popular in the girl community.

"I'm going to say you're a gift I bought for her," I said.

"Like a whore?" she asked in her witchlike voice. Before I could come up with a nicer synonym, like "masseuse," she blurted out, "I love it!"

Genevieve is half-Filipino, which means you get to have your cake (Asian) and eat it too (fat ass). Not only had she avoided the Asian curse of no butt, she could drink like Dean Martin. She was small and cute and looked like a squirrel would if it modeled for fashion magazines. Oh yeah, she also came from being fucked in the ass.

The hotel was a new, overdesigned, fancy-pants joint called the Saint Paul in Old Montreal, and when I got there, Sally was already sitting in the lobby on a strange spherical chair. I checked in without saying hello and then silently pointed to the elevator, where she was instructed to join me. We rode the elevator in silence. I was pretending to be furious and it was turning her on. I was thirty at this point and old enough to know women like to be abused. Not "Cook me some fuckin' eggs, woman" abused but "Get on your knees, slut" abused— BUT there needs to be some moderation employed. You can cum all over a bitch's face while telling her she's a fucking whore as long as you get out of that zone immediately afterward and run to get a towel so she can clean up. It also helps to ask, "Who did this to my baby?" as she wipes it off so she knows the bad man is gone.

But the bad man had just arrived so I walked into the room, slapped the smile off her face, and told her to get some fucking shoes on. "Ankle socks first!" I commanded as she scrambled around the room getting set up. I made her take everything else off and then said, "Bend over and show me your asshole," which looked delicious. Then I walked around the room staring at her as she waited for her next command. "You like to show me your ass, don't you, you fucking pig?" I asked with a schlong so engorged with blood, it could easily have smashed a coconut. She obediently nodded and I pretended that set me off. I grabbed her by the arm and pushed her on the ground, where she got her mouth impersonally fucked like she was a blow-up doll. The gagging sound was so "out of order," as the British would say, that I almost blew my load right there and had to stop. "Is something wrong?" she asked. You can't break character during these things and I couldn't say, "Oh, sorry, that just felt so nice, I nearly ejaculated," so I dragged her to the bathroom and made her get on all fours with her head over the toilet.

As I nailed her from behind, I decided it was time I took this shit to the next level and actually push her head in the toilet. That would be a new level of degradation and my cap could do with the feather. But for the first time ever, Sally resisted. The harder I pushed her head down, the harder she pushed it back up. This is a tricky situation. You have to say the Serenity Prayer and try to figure out if forcing it would make her cry—thereby ruining everything—or if she is testing you to see how much of a man you are. Sometimes tests like this can pull both of you out of it and the whole thing is ruined, like in *Bitter Moon* when

Emmanuelle Seigner pushes the guy in the pig mask off her and says, "You ruined it! Pigs don't talk."

I decided not to push it and pulled things back a smidge by positioning her on her back next to the sink and drilling her like a fucking jackhammer until I felt that telling tingle and it was time to give her eyes a pearl necklace.

The whole event looked like a disgusting rape movie that turned out to be a snuff film, but as soon as that last Silly String of jizz hit her eyebrow and I finished my ten seconds of postorgasm twitches, we were Ken and Barbie. I passed her a hand towel and washed the ass juice off my face in the sink as she took off her stilettos and found *Finding Nemo* on demand. Sally was not a member of Mensa and this wasn't a kid's movie for her. Within minutes she was completely engrossed. Fine. I ordered burgers and we sat there like a married couple with a deep, dark secret. We had set back feminism a hundred years.

By the time Nemo was found, it was getting dark and I had to go meet Genevieve. It was also time to get some fucking coke. This was supposed to be a party, not a Pixar film festival.

Dinner with Genevieve was pleasant, but I was severely distracted by the imminent orgy keeping my dick hard under the table. The fact that she had no idea made things about thirty times hotter. "Let's go back to my hotel," I said after settling the dinner bill. Genevieve had a pretty good buzz on and I could tell she would be up for anything. I sent a text to Sally telling her to go to the bar downstairs.

In the taxi, something hit me hard. I still didn't have any coke. "Do you have a guy?" I asked Genevieve. She reached into her purse and showed me a small bag of cocaine. I was so happy I grabbed her and we started making out.

By the time we got into the room she already had her shirt off and her bouncy little tits were winking at me like two innocent little Bambis. "Wait," I said after stopping a French kiss with my tongue in midair, "I have a surprise for you." I texted Sally the word "now" and got back to making out. Genevieve said, "What's going on?" with my tongue in her mouth, and before we knew it, the door opened.

Like I said. Sally isn't a genius. She was supposed to knock. Why would a sex worker already have a key? Genevieve was startled by the stranger and I broke the tension by being gregarious and jolly like the owner of a Greek restaurant. "Ah, great, you must be Sally," I said, greeting her with open arms.

Genevieve hid her tits with the blankets as I explained what was going on. "I got you a gift," I said. Genevieve was confused and Sally smiled awkwardly. "She's a masseuse," I said as I undid her dress. "Let's do a line," I said to break the tension. I had pulled Genevieve's bag out of her purse and was disappointed to see it was only about a quarter-gram (about as much as half a crushed-up Tylenol) but it still broke the ice. Genevieve dropped her guard and let the sheets fall from her boobs as Sally walked over without doing her dress back up. I laid out three reasonable lines and feasted my eyes on the four smiling little tits around me. When Sally's turn came, she stopped about a tenth of the way in and pulled back holding her nose. "I don't know how to snort coke," she said, wincing. "It hurts my nose."

"No problem," I said, vacuum cleaning the rest up my nostril. Genevieve cheerily went to open the minibar but it was locked. I called downstairs and after providing my room number the guy said, "Wait, are you THE Gavin McInnes?" What an awesome thing to hear right after two giant lines of blow.

"Fuck yeah," I said, remarkably full of myself.

"You want anything else besides your bar key?" he asked.

"Whaddya got?" I suavely replied like Marlon Brando leaning on the bar in *The Wild One*.

"I'll be right up," he said before quickly hanging up the phone.

Both girls were now standing next to each other. I sucked Genevieve's right booby, then her left one, and did the same to Sally. Halfway through Sally's left one, there was a knock at the door. Sally closed her dress and Genevieve grabbed a bathrobe as a dorky redhead with a scruffy beard and glasses pushed in a cart with a pile of beers on the top and a bucket of ice. He also opened up the minibar. We shook hands and exchanged niceties and he asked me if I'd "like to do any of this." He was holding a pillowcase-sized bag of coke. After dumping out at least a gram onto our little coke area he rolled up a bill and handed it to me. I did the first one and everyone but Sally took their turn. "Her nose hurts," I told him. He asked me some boring questions about Vice and we all bid each other adieu. Later, Whatsyourname. I got shit to fuck.

The second the door clicked shut, I tossed Sally on the bed and threw Genevieve on top of her. They began making out and I ripped their panties off—literally (chicks love that). Genevieve grabbed my neck and pushed it into Sally's face. Fine. So we began kissing as I wrestled my pants off and my boner popped out. I flopped over onto my back and then sat up as Sally mounted me. Genevieve was behind Sally and just kind of kissing Sally's neck and rubbing her tits on Sally's back. It was AWESOME. I was frantically videotaping every detail with my eyes like Robert Conrad told me to but it was pretty difficult because I was wasted. Wait, where's Genevieve? I reached behind Sally and couldn't find her. I kept going down her back until I realized she was eating Sally's ass. I was excited as a puppy on meth but the secret to good sex is to treat it like a girl's record collection: no Rush. As Sally slowly rode up and down my wiener, she had Genevieve's face buried between her cheeks. If there's anything better than that, I would like to meet it and make sure it becomes president. I put my hands on the back of Genevieve's head and pulled it so deep into Sally's rear, she almost disappeared.

I pushed Sally off and rewarded Genevieve with some serious punitive boning. We covered all the bases. I had Sally sit on Genevieve's face so we could make out as I fucked Genevieve on her back in a triangle position. I got both of them on top of each other and went from vagina to vagina, making sure every STD in the room was divided up evenly. The coke and booze made me last way longer than the thirty seconds I could normally summon in such a situation, but we all have to die sometime and my *petit mort* came around . . . now. I pulled out and committed my final act of brilliance, the snowball. Snowballing is when you cum in one girl's mouth and she keeps it there so she can French-kiss the other girl.

"Don't swallow it!" I blurted out as I filled Genevieve's mouth with about a quart of melted wax. They were both sitting up and Sally knew what was to come next. "Now kiss her," I commanded. As they began a cum-soaked smooch session, I switched my mental recorder to HD and recorded about seven thousand frames per second. Since this went down I have probably beat off to it 3,030 times. That's enough jizz to fill an ocean liner and it only took five seconds to "film."

The girls showered individually and we listened to music on my computer, drank beer, and finished the coke. Peppered in this two-hour experience was occasional soft-dick sucking and numb-pussy eating and I think one of them even sucked my toes, but it was real sloppy and more like Sid and Nancy than an interesting porno. I'm happy it happened but after the initial decadence, it got old. Two days later, I booked the next flight home and thought about Blobs the whole time.

# Circles or Strokes? (2001)

Before settling down, however, I had some unturned stones. Back in high school there was a mind-boggling knockout named Tricia who was so far out of my league, she got insulted if I looked at her. She dressed like a wealthy librarian and looked like Jessica Alba with a drinking problem. She was also a cunt, which made her twice as appealing. I love cunts.

As the years crept on, her currency went down and mine went up. By the time she was in her early thirties she had packed on some lard and I was a successful media mogul stationed in New York, center of the galaxy. It took almost twenty years, but we were finally on the same level. We started flirting via e-mail and talking about the old days and I made the commitment to hang out with her the next time I was in Toronto, where she now lived.

A month later, I was in town visiting Pinky, who had just recently moved to Toronto. He and I convinced Tricia and her friend to meet us at a reunion of a cheesy Canadian metal band called Helix. When we got there, I was chuffed to see she still had that cute doe face with her upturned lips and huge eyelashes but I was a little bummed to see her bum. It had become so large, her front side had grown a gunt (gut that goes to the cunt) just to balance it out. The hottest girl in high school had turned into a Weeble. She wore clunky platform sandals that were a far cry from the stilettos that are my boner's bread and butter. We hugged and grabbed a drink and after a few comedic jousts I realized she was really fucking boring.

The night was a bit of a slog but having the opportunity to bend over the greatest missed opportunity of my high school career made it worth it. After a slew of venues and dull conversations, Pinky took Tricia's friend home and I got to work on the head of my high school's in crowd.

Her apartment was a studio with a bed on the floor at one end and a couch with a coffee table at the other. Unfortunately, she also had two very furry cats, which put a huge dent in my plan because I am allergic as fuck to cats. Within minutes, I could feel hives on my face and a lump in my throat, and my eyes felt like they were wearing fur sweaters made of itchiness. Oh well, still worth it. Tricia said she had to slip into something more comfortable and I sat on the couch awaiting the lingerie show.

What I got instead was a frumpy bore in glasses, a ponytail, and sweatpants. No worries. I could still work with this. I dragged her over to the bed and started Frenching her with all the enthusiasm of a rejected tenth grader. "I look gross, right?" she asked, holding her glasses in front of her face. Before I could try to pretend she wasn't a human letdown, she uttered, "We can't have sex."

Sometimes when girls say that they mean, "I only want to fuck if you're really into it and you get me nice and horny because I don't want to feel bad about myself afterward." In college we were taught "'no' means 'no,'" but my experience has been more like "three 'nos' mean 'no.'" I took off her pants and tried to do the same with her shirt, but she wasn't having it. "No," she said, refastening her bra after I popped the clasp. We were still kissing, so I assumed it was still on, but when my hand slowly made its way to her bulbous mound, she uttered a second "no" and added, "Like, literally." I told her "Like, literally" is a contradiction as I rolled her over to massage her back. Eventually it was time to try feeling her substantial ass. This went well, so I rested my boner on her butt like a content lizard, and even though we both still had our underwear on, she issued her third "no," my third strike.

Frustrated, I rolled off her and lay on my back. She explained she had just ended a long relationship and wasn't ready. I looked down, and my dick yawned at me. She could see I was about to walk out the door. "But I'll give you a blow job!" she said enthusiastically. This seemed like quite the jump from "Like, literally," but I'll take it.

Then she sat up and got a condom from her night table. "You need to put this on first," she said like a brainwashed teenager.

"Are you kidding me?" I asked. "That's what prostitutes do." How did an educated woman in a big city in the twenty-first century get so fucking square? "I'd rather just not have one, thanks," I said, cringing but angry.

"All right," she said, "want me to masturbate you?" Ew. Is there a worse phrase in the English language? Say you want to jerk me off or better yet, don't say anything and just grab the fucking thing. "Masturbate you" sounds like you work on a farm and need a sperm sample for the sows because they're in heat.

"Yeah," I said, desperately trying to make the situation less clinical.

"All right," she said as she knelt next to my crotch and put her hand on my pelvis like a nurse. Then she looked up and asked one of the grossest/weirdest sexual questions I've ever heard: "You want circles or strokes?"

I was traumatized. I still am.

What the fuck are "circles"? You rotate my knob 360 degrees until the cum sprays out in a giant circle? You cup your hand around my dick and then spin around me like it's a brass pole? Vaginas don't Hula-Hoop. Where does the uppy-downy motion come into play? You *do* know how a dick works, don't you? And what are "strokes"? Do you wrap your hand around the dick at all, or do you just "wax on/wax off" like the Karate Kid painting a fence? I didn't say any of this but instead condensed it all into, "You know what? Forget it!" and rolled over in a rage. She shrugged and lay down facing the opposite direction. As I was drifting off and hating the entire universe, she quietly said, "Just because I'm a sexual lame-o doesn't mean we can't still be friends."

I sternly replied, "Of course," and then added, "it does, you stupid bitch," in my head.

# September 11 (2001)

$S$hortly before the day that polarized the world, I had met Blobs at our local bar Max Fish and she went from unicorn-I-will-never-see-in-real-life to kind-of-girlfriend. I was still getting blind drunk every night, however, so the courtship wasn't as romantic as it should have been. From the day I met her to a few months before I married her five years later, we had a turbulent relationship where she was constantly dumping me for not being "boyfriend material" and I was constantly trying to get her back by pretending I was.

On the night before September 11, Pinky was in town again, and bringing apologetic flowers to my new lady was far from my mind. The beer pounding started the second he got off the plane and we were already slurring when we caught up with Matt Sweeney, musician Andrew W.K., and ex–Hole bassist/fellow Canuck Melissa Auf der Maur. They had rented a karaoke room and we all sang, danced on the couches, and poured beer all over the place until we got kicked out. It was a night of relentless partying and by six A.M. we were so hoarse we couldn't say "good night."

A mere three hours later, someone was pounding on my front door. It was Blobs. I figured she must have been furious I didn't call her last night. I opened the door and she frantically said, "Turn on the TV." She wasn't mad. She was petrified. Pinky was asleep on the floor. I turned it on and saw the World Trade Center shooting out smoke. As usual, the sensory overload gave me gas and as Pinky sat up to see what was going on, he was greeted by a dust bowl of shit wind blowing right in his face. He pounded me in the leg harder than I deserved, and as I yelled, "I couldn't help it!" he said, "My mother's in there, you fucking prick!" I had forgotten his mother lived in New Jersey and worked there. I'd just huge-farted in a guy's face as his mother died. This is what the whole day was like, a juxtaposition of hungover jokes and the worst thing in the universe. It was like Beavis and Butthead do the Holocaust.

We ran up to my building's roof to get a better look. My apartment was above Max Fish, which is only about a mile from Ground Zero, and when we got to the roof we were gobsmacked by the carnage. "It's just a really big fire," I conjectured, and before Pinky could chime in we noticed another plane flying way too low. It silently disappeared into the other tower and a huge explosion engulfed the hole. "Holy shit!" we both yelled. Blobs was trying to call her mother and our roof was filling up with other tenants. No one knew what was going on. They were all walking around like catatonic zombies.

Blobs trying to get through to her mom. (2001)

## September 11 (2001)

After about twenty minutes of watching the towers pour smoke into the sky like a broken underwater oil pipe, we ran downstairs to watch the news. The anchors were all guessing at this point, but the consensus seemed to be it was an attack. Pinky's brown face was ghost-white. He looked at me and asked if I thought his mom was alive. It was a rhetorical question, but I played along. "I'm sure she's fine, dude," I lied. "It's just one or two floors in each building."

It had been just over half an hour since Blobs woke us up and as we were starting to get a grip on what was happening, a plane smashed into the fucking Pentagon. Then they cut back to the WTC and we saw people holding hands and jumping to their deaths.

Construction was going on in the apartment next door and we couldn't hear the TV. We ran back up to the roof, which was now filled with everyone in the building. People traded what few facts they had and as I spoke to my upstairs neighbor I heard a shout. I looked at the horizon and watched the first tower collapse. Pinky sat on the ground. I put my hand on his shoulder and told him his mother had plenty of time to get out. I was bluffing.

We ran downstairs and heard talk of a fourth plane. We also heard talk of the air force having to take it down. Then it crashed into a field. The construction was still going on next door, so I ran over and pounded on their door in a rage. A perplexed-looking man with a Polish accent answered and said, "Yes?"

"Do you fucking idiots know what is going on!?" I screamed.

"Yes," he said, motioning for me to calm down while pointing to the radio he and the other workers were listening to. "Two buildings go boom." He was making a collapsing gesture with his hands and I yelled, "QUIET!" before running back to my apartment. When I got inside, I saw he was right. It was buildings, plural. When was this going to end?

By eleven A.M. the terrorist attack was complete. They spent a few hundred grand separating the world into two groups and we would spend trillions trying to put it back together. We were in the center of our generation's Pearl Harbor and didn't know what to do. So we went to a bar.

The streets were deserted but for the occasional tank crawling down

Houston Street. Max Fish was closed so we made our way up Avenue A, where the bars were already packed and everyone was glued to the TV. The elephant in the room was Pinky's dead mother so I kept talking and talking, hoping he wouldn't stop to think about the odds.

"I know people are going to say we deserved this," I said, "but that's implying these guys are rational. They're madmen. They're kamikazes. What do they know about fair?" Pinky wasn't interested, and we walked to a bar called Doc Holliday's on Ninth Street and Avenue A.

A lot of Blobs's friends were already there and more friends started to come in and sit with us. We watched the news with one eye and shared theories. Soon Pinky's situation came up in the conversation and quickly made its way around the bar. People put their hands on his back to console him and I continued pretending everything was dandy.

The whole thing was very scary and sad, but the way all these strangers came together was something else. I've always said that people are inherently good. They may be selfish and lazy at times but when they need each other, they cooperate. Pinky kept checking his phone and making sure it was working. Reception was bad and few people could make calls, but anyone who got a few bars on their phone would hand it over to him so he could call. He was also calling his brother up in Toronto every thirty minutes from a pay phone. His brother had no news.

It was now well into the afternoon and things were looking grim. Lots of people had heard from their relatives by now and Pinky was still coming up empty. It was becoming impossible to pretend everything was okay. We could have made a "missing" poster for her but we weren't quite that naïve. It was over. She was dead. Then, out of nowhere, he got a call. It was his brother. He had heard from his mother and she was fine.

The whole bar cheered, and everyone at our table was crying and hugging him. He was in tears, too, and after thanking everybody and hugging us back, he ran out of the bar to go be with her.

We found out later she had escaped death by minutes. She got to work in Tower One early that day and was furious to discover her secretary hadn't done the photocopies needed for a big presentation. She was going to have to go all the way to another building to get everything ready. She left her purse on her desk and went down with a file folder full of important documents. The first plane hit as she was doing her photocopies. Her purse, along with her desk, along with people she had worked with for almost ten years, were all obliterated. Then she watched through the window as the second plane hit. She walked outside and was covered in dust. Then she walked like a gray ghost down through the Holland Tunnel and up into Jersey, where she eventually got it together enough to call her sons.

While this was going on my friend Sprague, a photographer who did fashion shoots for Vice, was in the thick of it. Just before the towers collapsed, a firefighter grabbed him and told him to help clean up. He was happy to oblige until he started hearing these incredibly loud *pops* and realized they were bodies exploding as they hit the ground. "Cleaning up" meant picking up body parts and throwing them on palettes that were then lifted away. He did this for twenty-four hours and has not been the same since. Every time I think about Sprague I think of what many call a "religion of peace" where a good 25 percent think suicide bombing is sometimes or often justified. Twenty-five percent of the 1.5 billion Muslims in the world is 375 million. Holy shit.

After Doc Holliday's, Blobs and I headed over to visit a guy we sarcastically called the Wolf because he always managed to pull an "Irish good-bye" by sneaking out of parties without telling anyone at the end of the night. As a game, we'd try to keep an eye on him all night but no matter how hard we tried, *poof.* He'd be gone. The Wolf was at his apartment with his girlfriend Marcie and like most of the world, they were watching the news. The Wolf was a heavily tattooed gigantic guy who had the same life history as me. Our bands were even in the same issue of the punk zine *Maximumrocknroll* back in 1990. In 2001, he was managing bands and he worked out of our office because we were all drinking buddies. He had seen the whole thing from his roof on Avenue B and was still reeling after seeing Puerto Rican teenagers across the street cheering and yelling, "Yeah, nigga! *Bomb* that shit!" That part still makes me mad.

As we sat in the Wolf's apartment in a state of shock, I broke the silence by suggesting we buy a huge pile of cocaine. The Wolf was disgusted at first but came to love the idea more than I did. "Think of all the times we sat here doing lines all night and talking about stupid shit like how owls are cool," he said to me, Blobs, and Marcie. "Well, now we finally have something to talk about!" He was right. We really had spent hours previously discussing how cool owls are. We spent the next nine hours inhaling mountains of blow, watching the news, and talking our jaws off.

The next day, the city was completely shut down. You needed a copy of your utility bill to get past the barricades to your home and the only places open were bars. Blobs was asleep but I was too jacked up to join her, so I stuffed my pockets full of mail and ID and went on a bike ride by myself. It was about nine A.M. on September 12 and I rode south down an empty Ludlow Street and toward the Williamsburg Bridge to Brooklyn. The enclosed bike path above the bridge was closed and so was the main part cars go on, but I dragged my bike under a barrier and rode across the "cars only" part to Brooklyn. It feels weird to be on that bridge with no protective cage around you. At any moment I could have turned a sharp left and disappeared into the East River forever. A strong wind could have resulted in the same. I made my way past the hump and coasted toward Brooklyn. A plastic bag blew past me in a loop and then disappeared over the edge.

I turned around, went back home, and crawled into bed with Blobs.

e-mail contact he wrote ryanmcginley@internet.com because he didn't have an e-mail address but didn't want to look unprofessional. I'd go over to his tiny apartment and root through boxes trying to find images for the magazine. It's what cheap people do when they don't want to pay real photographers, and the kids love it because they get exposure. Besides, you get better pictures from amateurs. They're more honest and daring and there's no ego involved. It's "This is my friend Mark jumping into garbage" instead of "This is an old black man's hands as he plays the blues" or "This is a model on the toilet" (I must have seen those last two dozens of times). Unfortunately, once you turn a bitch out, she gets hungry for more and within a few years, Ryan had gone from photo intern to photo editor to darling of *The New York Times*. He used to be honored to be in my magazine and now he was blowing off my phone calls? It was time for a talk.

I was still dating Blobs and planned to meet her at a party called Smiths Night in Tribeca but told her to come late as I was going to meet Ryan across the street first. We met at a crappy Irish bar and as soon as he walked in the door, I explained to him what loyalty is and how he'd be nowhere without me. He said I was just jealous of his newfound fame and it wasn't Vice that got his career going, it was his photo zines (handmade booklets he put together with his best photos, which he passed out to magazine editors and industry types). The truth is, we were both a little bit right but the real thing that made Ryan is what makes everyone: He worked his ass off. Everyone gets their fifteen minutes, but the secret to success is to bust your ass during that blip and establish yourself as someone worth everybody's time. When Ryan felt the first fish nibble, he yanked the line as hard as he could and didn't stop reeling until the entire commercial, editorial, and high-end art worlds were in his boat. When *The New York Times* asked Ryan to shoot Olympic swimmers, he rented all kinds of underwater cameras and strange lenses, staying at the pool for days on end. He shot hundreds of pictures and the dozen or so he kept are still some of his best work. He was invited back and soon had his own show at the Whitney Biennial. The pictures we used from his early days were what they call "documentary photography" and featured New York kids snorting coke, getting laid, and puking their guts out. He even did a series of puking self-portraits that I can't look at without dry-heaving. Almost half of his pictures were of his best friend, an orphan of sorts named Dash Snow whom we declared our unofficial mascot. Ten years later *New York* magazine put Ryan and Dash and their friends on its cover under the title "Warhol's Children." Eventually, however, that whole crew imploded when their hijinks landed two in jail. They stole a picture from a gallery and ran out laughing. "It was a spur-of-the-moment act, a juvenile prank, but one that had far-reaching consequences," as *The New York Times* put it in a huge article they did on the incident entitled "Unmerry Prankster."

Ryan survived the prank and didn't go to jail. Instead, he grew up fast and continued to grab his career by the balls. As I write this, he is finishing a Levi's campaign, which, in the world of photography, is like becoming president. It pays something like seven million dollars. You see? That's how you do New York. People say it's like riding the bull, but it's more like riding the bullshit. You gotta do the hustle and work hard for the money and don't stop 'til you get enough and a bunch of other disco lyrics.

When I had my sit-down with Ryan, all this was yet to happen and I was under the impression I could keep him under my wing like a baby chick and never let him leave the nest. As he scoffed at my allegations, I noticed he looks exactly like Sid Vicious and I started to doubt myself. He dressed like all New York kids at the time, in a Travis Bickle army coat and huge sneakers, but his face was pure Irish trash, and those people don't take too kindly to being told what to do. I know. I'm one of them.

After about an hour, I realized it was very difficult trying to convince someone of something that isn't true so I threw up my hands and walked out of the bar. Ryan asked me where I was going and as I told him to fuc—*WHAM!* I felt a thuddening punch to the back of my head. This was the worst punch in the dictionary of punches—a sucker punch. I turned around and pointed to a parking lot without saying a word. Ryan obliged, and we met by the cars to have it out like real men.

What followed looked more like real *old* men. We had our hands up the way boxers did in the 1920s and were sizing each other up like two geriatrics standing over a broken shuffleboard pole. Have you ever been in a fight? It's surprisingly hard to actually hit the guy in the face. Wrestling is one thing and head-butting someone in a bar is another, but actually going toe-to-toe is about as easy as that medieval carnival game where you throw a beanbag through the hole in the wood thingie. Every time I sent one of my Thor-like fists of fury at his head, I'd hit some hair or a sleeve or nothing at all. Then he'd deliver a knockout punch that probably would have broken my nose if my shoulder hadn't blocked it. We were both fighting like we were in the back of an empty eighteen-wheeler that kept hitting potholes. Toward the end, there must have been a dozen blows delivered by both sides and all we had to show for it were one red ear and a cramp. How do you end this type of fight? It's like one of those poos where after about a hundred wipes you say to your asshole, "All right, buddy, shit or get off the pot. I have a life to get back to." In this case, my asshole was Ryan and I told him to stop by putting my hands on my knees and panting. He was also too exhausted to go on and just nodded while patting me on the back.

A small crowd had gathered to witness the brawl and I was mortified to discover Blobs was included in this mess. This pathetic display would surely set me back several weeks of courtship. Instead, the opposite happened. Blobs came over and kissed my lips off before saying, "Oh my God, seeing you fight makes me so hot." That's right, gentlemen, you don't have to win or even get one good punch in to impress the ladies. Simply stepping into the ring gives women a wide-on.

The three of us got in a cab and headed to Max Fish. While Blobs molested me in the cab, Ryan and I continued to pat each other on the back and say, "I love you, man," to each other. But Ryan kept adding, "And I've always wanted to fuck you," which was weird.

It was a perfect autumn night and about half of Max Fish was on the street smoking cigarettes and telling jokes. This was our *Cheers* bar and Ryan immediately struck up a conversation with a very pretty girl who hoped he wasn't gay.

# A Faggot Kicked My Ass (2002)

I was about fifteen feet away and couldn't help but notice he was sitting on a car hood, laughing the same way he had laughed at me back at the bar. I never got him back for that sucker punch. So, I marched toward him with every molecule of force I could possibly summon from all the gods of Hades and delivered an earth-shattering blow to his face that sent him sprawling off the hood and into the street. Ryan was down for the count and I felt kind of bad but that's what you get when you sucker-punch dudes—a sucker punch.

A few seconds later, Ryan was still slumped over and just as I was about to ask him if he was OK, he looked up with a huge smile that went from ear to ear and was filled with blood. His face would have made Batman go to the restroom on himself. He also had a gigantic hole in his cheek where one of my rings had punctured his skin. Jaguar McGinley then leapt at my chest with so much agility, it sent me flying through the air like an anorexic who just stepped on a land mine. They say you're not supposed to let bull terriers fight because they'll learn how fun it is and never want to stop. It's the same with pet rats. You can never let them try meat or they'll get bloodlust and start biting their owners. Ryan's bleeding face was like a breath of fresh air to his pugilist instincts and the old man with his dukes up in the parking lot was now someone you click on after hitting the two-player button in *Street Fighter*. As I scrambled to get up from the first toss, he picked me up and hurled me into a pile of garbage cans. Where did all this strength come from? One of the best descriptions of the fight was from a guy we called Fatboy, who said, "Man, he threw you around like a rag doll." I careened off metal gates and bounced into parked cars. At one point, he wrestled me to the ground and sat on my chest, setting my face up for a bashing of Elephant Man proportions. I barked out, "Ryan, I'm in love with you!" to distract him, and his confusion bought me the tenth of a second I needed to scurry out from under him. This got huge laughs from the crowd that had gathered. I was kind of hoping someone would break it up, but this wasn't that kind of crowd. They were frantically taking pictures and shouting out advice, like "Kick his face!" and "Bite!"

We used one of the photos for our table of contents. That's
Ryan with the hole in his face, me buried under his arm,
and a guy named Steve who popped in to pose for the photo.
(2002)

I've been in a lot of fights over the years and they usually go like this one. I will take on any motherfucker who has a problem and I will almost definitely lose. I will, however, get at least one good punch in, and that's all you need.

During a pummeling, your adrenaline pumps so hard, you can afford to have dual thoughts. While half of me tried to avoid getting swollen shut, the other half calmly wondered what the hell a grown man was thinking punching a teenager in the face. Ryan was barely twenty at the time. He had a rough childhood and grew up in a house full of brothers, a Jersey kid who had been fighting his siblings since the day he was born. In fact, he's still fighting right now. Whoops, there I go over another car and into some boxes.

Finally, Ryan too was running out of steam and when I finally managed to not be flying through the air, I grabbed his coat, pulled it over his head, and gasped, "Please. We're done." For the second time that night, Ryan agreed. Then he smiled and roared, "Yeaaah!" as a kid called Kid America held Ryan's arm in the air and yelled, "Ladies and gentlemen, we have a winner!"

I stumbled upstairs to my apartment, where Blobs ravaged me so vigorously I now know what it's like to be food. I may have lost the battle but I won the war against not getting laid.

The fight became the talk of our tiny circle and photos of it were everywhere, including my magazine, where I used one for our table of contents.

A few days later at a different bar, Dash and his friend Earsnot took me aside to ask a few questions. Earsnot was a homeless black graffiti writer who grew up on New York's streets and used his gigantic arms to hospitalize anyone who made fun of him for being gay. Dash came from money, but his parents gave up on him at fourteen and sent him to a boarding school for bad kids. He got out two years later and never moved back home. He was alone in the world from a very early age and took fighting way too seriously. They both did. "The thing I don't get," Dash said like we were in a juvenile detention center together and this fight had lost us both our TV privileges, "is why his face is all fucked up and you look all right." I explained that Ryan's facial hole was my only good punch and the rest of the fight was nothing but me flying into things. Dash eventually accepted my explanation and was no longer dubious of his friend's victory. "Just one more question," he asked with his arms around my shoulders. "What's it like to get your ass kicked by a faggot?"

# Bigger Than Texas (2003)

V ice started making trips to South by Southwest back when we were still *Voice of Montreal*. We instantly fell in love with Austin. Austinites were rednecks because they lived in Texas but they were smart because it's a university town. That's what our favorite kind of hosers are: educated drunks. We were a match made in heaven. The city's motto is "Keep Austin weird," and our hosts regularly drove up and down the street yelling, "Don't move here!" at the music journalists who were visiting their lovely town for the festival.

We started going there to meet fellow publishers and get to know which bands were going to be big next year, but after one or two visits the party subsumed all other activities and the whole trip became devoted to getting really, really fucked-up.

Trace was the first guy we met there. He's one of those preppy-looking dudes with a side part and an argyle sweater who grew up going to punk shows and starting fights. He often wore knee-length tweed golf pants from the 1920s and fought so often he once got shot through the femur and now has a steel bar holding up that part of his leg.

By 2003, we had been going to SXSW for almost a decade and had the art of alcohol poisoning down to a science that Trace summed up in an acronym: DOWNER. It's broken down like this . . .

**D**on't cockblock: It's obvious when she likes one more than the other so back off if you notice you're number two.

**O**nly fifteen hours: If you start as early as nine A.M., you're going to have to pack it in by midnight.

**W**ater aplenty: It takes real discipline but almost every time it occurs to you, order a glass of water. If you forget this one too many times in a row, you need to get Roman on your ass and make yourself puke.

**N**ever after four A.M.: This supersedes the fifteen-hours rule so if you start at midnight, you only get four hours of partying in.

**E**at your dinner: Even if cocaine shits out your appetite. Force yourself to eat at least a burger an evening.

**R**egulate your bumps: If you get too greedy with a line, you're going to ruin your drunk buzz, so before you do a bump, take a step back and ask yourself, "Am I not already wasted enough?"

Blobs and I were on the rocks after I went on a particularly long bender so I booked a six A.M. flight with my booze partner Sharky and we started the trip by partying all night in New York. We liked to go to the worst strip clubs in Queens rather than fancy ones in the city because trash is more colorful. That night we went to a now-defunct club in Long Island City called Foxes and the first thing I noticed was a Puerto Rican single mom with deliciously droopy tits in black dad socks.

"I like your socks," I said sincerely over the very loud R & B.

"They're for medicinal purposes," she answered back, assuming I was making fun of her. Soon we were sitting with a girl named Maria who knew we were too cheap for lap dances but hung out with us anyway. "This nigga's better-looking," she said, pointing to Sharky before switching her pointing finger over to me and adding, "But this nigga's balls-out." An hour later she was giving me a free lap dance, which in New York entails a woman taking you to a private booth where she removes her neon-pink underwear to reveal . . . a matching pair of the same underwear. Nude dancing is illegal in New York and this panties ritual is a totally ineffectual way around it. "How come you ain't hard?" Maria said angrily, hitting me in the chest.

"I don't know," I said, and then asked, "Coke?" The bar stayed open until five A.M. and if we had been a few seconds later, we would have missed our flight.

"I have some bad news," I told the stewardess while panting after a long run to the gate. "My friend here is petrified of flying so I was wondering if we could just grab a drink from you before we take off." She hesitated and I told her it would make everything easier for everyone. She said she couldn't and Sharky thanked me for distracting her while he grabbed two tiny bottles of gin.

By the time we got to our connection in Houston, we were at a level of drunk that was poetic. It was too early for bars so I told him to wait around the corner and join me in exactly one minute. Then I walked over to the VIP Gentleman's Club and said, "Hello, I'm Chris Isaak's manager—has he shown up yet?" Then Sharky, who looks a little bit like Chris Isaak, turned the corner and I yelled, "Chris!" He was familiar with this gag and began following me into the VIP room when a black lady from the counter stopped and asked for our membership cards. Her white coworker then rolled her eyes and said, "I've got this, Cheryl," while waving us in. How culturally ignorant of that African-American woman not to know she was talking to country music royalty.

The VIP room went smashingly despite the fact that we had to work the taps ourselves due to a lack of bartenders. When we finally got to Austin after a good fifteen hours of partying, a wealthy entrepreneur we call Stockbroker was waiting for us at the airport in a Cadillac convertible with large steer horns on the front. "Hey, ladies," he said in that strangely effeminate tone all Southerners have, "let's get some drinks." Stockbroker owns two of the best bars in Austin. He looks like a balding old queer with anorexia but he parties like a biker.

I insisted we take a break, as it is number two in the DOWNER rule book, but we both convinced ourselves that landing in a new city wipes the slate clean. When Stockbroker stopped to get gas I was gifted with an idea that was even better than the Chris Isaak ruse. "I'm retarded," I told Sharky, and jumped out of the car with my eyes crossed and my arms crumpled against my chest like a grasshopper. "I'm Timmy," I said to him in Down syndrome. "And you're my brother." I ran away from the car and Sharky chased after me calling, "Timmy, Timmy, get back here."

Timmy was powerless after his new leaf blower became
unplugged. (2003)

At the back of the gas station some Mexicans were using a leaf blower to inflate a large bouncy castle for the kids. Timmy grabbed the leaf blower and started running around the lot shooting garbage into the air and turning everyone who tried to stop him into a Maxell cassette ad. As the Mexicans closed in for the kill, Sharky tackled me and got the leaf blower out of my hand. "No, Timmy! Bad!" he said, handing it back to the illegals. They felt bad that Timmy got in so much shit and assured Sharky it wasn't a big deal. Sharky escorted his handicapped brother back to the car and we explained our discovery to Stockbroker as he pulled out of the gas station and back to the highway.

"I love it," Stock hollered while laughing. Then he started yelling at me, "Goddamnit, Timmy! Stop it! TIMMY!" When we met up with Trace he was equally enthused. Timmy was now the trip's mascot and for the rest of our time there I was Daniel Day-Lewis preparing for the role of Timmy in the Oscar-winning film *Timmy Goes to Texas*. I grabbed women's asses, stole drinks, knocked over tables, and ran away with people's food. People would be furious at first but as soon as they saw my handlers chase me yelling, "Goddamnit, Timmy," their rage turned to sympathy. I could all but murder somebody and it always ended with the victim telling Sharky that everything was okay and no, they wouldn't be pressing charges. Timmy was sent from God and we used him regularly until my wife banned his existence for good shortly after my marriage. I still miss that little guy and his weird little Tyrannosaurus rex arms.

That night, Trace brought us to his friend Amy Rodger's house. Timmy was temporarily retired and we were ready to dilute this testosterone festival with some tits. As we walked in, we were thrilled to see at least five or six very fuckable girls there and most of them had cowboy hats on. Everyone was covered in tattoos, including a fat chef named Chin who had an angry cartoon chef with a cleaver chasing petrified vegetables up his right arm, across his back, and down his left arm. The music was blaring and the house looked like it was used to parties. Austin girls make Glasgow girls look like Islamabad girls and I had no problem getting a girl named Shelly to come into a broom closet with me and pull her pants down. We quietly pumped away with people hooting and hollering in the living room and I pulled out and ejaculated on the ground. She turned around and kissed me before pulling up her pants and saying, "Thanks, I was really fucking horny," as she fastened her belt and confidently walked out of the closet. "This is the best town in the world," I thought.

When we got back to the living room, Trace was having an argument with a guy named Cooper about cyclists shaving their legs. "Are you trying to tell me it's aerodynamic?" Trace asked rhetorically.

"Hell no," Cooper replied. "It's for infections. You get hair in your road rash and it gets infected."

Trace and I both laughed in his face. "When was the last time you ever heard someone saying, 'I would have been fine but I got a leg hair in my cut'?" I asked Cooper.

"Yeah," Trace added, "we're the only mammals not covered in hair. You think bears are running around with infected cuts because they got hair in them?"

Cooper was getting mad and jumped up pointing in my face. "Don't make me kill you, because I might have respect for you later," to which I replied, "Don't make me respect you, because I might have to kill you later."

"That's it!" Trace said, separating us and declaring a truce. "Let's let science settle this. Let's shave one of Cooper's legs and we'll scrape both to—"

Cooper jumped in waving his hands back and forth saying, "Oh hell no. You aren't shaving shit and you ain't cutting shit."

I ran to the bathroom, grabbed one of the ladies' razors, and came back to the living room holding it up like a trophy. "I'll do it," I told the party. "I'll shave one leg and then I'll cut both of them open and we'll see what heals faster." I shaved one of my legs completely bald and grabbed a huge steak knife.

"Now, the cut you make on the shaved leg has to be exactly the same on the hairy leg," Trace said.

"I know," I replied while making a thread-deep cut on the shaved leg.

"You chickened out a bit there," Trace said, pointing to the tiny scratch I'd just made.

"I know," I replied while digging the knife so deep into the other leg that I saw white on either side of the wound before a torrent of blood poured down my leg and into my shoe.

"Goddamnit, Timmy," Trace yelled, and all the girls ran to the first aid box. Blood was everywhere and out of nowhere Cooper got it all over his hands and then rubbed it on his face. We were all completely out of control.

Soon I had three pretty girls using Band-Aids and rubbing alcohol to make a really bad cut much worse. I don't know why but the whole thing made me want to see their vaginas so I said, "How about you guys all piss on me?" Nobody had ever said that to them before and it became a dare that none of them were prepared to back out of. Ten minutes later I was lying naked in the bathtub with blood-soaked bandages on my leg and three exposed pussies aimed at my torso.

They were laughing too hard to let a real torrent come out but I did definitely get a good cup's worth splashed all over me. When they were done they fell over each other laughing and Sharky and Trace came in brandishing their hoses, ready for round two. I leapt up while throwing punches toward their nuts and they ran back out of the room. It was one of the funnest parties of my whole life but we had started this abuse twenty-four hours ago and I for one was running out of steam.

Sharky and I had booked a cheap motel outside the city limits and Chin and Trace were happy to take us there because they wanted to use the pool. We rolled in at three in the morning and changed into our bathing suits for a dip. I was still bleeding a little but figured the chlorine would be good for the wound. The pool was packed with other guests wasted out of their minds so we sat with them in the tepid water drinking even-more-tepid whiskey until I worried about passing out underwater.

Trace and Chin stayed in the water with our new friends but Sharky and I retired to our room to pass out. He pulled out a bag and suggested a late-night bump, which is like a guy on death row requesting one more murder as his last meal. "Dude," I explained to my fellow DOWNER practitioner. "It's five minutes to four. We're done."

Sharky looked at his watch and was horrified. "It's three fifty-nine!" he yelled before inhaling a huge fucking line of cocaine on the dresser and chugging about twelve ounces of hot vodka. When the clock struck four he exhaled a sigh of relief and said, "I made it." I wanted to explain to him that bending your own rules kind of defeats the purpose, but I passed out.

A few hours later I woke up to see him on the edge of my bed jamming out to "Sussudio" by Phil Collins on his headphones really loud. Four hours after that, I woke up and could tell the bed next to me had not been slept in. I got a taxi and caught up with the gang, who had not stopped all night. Sharky was now running at thirty-six hours straight. I couldn't believe it. He was slurring a little bit but he was alive. We had Bloody Marys at breakfast and said "yes" when the waitress offered shots, because that's how it's done in Texas. Then, a homeless man came up to our table and gave me some rambling story about how he needed money for batteries because his flashlight was dead and he needed to see into the abandoned building he slept in blah blah blah. I interrupted him and said, "What a coincidence, my Care Machine has also run out of batteries," and we all erupted into thunderous laughter. We were the biggest assholes in all of Texas and I pity the fool who got in our way.

This was our ten-year anniversary of visiting the place and the traditions were now written in stone. Everyone had to remove his shirt when entering the bar and soon our bare backs became our gang vests. Slapping each other was also big so each vest inevitably had red handprints all over it. Another fantastic tradition I can't say enough about is clapping. One guy just starts randomly applauding for no reason and when another dozen or so shirtless guys join in, the cacophony is deafening. It sounds very cheery and social but it makes people furious.

Stockbroker was having a Pink Party that day to celebrate some Austin politician being caught trying to fuck his male interns. Everyone had to wear pink but Sharky and I only had white clothes with us, so we drenched them in red wine and it worked perfectly. The drunkenness was off the fucking chains and before long Stockbroker and Chin were having a fistfight about a croquet game that went bad. Chin won the fight and Stockbroker retaliated by pouring pink house paint all over Chin's hair. As if things couldn't get any funnier, I managed to convince Chin that the best way to get out oil-based paint was to add

*From left to right:* Totti, Cheese, Szabo, Skeeter (hidden), and me eating lunch in the suburbs. (1984)

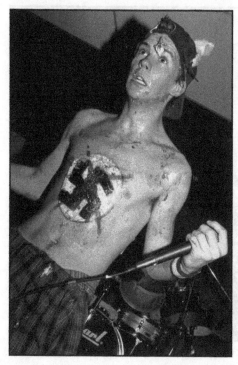

Taking a photo with the cops for a scavenger hunt. (1984)

Singing "Use Your Brains Now" with my band Anal Chinook while covered in cow brains. I had a crossed-out swastika on my chest, but the *X* sweated off and by the end it was just a swastika. (1988)

Working on a zine with a French Canadian punk we called Spam. This was before computers. (1988)

My baby brother, Kyle, hanging out with the punks. (1989)

Bringing planters their trees as a foreman. (1991)

Teaching in Taipei. The board says "GOTTA TAKE A DUMP" with "pee pee" and "poo poo" below it. (1992)

A page from issue no. 10 of my comic book *Pervert*, wherein I told the "He's Gone and Got a Bloody Tattoo" story in pictures. (1993)

Hanging out in Montreal at the peak of my philandering days. My hair is blue and that high-waisted-pants joke always did well with the ladies. (1993)

Meeting Bill Maher for the first time on his show. (2000)

*New York Post* article where Shane was a British soccer hooligan, I was a skinhead, and Suroosh was a recent hate crime victim holding a bloody bandage on his head. (2002)

Partying in Tokyo during the launch of Vice Japan. (2004)

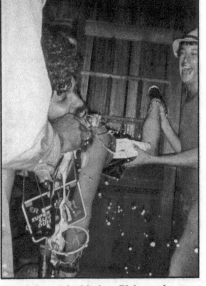

*From left to right:* Markus, Blake, and Dogboy doing keg stands at my stag. (2005)

*From left to right:* Me, Trace's brother, Blake, Markus, my dad, and Pinky dressed as klansmen at the denouement of my stag. (2005)

We went on a tour of Europe for our honeymoon. This was in Genova, Italy. (2005)

Me streaking through the Vice office. (2006)

Getting knocked out by a professional MMA fighter while shooting a pilot called *The Immersionist*. It got canned and I ended up in the hospital. (2008)

Signing the various contracts needed to sell my *Vice* shares. We re-created a famous photo of the Sex Pistols signing to A&M outside Buckingham Palace back in 1977. I played Steve Jones (signing), Sharky was Paul Cook, Pinky was Sid Vicious, and various Street Carnage staffers played the rest. (2008)

With my kids in England at Dial House, visiting the founders of *Crass.* (2009)

Onstage with Sebastian, representing Rooster NYC at a marketing seminar. Here I'm explaining our "How to Piss in Public" ad and showing attendees how to urinate under a car. (2011)

Wearing Pinky's WATCHOO TALKIN' BOUT MONDAYS?! Garfield Coleman shirt on Fox News with my homegirl Ann Coulter. (2011)

A puking view of my tattoos today. I may have overdone it. (2011) *Photo: Chelsea Skidmore*

hot water. This lie had him leaning into the laundry sink spreading the paint into every corner of his hair, permanently. "You're going to get fired," I said, laughing so hard a tiny bit of pee came out. "You're fucked."

I took a cab back by myself relatively early because it had been fifteen hours and rules are rules. Sharky said he'd catch up in a bit. The next morning I woke up and saw, yet again, the bed next to me had not been slept in. I called Sharky and got a taxi to Stockbroker's bar, where the party hadn't ceased. I couldn't believe it. We started Thursday night, did all of Friday, all of Saturday, and we were now into Sunday morning. When I saw him he was outside and talking to a girl named Jamie who was still wearing her pink wig from the day before. "What the hell are you doing?" I asked, in awe of his abilities. "You've been going for SIXTY HOURS."

"Well," Sharky replied with a wandering eye and the strange perm his hair had become, "you godda go wr yoo godngni dniad hiwd blllh."

"What?" I asked.

"It's all rebidding roor to the brrrss sss."

I tried to tell him that Timmy was kind of my thing and although I'm not against other people stealing my bit, he should probably ask first. He laughed and said, "Ha! Timmy weer chindst brr brr brr bah." He was still alive but the coke was doing all the heavy lifting. I said as much to Trace and he agreed. "My God," he said to Sharky, "you are one bump away from a feeding tube. Soon as this guy's done his last bag we're gonna have another Terri Schiavo on our hands." We both laughed and Sharky said some more stuff in Cambodian. It took a long time to recover from that trip but before we knew it, a year had gone by and it was time to give it another go. Then we all got married and had kids and closed that chapter for good.

My shirt says DON'T LET ME DO SHOTS OR COKE. (2003)

I went down to SXSW last year for a promotional thingy with Ray-Ban and was so bored I almost blew my head off. The music was too loud, the drugs didn't work, and the booze made me sleepy. Sharky wasn't there either. He was preparing for imminent fatherhood by spending two months at the Cottonwood holistic behavioral health and addiction treatment center in Tucson.

# Don't Let Your Mom Get Stoned (2003)

One of the upsides of being in the Slacker Generation is all your friends have really good pot. I have plenty of acquaintances who, despite being forty, still play video games, cup their farts, and play in joke bands with names such as Hot Piss. They also grow their own hydroponic.

Boggs and Lester's growing operation. (2003)

When I was back in Ottawa visiting my folks a few years ago, some friends we'll call "Boggs" and "Lester" showed me a secret room in their ridiculously decorated apartment that had about two dozen pot plants in it. They had spent years perfecting their crop and had botanically engineered what they called "Unicorn pot." "It's a level of weed we thought was just a fantasy," the abnormally shrimpy Boggs told me through his giant beard, "then it became a reality. It's magical." I tried a few tokes and they put in a VHS tape of Lester on *The Price Is Right* from 1989. It was so funny I forgot to laugh and realized I had become way too stoned. It took about an hour to be not stoned enough to drive home and Boggs gave me a sandwich bag full of Unicorn to take back with me.

I like pot as much as the next guy. It makes horror movies way scarier and joking with your friends way more amusing. However, with the caliber of pot they're creating today, I'm good with about a gram every few months. Boggs gave me at least a quarter-ounce, and I was leaving to go back to New York the next day. There was no way I was going to risk losing my green card by smuggling a year's worth of pot across the border, so I did what most of us would do. I gave it to my dad.

"Now, I need you to listen to me," I told my old man while holding the bag like it was a dangerous weapon. "This is not your father's pot." My dad told me his father never knew what pot was. "Yeah, I know," I said. "It's an expression. It means things have changed. This stuff is very potent. You can't go rolling some big, huge joint like you did in the seventies. Roll a pin-sized joint, take one quick puff, and put it out." I would have preferred his using a one-hitter, but sixty-year-old men tend not to have a lot of drug paraphernalia lying around the house. I considered smoking some with him that night but I'm sorry, that's too weird.

The next day, I hopped on a plane free of worry and left my parents to their own devices.

"It didn't go well," my dad told me a week later on the phone.

The evening after I'd left, despite crystal-clear warnings to the contrary, my dad decided to roll a joint as big as a Magic Marker and even convinced my mom to help him torch it. Neither of them had smoked in at least thirty years, so they carelessly consumed the reefer like back in the days when you needed to smoke a garbage bag full of the shit to get a tiny buzz. As my mom inhaled enough to give Willie Nelson a panic attack, my dad noticed the golf game he was watching on TV was the most beautiful thing ever created. "How wondrous man's rule of nature is," he thought, "that we can bend her will to make luxurious carpets and rolling hills. Who is dominating whom? Is it a battle or is there a symbiosis where both prosper?" As homo-sounding questions like that danced around in his head like sugarplums, my mom started to get pinhole vision. What the fuck were they thinking? Modern pot is just LSD in leaf form. You could probably die from it. "Jimmy, I can't see," my mom shrieked in a worried Scottish accent. "I cannee see a bloody thing!"

My dad wrenched his eyes from the television and told her to calm down. He explained that she was just very stoned and it would pass. He also encouraged her to inhale through her nose and breathe out her mouth, which she did. Unfortunately, that worked and her vision returned. "WHAT WAS THAT!?" she exclaimed, mortified by what she saw at the window. My dad was startled by her startle and walked over to the living room's bay windows to see what she was talking about.

"There's nothing there," he assured her after looking at his front lawn. "What did you see, a raccoon maybe?"

My mother's face was alabaster. "THERE IT IS AGAIN!" she wailed, pointing at a different window with nothing on the other side of it. As my dad peered out into the darkness, my mom shot up from the couch and ran upstairs. For the next fifteen minutes he heard stomping and slamming and clicking. She was locking every window and door in the house. Entrances were getting blocked and the house was almost completely secure. But from what?

"Jesus fucking Christ, Jimmy," my mom yelled from the kitchen. "He's staring at me!" My dad came into the kitchen to see his wife delirious with fear.

"What?" my dad asked, trying to calm her down. "What's looking at you, an animal?"

My mother was now in tears. "It's a creature," she sobbed. "A goblin or something. It's a tiny man. He's a gremlin."

"You mean a midget?" my dad asked, hoping she'd realize how ludicrous this notion was.

"No!" my mother said angrily. "He's only a few inches tall. Wait, there's more!"

At this point, my dad made a huge mistake. He threw up his hands and went back to the TV. She was ruining his groovy nature trip and he knew if he kept talking to her, he'd start bad-tripping too. "It'll pass," he said to her as he left the kitchen. "Just wait it out." What he should have done is explain to her how irrational her fears were. "How many of these creatures exist?" he should have asked. "Are they taking over the entire planet at the same time or has this one tiny handful of monsters decided to focus all their attention on a retired teacher and an engineer who live on the outskirts of Ottawa?" I've done this with people who talk in their sleep and it usually snaps them out of it. When a tree-planting buddy named Jamie sleepwalked over to my tent one night, he told me a stampede of married women was chasing him. This was before Facebook, and after I explained how impossible that would be to coordinate, he said, "Oh yeah," and went back to bed.

My dad enjoyed another ten minutes of lawns until he heard her talking to someone. He tried to ignore it at first but she was getting louder and it didn't sound like "talking to yourself" talking. It sounded like "responding to questions" talking. Did the goblin get in? Was she talking him out of murdering her?

My dad walked over and put his ear against the kitchen door. "This might be funny," he thought.

"Yes, McInnes. Yes," she said while giving out her address, "he's trying to kill me!"

This wasn't what my dad was expecting, so he opened the door. Oh, no. Mom was on the phone.

"Who are you talking to?" my dad asked in one of those whisper-screams people do when they're panicked but want to remain quiet.

"I called the police!" my mother replied, incensed. "You left me no choice." My dad started pacing around the kitchen in terror and pulling out what was left of his hair while silently and frenetically making "Hang up the phone!" gestures at her.

Then my mom made things a whole lot worse. She said, "I've made a huge mistake—I'm sorry," and hung up the phone. Shit! My dad knew the cops were on their way and he also knew the house reeked of hydroponic skunk weed. He ran to the living room, grabbed the couch cushions, and started fanatically trying to fan out the room. He was only able to do this for about a minute before a squad car screeched into the driveway and two cops began pounding on the front door. "Open up!" they yelled. "We know you're in there!"

My mother was mortified. She dropped to her knees and put her hands on her face like the kid in *Home Alone*. "What have I done, Jimmy?" she pleaded. "What do we do now?" Things were so bad at this point it actually would have been best to tell the cops the whole thing was about tiny monsters—not that they would have believed her. Instead, my dad told her he'd handle it and went to the door. When he opened it and asked the officers if he could help them, they saw a drunken bastard who ruled his roost with an iron fist and regularly beat this poor, innocent woman. "We'd like to ask your wife a few questions," they said to my dad.

"Helloooo!" my mom said like some best friends had popped by to play cribbage. The cops pushed past my dad and asked my mom, "Is there somewhere we can talk?" My dad's heart sank as my mom escorted the two cops into the dining room before closing the door behind them. Like when Steve dropped into the huge pile of shit, the adrenaline had chased the high out of her system, and she was now more worried than baked.

He listened through the dining room doors as best he could but all he could hear was the tone of my mom pooh-poohing her domestic abuse and the two officers insisting they'd protect her. He heard quotes like, "Your husband isn't the boss, we are," and "There are places we can take you right now where you'd be safe." If only they knew the person they were protecting her from was as small as he was and nonexistent. After another twenty minutes of questioning, the cops realized my mom wasn't going to press charges and they gave up. God bless them by the way.

As they walked out of the dining room they stared at my dad like he was everything that's wrong with this country. "Thank you, gentlemen," my dad said to break the silence.

The cops ignored him and turned to my mom. "Remember, Mrs. McInnes," they assured her, "we are always a phone call away. Whenever you're ready." My mom said thanks and closed the door. Then she put her back up against it and slid down to the floor with her head in her hands.

She hasn't smoked pot since.

# That's What I Get for Teasing
# Junkies (2003)

I hate when magazines have an article about drugs and they use an obviously fake picture. Don't show me a pile of sugar when you're talking about cocaine. It makes you look like a nerd. So with a name like *Vice*, we weren't about to use cinnamon and oregano to illustrate our cover story about heroin and pot.

I hired our editor TJ on the condition that he quit heroin. He did, but it wasn't easy. For ten days his scrawny body writhed in pain because it no longer knew how to release dopamine. In heroin withdrawal, every nerve ending stings like a third-degree burn. Once he emerged from hell, he attended several weeks of nightly meetings and was finally ready to hold down a real job working for me.

I walked over to his desk, which was only a few feet from mine. Vice had an open floor plan but I made sure editorial was far away from marketing. I wanted our writers to be as unhinged as possible. As old-timey journalist Theodore White once said, "When a reporter sits down at his typewriter, he's nobody's friend." If editorial was happy, marketing was mad, and vice versa. That's the way I liked it. It was a fifteen-hundred-square-foot warehouse space with about fifty people tapping away on keyboards and quietly talking on the phone to writers all over the world. TJ was spell-checking a piece while dressed in ratty jeans and a BMX shirt that said "FOX" in huge letters. He still resembled a junkie and his thin arms looked like Kermit the Frog's. "I've got some bad news," I told him.

"What?" he asked without looking away from his computer.

"I need you to buy some heroin."

"WHAT?!" he blurted out while pushing away from his computer and turning to face me. Sweat droplets had begun to magically appear on his forehead.

"I need there to be real heroin in the photo," I said, "and you're the only guy I know who knows a guy."

TJ looked around the room hoping to find another junkie. There was his other boss Suroosh, but all his connections had dried up well over a decade ago and even then, they were from Montreal. "Fine," TJ said while angrily wheeling his chair back to his computer.

"When?" I asked.

TJ turned to me and exhaled an exasperated sigh. "Today, I guess?"

"I think now would be ideal," I said.

TJ got on the phone and called a guy he used to call several times a day. This is someone he would yell at and cry to and sometimes fear. For years he was TJ's archenemy and best friend simultaneously. They agreed to the drop-off spot and I rubbed my hands with excitement. An hour later, TJ and I were putting on our coats and heading outside. I'd done heroin before but I'd never seen a deal go down. "How does it work?" I asked, expecting a guy wearing a trench coat with a dozen syringes attached to the inside.

"I drop a hundred dollars in a phone booth then walk around the block," he replied. I'm fucking cheap, so leaving that kind of money in a pay phone's change hole felt like abandoning my baby in the middle of the road. I reluctantly gave him five twenties while asking why we couldn't get a smaller amount. He told me we couldn't, then walked over to the pay phone across the street. TJ pretended to make a call and stuffed the money into the hole. "We're not walking around the block,"

I said after he came back. "Let's go hide in that store." I watched the phone like a hawk and fifteen minutes later a nerdy Asian guy in a new ski jacket walked up to the phone and made the same pantomime phone call TJ did. "I hope that's him," I said to TJ, who nodded that it was.

After Chinese Downhill left, I trotted over to the phone and grabbed the bundle. It was ten tiny plastic bags of beige powder. They were wrapped with wax paper and stamped with a skull and cross-bones. Dealers like branding their product as much as any small business owner and want you to know exactly who it was that got you so high. Suroosh told me that whenever he heard someone OD'd, he and his junkie friends would run over to the guy's house hoping to find out what brand the guy was doing, because it must be some really good shit.

I hurried back to the office completely ignoring TJ and when I walked through the front doors I yelled, "Who wants heroin?" to the whole office while holding up the bags. For nonaddicts like myself, heroin is just some stupid powder that kills sad people. For recovering addicts it is an omnipresent force that haunts their dreams and is constantly floating through their minds. Suroosh hadn't gone near any drug or booze for a decade, but he still had to attend meetings regularly and told me about frequent nightmares. "Hey, man," I said, walking over to him with all ten bags, "you love this shit, right?"

Suroosh pushed away from his desk the same way TJ had. "Is that real?" he asked like I was holding the three-inch-tall goblin that tried to kill my mother. TJ had walked in behind me and was nodding. They both stared at it with scared smiles. Then they said, "Holy shit," at almost exactly the same time. I looked at my watch and realized it was time to take this to the next level.

"So it's valuable to you guys, right?" I said as I tore open a bag and let it slowly sprinkle to the dirty floor. For years they'd been trained to worship every granule of this stuff, so their Pavlovian instinct was to yell, *"No!"* and try to stop it from falling. As they clamored to protect it, I spread the powder all over the floor with my shoe while saying, "Oooopsie!" Then I danced around like an asshole holding the other nine bags and singing, "I have heroin! I have her-o-in!" TJ and Suroosh couldn't wrench their eyes from the floor.

I pulled out a key, dipped it into the bag, and scooped out a bump. "Come on, guys," I said, holding the key to their noses, "just one sniff." Again with the "holy shit." Can't junkies come up with anything better than "holy shit"? Before I knew what I was doing, I had snorted the heroin up into my own stupid head, which destroyed TJ and Suroosh. I basically had shoved a cross in Jesus's face and said, "Remember this?"

They staggered back to their desks and tried to get on with their day and I laughed at them and . . . wait a minute . . . why am I wearing an anvil for a hat? Why is my face itchy? Why do I feel like I'm going to barf? I mumbled something to our secretary about making sure nobody touched those bags—especially TJ and Suroosh—and walked in slow motion to the bathroom, where I barfed so violently, I was worried the toilet would split in two. It didn't feel bad, though. It felt like taking a big shit out of my mouth.

I wobbled out of the bathroom and spent the next two hours doing the two-minute job of snapping one picture of the heroin before flushing it down the toilet forever. I had only done a bump the size of a pencil tip, but I felt like I drank a salad bowl of vodka. "I gotta go home," I said like a sleepwalking Orson Welles, and TJ nodded while shaking his head.

When I got outside, the entire city was underwater. Everyone was speaking backward and the sidewalk was moving. I was only a few blocks from the train but I might as well have been stranded on the top of Mount Everest. Then Blobs called. "You ready?" she asked in the perky tone of someone who wasn't on heroin.

"Whuuu?" I replied like a talking snail.

"For dinner—we gotta go meet David. Did you already forget? Jesus." She said a bunch of other stuff, but people talk fast when you're on heroin and I was still trying to wrap my snail antennae around the first part.

I had recently started hanging out with comedian David Cross and didn't want to risk our delicate new friendship by blowing off some dinner plans he had made weeks ago. David is so into barbecue, he has a tattoo of a pig who just ripped his own ribs out and is handing them to you on a platter. The dinner was at a popular soul-food place in Chelsea called Maroons and I was already late. I ran down the stairs before realizing I wasn't running at all but barely walking, so I stumbled back up and called a car service. It showed up almost immediately and after mumbling the address to the driver, I slumped into the backseat and fell asleep with my eyes open. It was like being in a music video made for dead people. When we crossed the Williamsburg Bridge I looked at the Manhattan skyline with the Chrysler Building and the Empire State Building standing above their peers like steel gods and thought, "That's nice." As we drove through the East Village and passed ratty dope dealers and Puerto Ricans on their third generation of welfare I thought, "That's nice." As we crossed town on Fourteenth Street and passed methadone clinics, I remembered the thousands of junkies who had already died in this town and thought, "That's nice," and I was there. I was relieved to see Blobs standing outside because the only way my driver was going to get paid was if I could spit out the words "Please pay him" as I handed her my wallet.

David was inside dealing with the table and before I could greet him he said, "What the fuck is the matter with you?" I had no idea I was doing anything unusual but Blobs told me later I was standing like an ape with bended knees and my knuckles dragging on the floor. I tried to get it together and snap out of it but fuck, man, the air was made of transparent licorice. How's a guy supposed to move around in that? Getting to our table was a huge imposition, and Blobs had to order for me as well as handle all the conversating.

I couldn't believe how fucking fried I was and there were no signs of its wearing off. When you do cocaine, you're high for ten minutes and then things go back to normal. This was more like changing into a different life-form. It didn't add a little spice to the evening. It swallowed the entire evening like a gigantic bullfrog.

When our meals arrived, Blobs and David were thrilled. Apparently fried chicken is delicious or something but I might as well have been gawking at a sweater knitted to look like a meal. I didn't want to put anything down my throat besides my finger, which reminded my stomach that it was again time to hurl. "Excuse me," I stammered while heading toward the bathroom. I could feel barf walking up my throat and I almost knocked over a table near the bathroom door as I threw the door open and dropped to my knees. The restaurant was very small and this tiny bathroom was a few inches from the nearest couple. A waiter politely closed my door and an earsplitting vomit geyser came hurling out of my guts, splashing against the bowl. Before I could inhale some oxygen and recover, another pile of vomit roared out of my face. I couldn't stop. After a half dozen monster pukes, I rolled off the toilet and let my face enjoy the cold tile floor. I was lying in the piss of a thousand New Yorkers and it felt great—so great, it was putting me to sleep. As I dozed off, I wondered how many meals were ruined by my 120-decibel barf concert.

When I came to, I crawled up the wall and tried to steady myself. I opened the bathroom door and apologized to the couple who was inexplicably still sitting there. Apparently some time had passed because the check was paid for and my meal was waiting in a doggie bag. Blobs was not impressed and David was laughing and shaking his head. "You are a piece of work," he said, handing me my food. I tried to think of a witty comeback but all that came out was, "That's nice."

# Yet Another Asian Threesome
## (2003)

$\mathbf{A}$s I let on earlier, Blobs had no faith in our relationship and every time she succumbed to my advances, she'd kick herself and tell me to get lost.

These "breaks" were often lonely places to be, but then the phone would ring. This time it was my partner in sex crimes, Sally Woo. It's not considered very cool to be into Asian chicks. It's usually a pursuit reserved for weak nerds with tiny dicks, but my dick is so big, it makes "my person is so small" jokes. Pair me up with an Oriental, and it's like a happy person popping Prozac.

I had been in a particularly long dry spell so I got right to business. "I'm so horny, I got a boner you could tie a bow on," I told her. She said she'd love to oblige and I upped the ante with, "I got a boner you could tie *into* a bow if it ever got soft, which it won't, so fuck your bow and fuck you." She seemed confused so I added, "And fuck me while you're at it because, like I said, I'm horny." Sally giggled and told me she was going to be in New York in a few days for her "requisite spanking." I told Sally I'd be happy to hang out and said it in a very standoffish way,

193

because chicks like that. I sat down on the couch and hatched a plan. I was going to set up a threesome with Sally and Yoo-jin.

Yoo-jin was a shy Korean girl who didn't like me as much as I liked her. Luckily she was also an alcoholic so if I could pour five beers down her little yellow bird beak and convince her to come home, I was in for some of the best fucking this side of the Pacific Ocean.

When Sally arrived, I told her my genius idea. She was going to find a bar near her hotel. Then she was going to text me the location and I was going to show up there with Yoo-jin. "After a few hours you're going to walk in," I told Sally, "and I'm going to shit my pants. 'Sally!?' I'll ask incredulously. 'I haven't seen you since high school. What the fuck are you doing here?' Then we'll have some more drinks and a few shots and eventually you'll convince Yoo-jin and me to come up to your hotel room because it simply has to be seen to be believed." Sally liked the plan as usual but she was worried about her lackluster hotel room. "Of course, your room isn't going to be that impressive," I assured her, "but once we get Yoo-jin into the hotel, all questions will be flushed down the toilet." The plan was multifaceted but I was at the point where I needed something that interesting to keep it interesting.

It was colder than a dead slave's eyes that night so I made sure I met Yoo-jin at a bar that was a quick walk to where I had planned to meet Sally. Yoo-jin's a tiny girl who looks like a movie star but dresses like an old lady right down to her beige orthopedic shoes. She had on green socks, a knee-length denim skirt, a librarian's blouse, and a wooly cardigan that matched her socks. After carefully monitoring the time, I headed to the secret spot and Sally walked in after about another hour of boozing just like she was supposed to. Sally was dressed like she was going to a senior prom with strappy heels and a long gown. Her hair was like Yoo-jin's, long and black, but she had lopped off her bangs so ridiculously short, it made her look almost comical.

I fake-freaked-out when Sally walked in and she seamlessly continued the gag by not recognizing me due to the mustache (nice touch). We all got along great because booze'll do that, but I must have looked idiotic pretending I couldn't believe she was there. "How long has it been?" I asked like we were on a Canadian after-school special.

"Oh, shit, fifteen years?" she replied without doing the math. Eventually, I'd be able to drop the charade and talk to them like human beings. A few drinks after that, Sally said, "You guys absolutely *must* see the hotel my company booked. It must be a thousand bucks a night." I said we could check it out if it was nearby and Yoo-jin shrugged before passively following us out.

As predicted, the room was a very small suite that was nothing to write home about. Yoo-jin was unimpressed. I could see my dick staring up at me, pissed off. I imagined him with a face like a very zitty Steve Buscemi saying, "You betta not blow dis!" Closing this part of the deal is like juggling on top of a moving car. You need to maneuver quickly and can't show any fear. With my stomach in my chest, I "confidently" told Sally to take off her dress. Yoo-jin was not so easy to manipulate. She seemed bored by Sally's perky tits and it was clear this juggler's vehicle was about to slam on its brakes so hard, my balls would be wrenched from my hands for good.

In a last-ditch attempt to rescue this dying scene, I grabbed Yoo-jin and started making out with her. Yoo-jin was FOB (fresh off the boat) so she was used to having curveballs thrown at her. She had only recently discovered the Rolling Stones, so my hope was that all these weird sexual opportunities would incubate long enough in her decision chamber for her to say, "Why the fuck not? Everything about this country is just as weird."

Sally could see we were losing her. I gave her a look that said, "Get out of here, NOW," which she did. Then I pulled out my defibrillator: pussy eating. As I munched on Yoo-jin's cunt, it felt like her pussy lips were the edge of a cliff and I would plummet to my death if I made one false move. After about a minute of Olympic-grade tongue figure-skating, I looked up and saw a Korean cadaver staring back at me. She was about as amused as Queen Victoria and it was throwing me off my game. I was getting bitter and her vagina was starting to taste like pinworm medicine. Buscemi gave me an evil eye that burned straight into my soul.

So, I stopped and threw up my hands. Sally walked back in all smiles with a bottle of white wine and three glasses. But I had totally given up. Fuck this shit. Fuck me. Fuck her. It's not like I'm here to rape anybody. I'm offering two women nothing short of an internal massage.

My main man in the sky decided it was time to intervene. Like Zeus entering our atmosphere as a swan, God floated down into Yoo-jin's body and took over. "You don't think I'm horny!?" she suddenly squawked like a child possessed. Sally and I both looked at each other in shock. Yoo-jin then did a strange dance where she tugged at her skirt like someone who had to pee bad and was ashamed of it. (This is giving me a boner right now.) I felt an enormous bucket of joy wash over me and I attacked those bitches like white on rice.

I grabbed Yoo-jin and we all started kissing and feeling and tugging on things. I fucked them one at a time and took pictures of them tangled together. At one point I had Yoo-jin stacked on top of Sally in missionary and pumped Yoo-jin until Sally made a guttural moan and her paraurethral ducts squirted out an enormous puddle of vagina juice. Even in the heat of mad passionate primal lust Yoo-jin and I sort of turned to each other like, "What was that?"

I came all over their faces and collapsed into a ball of "there I did that." They shot some more photographs and giggled as I sat there like a used condom. When it was time to go Yoo-jin asked what I was doing and I answered her by passing out. I asked her later what she thought of that night and she said I ruined the whole thing by not leaving with her. I tried to give a shit but it just wasn't there.

# Funnest Blackout Ever, You Guys! (2003)

On August 14, 2003, fashion photographer Terry Richardson turned thirty-eight and the entire Northeast sank into darkness. Forty-five million Americans and half the Canadian population were without power for two days.

I was at Terry's on that fateful day. Blobs and I had reunited after our longest breakup ever but she had to work so she couldn't join me. I love Terry and I respect the way he revolutionized fashion photography by replacing airbrushed fakeness with punk rock irreverence. I've had a lot of great nights doing drugs at his place one-on-one and talking about life but I gotta say, his parties kinda suck.

I used to think it was because he's sober and you're not allowed to bring booze, but even when he was a heroin addict his parties blew chunks. At his bachelor party, everyone was so strung out on smack, the strippers thought they had been invited to a morgue. The girls just sat there, nude and bored, watching TV and eating popcorn in a room full of sleeping men until a sober Iranian named Omid arrived and fucked their brains out. I was pining for something like that, at least, at

Terry's birthday party in 2003. I had smuggled in an Evian bottle full of lukewarm vodka and tried not to contort my face after every swig because I didn't want to tempt any of the Anonymous Alcoholics staring at my drink. I don't care about teasing junkies, but messing with alcoholics is simply NOT cool.

Terry lived in his photo studio, which was a huge loft that opened out to a large backyard that was really the roof of the building below him. It was one of the hottest days of an already sweltering summer. Terry was cooking hot dogs next to a picnic table full of pretty girls while old punks played Ping-Pong and made fart jokes. Dash Snow was drawing his tag all over a Dunkin' Donuts box and despite liking everyone there, I considered hara-kiri. How can you have a party without booze? It's like wearing a bike helmet. Only retards and kids do it.

Just when I was trying to think of an excuse to leave, the music cut out. I walked into the kitchen and heard the fridge shudder to a halt. The clock radio over his bed was dark, too. "Your whole place lost power!" I yelled out to the backyard.

I called Blobs, who was doing fashion publicity for the notorious Kelly Cutrone at the time. Kelly, who later got her own reality show called *Kell on Earth*, was refusing to let anyone leave. "I don't know what kind of work she expects us to do," Blobs whispered to me with dwindling reception. "Everything is dead." I told her to leave and she said, "Doy." After September 11 happened we made the plan to meet at Tompkins Square Park if there was ever another state of emergency. We had no idea it would happen in less than two years. We both agreed to head to the spot.

I made my way up Bowery and was thrilled to see people out on the street already figuring shit out. Car batteries were used to power TVs that sat on the sidewalk. Kids played next to open fire hydrants as parents strained to hear the news. New York's last blackout had been in 1977 when crime was at its peak. The entire city was looted and thousands of fires raged throughout the night. This was a different New York. Giuliani's zero-tolerance laws got rid of all the criminals and the Twin Tower attacks turned the remaining residents into the Get Along

Gang. Walking through the new, newer New York without power felt as safe as walking through your mother's house.

As I walked along Houston Street the sun sank behind the buildings and things started to get dark fast. For the next forty-eight hours the world was left wondering: Now that New York's gone black, will it ever go back?

Most New Yorkers seemed to be walking to the bridges and tunnels to be with their families, but a lot of people wanted to stay for the party.

About five blocks from the park, the street became totally devoid of light and I felt my way into a bodega to get beer. Inside it was the kind of pitch-black usually reserved for the forest. I couldn't see my hand in front of my face. The bodega wasn't empty and there was someone at the register, but they couldn't open it. The conditions were perfect for looting. Instead of taking advantage of our fellow New Yorkers, we all did the right thing. Everyone there formed a blind line that involved bumping our way to the fridges, grabbing a six-pack or two, and then making our way to the register, where we felt out what was probably about $20 for the cashier, who then stuffed the money in her pocket. The mood was cheery and people made jokes like, "Hey, that's not my hand!"

I made my way to the park. Soon after, Blobs showed up with Ben Cho and a bunch of other fashion fags. My eyes were getting used to the darkness and I could finally see this motley crew. Blobs's gay coworkers were dressed in ridiculous parachute pants with huge SpongeBob prints and wrestling boots. The girls looked like groupies from a Van Halen concert in the eighties and I was dressed like a homeless businessman in skintight white pants and a vest with no shirt. We all made rape jokes about the darkness while strangers hollered "yahoos" from the void. I discovered later that David Cross was having a horrible time with fellow comedian Todd Barry about ten yards from us. We never found each other. Hearing his version of the night is a great example of how one shitty attitude (Todd's) can drastically change the course of events.

After finishing our warm beers, we decided it was time to check out the city. We might have been killed or we might have died laughing, but it's better to regret something you *have* done than something you haven't. The terrifying Avenue A of 1977 was now more like Sesame Street. Instead of hiding indoors with their rotting groceries, people were out on the street grilling steaks and hot dogs and handing them to random strangers. Puerto Ricans blared salsa music out of their cars and kids had their beds made right there on the sidewalk.

We walked south and west through the Lower East Side, across the Bowery, and into SoHo, where bartenders were out on the street handing out free beer. If you saw this in a movie you'd say it was corny bullshit that didn't seem real and you'd be right. It was a scene from *Fame* but it was real. The only thing that could have made it better would have been some testosterone to balance out all this gayness. Just then an old punk named Eric appeared. He owned a bar called 6's and 8's that *New York* magazine described as, "Picture Blondie in bed with the Strokes," and he's about as balls-out as bros get. I met him through Terry Richardson and we bonded over Montreal because he and his buddies used to drive up there just to fuck French chicks.

Eric and I screamed at each other like excited frat boys and he handed me one of the three beers in his hands. Car headlights lit the streets and one or two generators provided the rest of the lights. It was like a post-nuclear New York where everyone had taken MDMA and we were all going to die soon from radiation anyway. Guys were double-fisting beers and the street was packed with scantily clad women dancing and making out with strangers. Bar owners seemed to think alcohol was milk and were furiously giving out free booze so it wouldn't curdle in the heat.

We left Spring Street and headed up Mercer, where a fire hydrant was shooting a ten-foot torrent of water across the street. People were competing for outrageous water dances and after a guy did the robot right through the blast, everybody cheered. He was followed by a guy carrying a busted boom box on his shoulder, which was ripped away from him when he hit the water. Again, cheers. I turned to Eric like a World War II soldier on D-day: "You know what we have to do, don't you?"

Eric closed his eyes knowingly and said, "Get naked."

I nodded my head. We went over to a less populated part of the street and undressed. I told Blobs to guard our clothes and she laughed in my face. Eric and I emerged from the crowd and put our hands in the air as everyone sort of cheered reluctantly. My adrenaline was pumping too hard to notice Eric and instead of dancing I got into the center of the jet and started a mime shower act. The crowd was now chanting, "No more nude guys! No more nude guys!" I washed my armpits and pretended to shampoo my hair and then, nothing. The water stopped. I was left there totally nude, dripping and wondering what happened as maybe a hundred eyeballs frowned at my heavily tattooed Grover body. I looked over at the fire hydrant and Eric was mooning it but unable to move. His face was devoid of color and had a grave expression. He looked like someone was taking a huge shit inside him. Then he wrenched himself up and moved out of the way as the water shot back at me so hard, I was catapulted into the scream-ing crowd. As a cacophony of laughter continued behind us, Eric and I walked back to our clothes to get dressed. I was giddy but he looked morose. "Are you OK?" I asked, rolling underwear up my wet legs.

"No, man, I'm not," he said, crouching down naked. "I thought it would be funny to put my ass on it," he groaned, "but the water hit me in the nuts like a fist." I started laughing so hard I couldn't get my pants on. "It was like being punched by a boxer," he said without smil-ing. "I'm not kidding." I was still having one of those silent laughs that drains your body of oxygen and incapacitates you. It took a while but I was eventually able to explain that his bagging denied me any water and left me standing there like a naked fool. He hadn't noticed and this got a bit of a smile but being punched in the nuts by sixty pounds per square inch is no laughing matter.

As I pulled on my T-shirt and headed back to our friends, I was blinded by a spotlight. I was worried it was the police coming to bust up the place but noticed a peacock logo after sheltering my eyes with my hand. "We're with NBC News," a silhouette with a microphone yelled out over the commotion. "What made you guys get naked in the street like that?"

In a bid to amuse my friends back home I yelled, "Because if we didn't, THE TERRORISTS WIN!" This was way too esoteric of a joke and ended up on the cutting-room floor. What I should have done is flexed my right arm for the camera and said, "'New York Muscle,' baby!" It was a great song by A.R.E. Weapons that we all loved and it surely would have become the motto for the whole blackout. To this day I lie in bed and kick myself for not saying "New York Muscle." It would have been on T-shirts and bumper stickers and giant banners at tailgate parties. I could have summed up post-9/11 New York in a life-changing phrase that may have even ended the war in Afghanistan, but I went for some sarcastic quip. Shit!

As I started to regret my NBC quote, we all heard the *Bwoop! Bwooop!* of real police sirens. The police drove past the fire-hydrant blast, which soaked their car, and stopped just in front of it. "Stand back," the voice on the loudspeaker said. Everyone got off the street and the music was cut dead.

The car just sat there with the loudspeaker pointed at us. Everyone stood motionless and dripping wet in the summer heat. It seemed the party was over. We were doing about a hundred illegal things and knew it was only a matter of time before it was all shut down. Then, just when we were all about to go home with our tails between our legs, the silence was broken by the cop's loudspeaker. "Sta-a-a-a-rt sprea-a-a-ading the n-ee-e-e-ews," he sang, building up to, "I'm leavin' today," and then an earsplitting, "I want to be a part of it, New York, NEW YO-O-O-RK!"

Everyone went completely fucking berserk. The fact that those genius cops let us doubt the party and then TKO'd us with that fucking song made our heads explode. As the cop drove off to hysterical applause, the music kicked back in ten times louder than before and the dancing and yelling was so delirious, we were acting more like deranged savages than partiers. I looked over at Blobs and we both shook our heads in awe of what we had just witnessed. I grabbed her wet hair and started kissing her, and it became very clear she would one day be my wife and this would always be my city.

# Lord of the Botflies (2003)

Racing around our property on my rice rocket
while nude. (2003)

The place we had in Costa Rica was called Montezuma but the locals referred to it as MonteFUMA, COCA Rica because it was known for smoking pot and snorting cocaine. The neighboring town is called Malpais, which translates as "Bad Land," and Montezuma should have been called "Worse." Doing a shot and a small line of blow in that town was like having an espresso in any other town. Everyone was wasted. We had a caretaker named Richie who was a six-foot-four surfer with half his body covered in tattoos. He was on the lam for drug charges and called the town his "Tropical Prison." Every vacation I'd go down, get him drunk, and catch up on all the gossip. It was always over the top.

"Remember that German dude who was always hanging out with the guys from Granola Funk?" he'd tell me. "He died of a hangover." Apparently being wasted for 365 days straight means the withdrawal symptoms are fatal. River Phoenix's dad, Juan, lives down there and there's the story about the little kid who died in his car during the six-hour drive to the hospital in San José. The hippies down there are weird about blood transfusions and there are rumors it was their bullshit beliefs that led to the kid's death. Juan was trying to save him but it was too late and they had to continue half the journey with a small dead child wrapped in blankets in the back. The rest of the town is just as disturbing. There's the Midwestern crackhead who got his mother addicted too by convincing her she'd lose weight. They both became paranoid lunatics who scared the father so bad he had a heart attack and died. He had been telling locals his family was trying to kill him but they assumed he was just as paranoid as they were. You're not paranoid if people really are out to get you. One year a Nicaraguan worker (Costa Rica's Mexicans) got in a fight with his brother and chopped the guy's hands off. I get one hand, but two? How does that work exactly? I always had so many questions during my catch-up sessions with Richie but he always had more to tell me. Infanticide, patricide, and fratricide are about as heavy as stories get but they were always being trumped by something more insane. It is a twisted and scary and decadent town but it's also beautiful and I love it there.

Before Richie we had an amazing caretaker named Robert Dean. This funny little British man was best known as guitarist of the New Wave band Japan, but he also played with everyone from Sinéad O'Connor to Gary Numan. I loved to get drunk with him and hear his amazing rock stories, like when Gary Numan insisted that his brother join the band and fake-play the saxophone on tour, or the time Numan got scurvy on tour after exclusively eating McDonald's plain hamburgers every day. Robert saw the Sonics play when they first started and even went to a Beatles concert when he was twelve. I could talk to that guy for days.

After Japan peaked and played Budokan, Robert looked down and realized he had become a total cokehead with zero grasp of reality. Not one for half measures, he chucked that entire life into the toilet and moved to Montezuma, where he became a world-renowned bird expert almost overnight. The dude is extreme. Bird-watchers write down every bird they see and try to outdo each other by discovering rarer and rarer birds, and Robert made short shrift of becoming the best.

One day, Robert decided he was going to break all records by spotting a keel-billed motmot. This required lying motionless in a swamp for twenty-four hours and staring at the same tree with binoculars. Within a week of coming up with this goal, he had pulled it off. He called whatever bird society you call and after tough questions like, "Are you sure it wasn't a blue-crowned motmot?" Robert Dean was in the history books as one of the few people to see the *Electron carinatum* in its ever-shrinking natural habitat.

There was only one problem. While he was lying in that festering bog, a fucking botfly laid eggs in his forehead. This is not unusual. In Costa Rica, everything is alive. If you get the tiniest cut in your finger it will instantly get infected because the very air around you is jam-packed with living organisms. And they aren't fucking around. I was stung by an army of fire ants once and it felt like riot police were rapid-firing rubber bullets at my legs. Being stung by a scorpion is also a wild ride. The sting itself feels like someone sinking a hot poker into your foot and for two days afterward, your lips are numb and your hands have pins and needles. The botfly is more evil and disgusting than all its rivals combined, and that's saying something. It reproduces by sneaking eggs onto a mammal's skin (usually cattle) until a larva gets strong enough to crawl deeper inside through the nearest pore. Are you puking yet? The larva then lives there for about a month, eating the fat around it and getting strong enough to turn into a bug and bust out through its host's skin.

When Robert came back and explained to me what the lump on his forehead was, I roared so loud the jungle exploded with scared birds. I was delirious. "How are you standing there telling me this?" I yelled incredulously. "If I had a fly fetus in my head I would carve it out immediately and then take ten thousand showers."

But Robert was blasé and muttered, "I don't really notice it." The only time he remembered he was harboring a motherfucking baby in his head was when it would wriggle around every few hours. He'd hold his head and wince for a second and then happily get back to work.

"R-Robert," I'd stammer, "it hurts because it just ate the area it was in and it's moving over to a new spot. You are being eaten by a parasite, you asshole. *Do* something!" I don't know if he enjoyed seeing me squirm or enjoyed feeling his own head squirm, but I was determined to solve this revolting problem. Blobs was coming in a few days and I knew I wasn't going to get laid if my friends were pregnant with insects. She was already very dubious of our on-again-off-again relationship and I needed to make this work. I took Robert to the local bar and broke it down after a few tequilas. "Robert," I told him calmly, "do you realize if you let this thing incubate and fly out of your head, YOU WILL BE ITS MOTHER!?" This gave him pause. "Your only progeny on this earth will be a hairy fly," I added, because he has no kids. While this tiny moment of sanity gripped my friend, I got a local farmer to convince him to suffocate the thing by covering the whole area with Vaseline—that's what farmers do to their cows. "All right, why not?" Robert conceded as if I was suggesting he give Diet Coke a whirl.

Robert went to bed with a big dollop of Vaseline on his head and woke up with a dead abortion hanging out of his forehead. (I just gagged remembering this.) After no longer getting enough oxygen, the larva had tried to make a break for it but suffocated halfway out of Robert's head. It was huge and fluorescent pink with thick, black, coarse hairs jutting out of its back. Seeing it made me do hollering dry heaves that went, "HwooooACH! Huuuh. Huuuh. Whoooo. WuuuuuACH!" As I stumbled around the room trying not to faint, Robert smiled and pulled the larva out. It made a quiet *schlooop* sound that was so nauseating, I ran out to the lawn and retched my last meal out of my stomach and onto the grass, where it was instantly covered in insects. Then, without looking back, I ran from the house like it was haunted and didn't come back until very late that night.

The next morning I got in the shower and was beyond horrified to discover Robert's dead child lying on the shower floor. I leapt out and ran over to Robert. I was completely naked and soaking wet with my eyes bulging out of my head. "Are you out of your fucking mind?" I asked. "How could you not BURN that thing? It's lying on the shower floor. What were you thinking?"

Robert didn't understand what I was so freaked out about and answered the question literally. "I don't know," he said casually, "when I saw it, I looked down and just thought, 'There you are. You're there.'" That's what he said: "There you are. You're there." I exhaled, shook my head, and got a towel. Then I opened a beer and went out to the porch to try to digest the fact that I had two aliens in my house: one dead, one living.

I've met a lot of eccentrics over the years, but Robert's botfly apathy is something I will never even begin to comprehend. Soon after this, he moved to the nearby town of Monteverde because it was better for bird-watching. Last I heard he got into bodybuilding and had become gargantuan. Like I said, the dude is extreme.

# Partying with Mötley Crüe (2004)

I had heard from a few people that one of my favorite bands, Mötley Crüe, were big fans of my DOs & DON'Ts book. Apparently their manager brought it on tour and they all passed it around the plane laughing their asses off and looking forward to the day we could all be best friends. The guy who wrote *The Dirt*, the band's life story, told me my book was a huge help because every time drummer Tommy Lee would get reluctant to tell a raunchy story he'd say, "Don't be a pussy. Remember that DOs & DON'Ts book you liked? He went way farther."

So, when Tommy Lee was in New York back in 2004, Matt Sweeney called me up and said he was with Lee and I should meet him. I hadn't read *The Dirt* and he wasn't a big reality star yet, so all I knew about him was that he fucked Pamela Anderson and played drums on *Too Fast for Love,* an album so metal it was punk. Tommy was staying at a hotel on Forty-second Street and drinking with his entourage in the hotel bar. Matt had to leave before I got there but he knew about Tommy's infatuation with my book so he set it up before leaving.

I hopped in a cab and headed to midtown. It's a strange place, Times Square. You always feel like you've been transported to a minimall in

Cleveland. The hotel's bar was in the basement and it was way too fancy to be a fun drinking spot. Tommy was easy to pick out. He was sitting at a table of dudes who were broken into two categories. There were the balding rock dudes dressed like pubescent pop stars but with way more tattoos. And there were the music industry guys who wore pressed shirts and corny leather jackets. Tommy had on a sideways baseball hat, a shredded jean jacket covered in bric-a-brac, and pants that looked like bondage pants for kids into metal rap. There was a lot going on with his look but anyone who's a friend of my jokes is a friend of mine so I was happy to see him.

As I walked toward the table Tommy stood up and opened his arms for a big hug. "My MAN!" he yelled from twenty feet away while waiting for an embrace like we were long-lost brothers. Now, if you act like a good buddy, I'm going to treat you like a good buddy and that's going to include fucking around, no? So, as I walk into his arms and we're pressed together like a panini sandwich, I holler to the table, "Hey! This guy's got a boner!" expecting a big wave of laughter, which I would then surf into and assume my usual position as big kahuna.

Only, nobody laughed. They were mortified. The whole entourage stared at me like I was a homeless man who had strayed into the hotel looking for discarded food. Their faces said, "How dare you call our boy a fag?" and my eyes said, "It's called a joke, fags."

Tommy unwrapped his arms and stared back at me speechless, like I'd just farted on his balls. For some strange reason, I involuntarily said, "Hey-oh!" with my fingers pointing down at my chair and sat at the table. Tommy didn't sit with us and instead walked over to a completely separate booth all by himself. All right. I looked over for a minute, wondering if he expected me to follow him but he clearly did not. When a waitress came to ask him what he wanted he pulled her into the booth and started chatting her up.

I sat down with people who didn't want me there and told our waitress I'd like a Bud. I had just lost one after all. The rest of the guys spoke to each other and continued to ignore me. I tried to make a few jokes but I may as well have been a Goth chick trying to join a frat. After a short while, I looked over at Tommy, who was holding the waitress's hand and leading her out of the bar and, presumably, up to his room. It was pretty clear this was not going to be another episode of the Get Along Gang, so I took a big swig of my beer, said a purposely obtuse "BYE! BYE!" and walked away.

In the cab on the way back, I got a text from Matt: "U guys still there- May come back." I responded with a "nope" and when he asked, "U already left, y?" I replied, "Made a boner joke he didn't like and he left." Matt texted back, "Can't tell if ur kidding or not," and I didn't get back to him.

Brooklyn. Today this area is known as the "hipster mecca" but it wasn't pretty back then. You're welcome for the conversion, or maybe I apologize.

Shane and Suroosh were stuck with putting out a lot of fires and I was happy to be left alone to focus on content again without having to worry about answering to strangers. All I had to do was keep costs down to zero and I did that by doing the whole magazine myself. I should mention that I'd been trying to get them to contribute writing since day one but it was like pulling teeth. Alas, our first Greatest Hits book had about one article from each of them and almost all the other bylines were mine (or a pseudonym of mine). I'm sure they resented me during this post-dot-com phase, and the fact that I took a ton of freelancing gigs to pay the bills didn't help. I always sensed Shane resented my being the star of the show and wanted to be there himself one day. Suroosh didn't seem to care about popularity as long as nobody embarrassed him. I didn't mind the way things had turned out because I always dreaded the idea of salesmen taking over the company, but I had no time to discuss any of this with either of them. A big part of my job was going out and meeting freaks at all hours of the night. To generate interesting content I needed disposable income, and the British press had deep pockets. So if it paid the bills to be England's New York rep the way Lester "Last of the White Niggers" Bangs had been three decades earlier, well, I had no choice. While I wrote cover stories about getting wasted with musicians, Shane and Suroosh ripped up invoices and got screamed at by debt collectors.

After a two-year grind, we got things going again and it felt great. It felt like the pre-Richard days in Montreal. I was letting people with Down syndrome guest-edit the magazine, and we had a cover that was a mirror with a line on it for cocaine users. This version of *Vice* was about Terry Richardson and Ryan McGinley and getting wasted and having fun. Dash Snow's gang Irak was in every issue and it felt like the magazine I had always wanted to make. My "DOs & DON'Ts" column had become so popular it was defining a new subculture that people were calling hipsters. A British television show emerged as a parody of us: *Vice* was called *SugarApe* and I was an irritating prick named Nathan Barley.

At our ten-year anniversary party I felt like we'd reached our peak. We had ten of our favorite bands play and gave everyone free Sparks, which was an alcoholized energy drink that is now banned (though a caffeine-free version is still available). I dressed as a Nazi skinhead and oversaw a midget-tossing (also now banned) while an enormous screen behind me played Japanese puke porn that was so graphic it made everyone puke.

This high continued for another five years. I started a TV division and sold a pilot to Showtime with David Cross. Suroosh used his golden-goose ear to run a record label, and Shane had us in seventeen countries with hundreds of employees and a film production company. Every year we were doubling in size and soon we were way bigger than we were during the dot-com days, and most important, it was ours again.

Things started changing around 2006 when Shane began discussing a merger with Viacom. The stakes got very high very fast and soon law-yers had to be consulted and releases had to be signed for every move we made. The show I had been pitching with Johnny Knoxville was mor-phing into a whole other MTV thing that I wasn't in control of. For a travel DVD we did with Viacom, Cross and I set up an elaborate prank where we went to China and used the cheap labor there to outsource apple pies that came with an American flag in the center and played "The Star-Spangled Banner." This ended up on the DVD extras. I was flabbergasted. There are times when you do something that you think is funny but you understand if others disagree. Our China footage was not one of those things. As David put it, "I know for a fact that shit was great and anyone who thinks otherwise is wrong." I did a web series with Eva Mendes that was canned. I shot bits with Jimmy Kimmel, Sarah Silverman, Zach Galifianakis, and dozens more but nothing took. It became pretty clear this was no longer the old Vice, or what Shane called "The Gavin Show." Pinky sees the world through TV metaphors and describes the Viacom merger as Les Nessman and Herb Tarlek tak-ing over WKRP from Dr. Johnny Fever and Venus Flytrap, but I see it as a band that woke up one day and realized they don't like each other anymore or, more important, they don't respect what the other mem-bers do. "It's a different company," the head of human resources told me, to which I replied, "We have a human resources?" I always hated the term "human resources." It reminds me of *Soylent Green*. Fuck it.

Throughout 2007, we negotiated a split and by the beginning of

2008 I had sold my shares for an obscene amount of money. I never spoke to those guys again. As a *Vanity Fair* reporter put it, "It's not like they had to get rid of Gavin, but they knew he would have to stop pissing on the furniture—and he just *would not* do it."

With the money from the buyout, I bought a couple of apartments in Brooklyn and built my dream house upstate on a big piece of land I bought with Cross. I got my parents a Jaguar and myself a Range Rover, along with a bunch of other toys, and I stuck the rest into the stock market when it was at its lowest ebb since the Great Depression. I set up a standard estate credit shelter trust or whatever you call it and included a last will and testament that, for no reason, included the provision that my gravestone say I HEARD A RETARD SAY "CUNT" ONCE.

For the first time in thirteen years, I had the opportunity to do absolutely anything I wanted. I was a multimillionaire but to be totally honest, I never really cared about money and the vast dark infinity of it all scared the shit out of me. Leaving Viacom felt like leaving *Images Interculturelles* and leaving Szalwinski, but this time there was no magazine to rescue. I didn't know what to do. I mentioned my plight to Will Ferrell while we were sitting with his manager, and my pal, Jimmy Miller at a Yankees game and he said, "You got out at the perfect time. I can't even look at *Rolling Stone* anymore. It looks like a pamphlet." I started bringing the family to Dial House every summer, where the founders of Crass lived, and they said the same thing, but they also told me to tell everyone to fuck off and drop out of society. I definitely didn't deserve any sympathy but I was confused and lost.

I could have retired but I'd seen what happens to people who retire early—they die. After the Clash, Joe Strummer lived in a cave in Barcelona and quietly lost his mind. Looking back on it later he said, "Without people, you're nothing." I had a family now, but as far as creating things and making money went, I needed a new gang. Besides, I was almost positive my wife would stop fucking me if I didn't have a job. Guys in sweatpants do not get blow jobs.

If you're ever in a situation like this, I highly recommend getting in shape. My fitness regimen had been boxing for a while, but after signing my good-bye papers, I really went apeshit on it. Boxing isn't only good cardio. It's a type of Irish therapy that's crucial to your mental health. Got an important meeting or a pitch or you're going to be on TV? Go boxing first and you will kill. It makes you feel invincible.

I stepped up my regimen from three times a week to every single day. I even built an outside gym at my place upstate. Then one day, two blocks away from Ground Zero at Church Street Boxing Gym, it hit me. It was after a bout with a cantankerous sparring partner ten years my senior who'd kicked my ass so hard it made me mad. "I know what I'm going to do with the rest of my life," I realized while taking off my headgear. "The same shit I've always done. And I'm gonna give 'er." The motto at Church Street is "Fighting Solves Everything" and they're right. As prominent NPR nerd Ira Glass says, "You've just gotta fight your way through. It is only by going through a volume of work that . . . your work will be as good as your ambitions." I'm out to make the funniest shit possible. I'm not out to make people laugh. It's not up to me if they laugh or not. As weird 1920s dancer Martha Graham put it, "It is not your business to determine how good it is, nor how valuable it is, nor how it compares with other expressions. It is your business to keep it yours clearly and directly, to keep the channel open."

Pinky, me, and a bunch of ex-Vice people started a company with the totally unremarkable name Street Boners and TV Carnage. Then I dove headfirst into a sea of failures and took my punches like the first half of a *Rocky* fight. I wrote two screenplays that didn't go anywhere. I started a hardcore punk cover band that broke up quickly. I convinced Comedy Central and Adult Swim to commission pilots they later canned. I got a gig writing for a show Justin Theroux was doing for HBO that never got off the ground. The Travel Channel bought eight episodes of a show I created called *America on Zero Dollars a Day* and then killed it after the first episode. I did a documentary about a movie-watching competition for Netflix called *A Million in the Morning,* which they later passed on, and I made that sketch comedy movie called *Gavin McInnes Is a Fucking Asshole,* which few people saw outside of the cornflakes scene. I also wrote a book of DOs & DON'Ts called *Street Boners* that crawled off the shelves (thanks in part to that totally unmarketable name). On the bright side, I broke even on my investment in a taco truck.

It was a humbling slog but sometimes the shit I threw at the wall actually stuck. I started doing stand-up and only bombed half the time. A short film I did called *Asshole* got into Sundance. I realized I'd need a new guy to handle the business and marketing side of things so I offered my friend Sebastian a commission on everything he brought in. Soon we had sponsors to pay for my viral comedy videos and after convincing Vans to let me urinate on their shoes for a comedy sketch called "How to Piss in Public" we got over a million hits on YouTube and a cover story in *Adweek* magazine. Sebastian quickly went from being my manager to my business partner. We called our new company Rooster NYC (after our cocks) and focused on funny commercials. We did a comedy sketch with Kevin Hart and T-Pain that garnered 12 million views, and soon our client list included Microsoft, Nissan, Kraft, and Levi's. Within a year we had become a full-fledged advertising agency that made "ads for people who hate ads," and a year after that we were acquired by a much larger company for a shit ton of money. We never changed or lost our "Piss in Public" attitude, and began making movies that reflected that. We made a documentary about a very raunchy stand-up comedy tour I did called *The Brotherhood of the Traveling Rants,* and Fox produced an outrageous movie I cowrote and starred in called *How to Be a Man* (both are available on Netflix). I also broke even on a Southern-food restaurant called The Cardinal.

No matter how big Rooster became I was still determined to write my incendiary political rants and was lucky enough to get a cushy job as a columnist for the eccentric Greek tycoon Taki Theodoracopulos doing exactly that. Then I got Jim Goad hired as editor, something I had been planning for a long time at *Vice*. The column later led to a regular spot on the Fox News show *Red Eye,* an uppity talk show that destroys CNN and MSNBC in the ratings despite being on at three A.M.

New York is a lot like the Lord in that it helps those who help themselves. A couple of years after ending a career where I ran a company, wrote articles, and made funny videos, I began a new career where I ran a company, wrote articles, and made funny videos. And, just like in the early days, there's no boss. When clients give too many notes and start to wreck the joke, we stop working with them. As the article in *Adweek* said, "Gavin McInnes doesn't care about your product." All I care about is all I've ever cared about: being able to do fun shit with my friends without anyone telling us what to do.

# Will You Marry Me, Blobs? (2004)

Updating the Vice story takes us so far ahead I forgot to tell you about getting married. Smack-dab in the middle of the last story, I proposed.

My friends often ask me how you know when it's time to pop the question but for me there was no question. When it was time I could just tell it was time and I set up the greatest proposal of all time to make sure she said yes.

I was partying so hard back then, life was still check-to-check, so I set up an interest-free payment plan at Zales where I had a year to pay it off. Then I booked two tickets to Paris and contacted some friends there about getting a French child actor to surprise Blobs.

I told her we had to go meet my parents and discuss a tax clause regarding their will. Visiting bombastic drunk Scots in the Canadian winter to discuss a death tax is the worst life has to offer so I was setting the bar low. The first time she met them, I showed her my old teddy bear and she sat in the living room staring at its mangled face as they stared at her the same way. "You like that?" my dad asked her loudly only moments after being introduced. Before she could respond he yelled, "I FUCKED Teddy!" You never know what's going to happen in their presence but it's never relaxing.

At the airport, we got in the Europe line instead of the Canada line. Blobs was used to my scams and cheats and figured this was just another shortcut so she went along with it. She didn't even check the sign on the gate to see if it said Ottawa.

At the bar, I presented her the tickets. "Thanks," she said apathetically. Then I went, "This looks weird. They spelled Ottawa wrong." Blobs hugged me as hard as she could and we began a weekend of nothing but ear-to-ear smiles.

Montmartre is our spot when we go to Paris. It's got the quaint hills you saw in the movie *Amélie* with the huge Sacré-Coeur church at the top, and just when everything is getting too nice, the disgusting sex shops and seedy bars of Pigalle lure you to the bottom. At the border of the two worlds is an incredibly corny bar called Aux Noctambules where an old man in a pompadour and a red suit named Pierre Carré sings songs about all the places he's been, like "*dans* MEXIC-O-O-O-O!" Only, he couldn't have been to any of those places because he's played at this bar every night of his life since he was a kid. He sings 365 nights a year there and every time we go to Paris we bask in his crazy anthems like the Catholics in Sacré-Coeur several hundred feet above us.

On our last Paris trip, we went to the Eiffel Tower at five in the morning to do cartwheels. I convinced her I could do one over a park bench and ended up unconscious on the brick with a broken collarbone. The rest of the night was spent going to various hospitals and eventually faking a seizure in order to be seen. Talk about romantic.

I had the whole proposal scheduled for the day after we got there and it was going to happen not far from the site of the collarbone incident the year before. After a pleasant brunch, it was time to take a taxi to the tower. I had scheduled a light-skinned black child (half–American Indian would have been ideal because she was supposed to represent our future kids, but this was the closest I could get) to run up to Blobs under the Eiffel Tower and hand her my ring at three P.M. We had exactly fifteen minutes and I couldn't find a taxi for miles. I was starting to panic. About ten minutes after I needed one, we crawled into a cab and I realized we were still going to make it. My adrenaline was flowing and I started playing air drums against my will. Blobs looked confused. "You like that?" I asked like a Scottish dad thinking of something controversial to say. "You like when I play the drums? You wanna hear me play the drums for the rest of your life?" This strange bit of dialogue is the only part I regret about the whole thing. I wasn't in control at that moment.

We got to the Eiffel Tower only a tiny bit late. I tried to act casual but knew we had to get underneath the tower where avenue Gustave Eiffel meets Parc du Champ de Mars. I held her hand and the mulatto girl started running across the grass toward us. She handed a crumpled-up paper bag to Blobs and said, "*Bonjour, madame, j'ai un petit cadeau pour vous,*" then she ran away. Blobs asked me what she said and I told her she said, "Hello, madam, I have a small present for you," and added, "Open it up." When she saw the ring, she started to cry and I managed not to cry while asking her if she'd marry me. I didn't get on one knee because I think that sends the wrong message. She said yes and we held each other and then we made out and walked around holding hands. It was fucking heavenly.

That night we sang karaoke in Pigalle and saw Pierre Carré perform his cheesy songs and a year later, we were married. Then two small people came out of her and we gave them American Indian names.

# A Dog Named Pancake Saved Our Lives (2005)

*F*our Brothers is a movie about some badass orphans who were all adopted by a nice old lady who got her fucking head blown off. The brothers come back to their hometown to get revenge and—holy shit—do they ever. I went to see it with my soon-to-be wife and she came up with the brilliant idea of bringing a flask of whiskey. Until then we had been following the New York tradition of sneaking beer cans into the theater, which makes for a loud *pksh!* every time you open one and a dozen "excuse me's" each time you have to go pee. A flask solves both problems, though it's not good for the Irish.

The movie is good in a bad way, packed with David-and-Goliath clichés and "doing what's right" peppered with car crashes and explosions. The ending is especially invigorating and as we walked out of the theater onto Tenth Street and Third Avenue, I felt like a righteous vigilante. One of the biggest differences between girls and boys is the way they feel after a movie. When the credits roll, the female files the movie away in her brain and is ready to move on. When the credits roll on a superhero movie, however, the boy who just saw it will spend the next three hours with his arms stretched in front of him as he flies around the neighborhood looking for crime to fight. It takes us as long to get over a movie as it takes to watch it. After *Four Brothers,* I steeled myself to throw every New York gangster back in jail where he belongs, consequences be damned. "I don't give a fuck," I said to Blobs, to which she replied, "What?"

A few blocks later we were walking on the south side of Tompkins Square Park, which is more than just a place Blobs and I meet during emergencies. It's also where junkies meet. There were two crusty punks in front of us walking a dog with a rope for a leash. Crusties are a punk subculture that takes the music and douses it in speed metal, puts everything in a backpack, then mangles the hippies' "dirty and smelly" aesthetic into "so unbelievably filthy you can smell my foreskin from across the street." Their clothes are just punk rags but they throw in some facial tattoos, dreadlocks, and vegan boots, then smear smegma and poop over everything to make it all their own. It's homeless chic with a big shot of heroin and it's such a bummer, it's a big part of why I gave up on punk back in 1992.

This couple was a slightly shorter version of Blobs and me if we'd bathed in manure for ten years and panhandled under a cemetery. They annoyed me but they weren't doing anything wrong, so I figured I'd let them be. Then the dog stopped to take a shit. Oh, HELL no. I became the Fifth Brother about to wreak some street justice.

"I assume you're going to pick that up," I told the guy with the Maori tribal tattoos on his chin (which, I'm pretty sure, meant "wife").

"What?" he asked.

"The shit," I said.

"It's not shit," his equally facially tattooed mate yelled with her floppy tits wobbling around inside her stained-brown white T-shirt. "She's taking a piss."

They got me. Stopping dog piss in New York City is a beautiful notion, but you might as well try to rid the city of the word "fuggedaboudit." I said, "All right, all right" and walked ahead. Blobs looked concerned and suggested we go home immediately.

The crusties followed behind us yelling things like, "Way to go, buddy!" and "It's the piss police!" I didn't let down my guard. One thing about growing up in an orphanage and having your mother's head blown off is your street smarts get polished to superhero levels. My Spidey Senses told me some shit was about to go down. It would only be a matter of time before a neglected turd was sitting on the sidewalk so I stuck around to take care of it.

About thirty seconds later, I turned around, and what did my eyes behold? The exact same scenario as before, only out the butt. The bitch's stinky parents were cooing and smiling as the turd oozed out, saying things such as, "Good girl," and "There you go." (I've seen other dog owners do this, and it's revolting.) They didn't notice me and I stood there giving them the benefit of the doubt until there could be no doubt the shit was going to be abandoned like the Four Brothers were. As Blobs sank her face into her hands, I walked over to make my first citizen's arrest.

"You're kidding, right?" I said as I got within punching distance. "You're laughing about my accusing you of leaving shit on the street and two minutes later, you do exactly that?" I pointed to the hot brown mound on the ground. This was shit, Sherlock. They knew I was right and walked off with all of their tails between all of their legs. I wasn't done with them yet. "Well?" I asked as they tried to move on by doing a strange walk that was curiously snobby. "What are you going to do about it?" I demanded.

"People will get it eventual . . . ly," the more male of the two mumbled. I insisted he speak up so he stopped walking and said, "People will pick it up. It's a job. Cleaning up the park. We're actually providing jobs." He was indulging in a bastardization of what economists call the Broken Window Theory and it made me shit a brick of rage.

"Oh, great," I said, like an angry teacher. "THAT's your contribution to society. You're the Shit Easter Bunny who leaves treats everywhere so we can all spend our tax dollars cleaning it up!" I couldn't stop. "Fantastic. Thanks for coming out. Hey, everybody! The people who leave shit everywhere are here. Who wants a job?" The crusties shook their heads and walked off, but I had a lot more work to do. I needed them to be as mad as I was.

Then I blurted out, "You got fucked by your dad." I'm not exactly sure where it came from, but it worked.

He stopped and turned around before asking, "What the fuck did you just say?"

I was happy to get his attention and leaned into his face, saying, "Everyone who has facial tattoos was molested. It's a well-known fact." It's actually not a well-known fact but a theory I've had for decades.

His lady friend then stepped to me. "You saying I was fucked by my dad, too?" she asked.

"Yes," I said, unfazed, "that's what it means. It says, 'Stay away from me,' as in 'Stop raping me . . . *Dad*.'" Then I pointed at her tattooed face and said, "Now. Go. Pick. Up. That. SHIT!"

I thought I was winning the intimidation game but she surprised me by getting even closer to my face and saying, "Oh, yeah? And what are you going to do if I don't?"

There's a scene in *The Sopranos* where Tony sees a guy wearing a hat in a restaurant and it pisses him off so much, he walks over and tells the guy to take his hat off. The guy gets a little snarky, so Tony leans in close and says, "Take it off," so intensely, the guy apologizes and quickly removes his fedora. I looked at both crusties as I thrust my hand into my pocket and said in my best Tony Soprano tone, "I will stab you both." But Tony Soprano is a six-foot-tall, three-hundred-pound Mafia boss. I look more like Rip Taylor's inexplicably heterosexual son. Tony had a gun. I had nothing in my pocket but some loose change.

Immediately after I made my idle threat, the dog's mom ripped open the front of her shirt and yelled, "Then go ahead, motherfucker. Stab me." As her gigantic smelly boobs slapped from side to side, I started to realize I was in way over my head. I'm not an orphan or a mob boss. I don't intimidate people and I don't even know how to fight. As her filthy nude torso disturbed me to my core, I noticed her doggie's daddy was pulling a motherfucking tire iron out of their large army backpack. He had a sort of "Here we go again" demeanor as he slapped the iron against his palm and walked toward me. I had nothing but a fictional knife and some previous courage to defend myself, and all I could think was how Blobs and I were going to get brained because a dog took a crap on the sidewalk. We would never have kids or a family. We had been blessed with three decades of life on this wonderful planet and it was all over in an instant because I got a bee in my bonnet about poo-poo. What was I thinking? Confronting homeless people is like saying "BOO!" to a cornered rat. Just before it all went black, everything turned upside down and I heard the most beautiful word in the English language: "Pancake."

Their stupid dog had become spooked by the kerfuffle and was trotting across the road dragging her frayed rope leash behind her. Both parents became petrified and dropped what they were doing to go save it. I grabbed Blobs and we speed-walked past the discarded tire iron toward safety as both punks ran in the opposite direction. I'll never forget looking back and seeing their rags flapping in the midnight air and a guy with his arms outstretched zigzagging across Seventh Street yelling, "Pa-a-a-a-a-ancake! Pa-a-a-a-a-ncake!"

# The KKK Stag (2005)

Prostitutes bore me. I tried it and it didn't work. I want a woman to be gagging for my cock, not gagging if my cock isn't wrapped in latex and attached to a $100 bill. Strip clubs are OK but there's nothing sadder than a bachelor party with a bunch of horny men sitting on fold-out chairs in a motel room while some ditzy young girl in a K-hole dances around naked.

For my stag, I wanted to get every bro I've ever had into one big house in the woods for the bender of the century. I scheduled it to be four days long because I was getting married on the fifth day and figured they'd all be so sick of booze by then we'd have a wedding without totally wasted people.

If you've ever seen old footage of biker rallies you'll see a lot of swastikas and a lot of guys making out. They weren't gay, they were drunk and enjoyed making everyone as uncomfortable as possible. Or maybe they were gay. We rented a gigantic hunting lodge in the upstate New York village of Bovina and filled it with enough booze and drugs to justify a DEA raid. I had my brother, Kyle, there; all the Monks from high school; all the SXSW dudes from Texas; old tree-planting buddies; and Anal Chinook, including Blake Jacobs and his best friend, an equally tiny drunk man we called Geddes. We had New York pals as well as David Choe, Pinky, one of the guys from the movie *FUBAR*, Vice employees from all over the world, Matt Sweeney, prank-call expert Jeff Jensen, and my cousin Mark from Scotland. Even my dad showed up.

The first night of drinking went on until the sun rose. By that morning, a group of old friends getting together to riff had transmogrified into an old-alcoholic *Lord of the Flies*. Nobody was allowed to wear a shirt and slapping each other as hard as you could had become the new "hello." We had water balloon fights indoors and the owner called the police regularly. We were building huge fires, making puke jokes, and kicking each other in the nuts.

The second day got more intense. Nudity had become de rigueur and fag jokes were no longer kidding. "Look at his scrumptious ass," I'd yell at the ballerina-tiny Blake before shoving my tongue down his throat. "I've never been this horny for a dwarf before!" Groping each other's buttocks slowly and passionately was perfectly normal. Grabbing a guy's crotch and holding on until he punched you in the face was also common. When a pizza guy finally brought food (I forgot to include food in this grand scheme) he told us the whole town was talking about a bunch of gays who took over the hunting lodge and were trying to kill each other.

By the third day, we were completely off the rails. My dad was bad at the keg-stands but he was the only one who didn't projectile-vomit, so maybe he wasn't. I got mad at him for not doing cocaine with us and that's something that still makes me cringe. We were filthy and grubby, with vomit in our hair and piss stains on our pants. Some tried to bow out and snuck off to their beds but as soon as one of us noticed, we all stampeded up to his room to pound him awake. Late-night sing-alongs around the piano sounded like crazed soccer chants and I remember something about locking Geddes in the oven and turning it on.

On the last night, everyone seemed particularly quiet and reluctant to explain why. I was hoping my plan had worked and the wedding was going to be a serene collection of hungover nice guys. When I walked into a room wearing nothing but rubber boots and underwear, people stopped talking. I did a line, rolled a joint, and took a sip from a bottle of warm whiskey by the piano. I asked why everyone was being so weird. Nobody answered so I passed out in my chair.

I woke up to a handful of guys partying their asses off. This was the fourth day. How were they still going? Someone found a saddle and everyone was taking turns riding li'l Blake around the living room but the majority of people were MIA. Then a voice yelled, "It's time!" and the stragglers with the saddle snapped to attention. TJ picked me up and handed me some pants. Cheese gave me a T-shirt, but it was wet so I refused.

I was marched out of the lodge down the back steps and into the darkness. From out of nowhere a bandana was wrapped around my eyes and I was marched even farther away from the lodge. I could tell from the twigs snapping beneath my feet that we were going into the forest. About a minute later we stopped and my blindfold was removed.

Pinky was standing in front of me with a gigantic watermelon slice in his hand. He was wearing a fluorescent orange jumpsuit with the Hooters logo on the front. "Do you," he said like a very loud James Earl Jones, "accept this new level of manhood?"

My heart was pounding because I knew whatever was about to happen might just be the most towering experience of my life. "Yes!" I yelled dutifully.

"And," Pinky continued, "do you understand that no matter what happens from this day forth, you will always stay true to the brotherhood and the values it holds dear?"

"Yes!" I said again.

"Repeat it!" he screamed in my face.

I repeated it word for word and Pinky plunged my face into the watermelon while yelling, "Eat!"

With my face covered in watermelon juice, Pinky and TJ flung me through the bushes and into a clearing, where I tripped over some roots. I looked up and in the moonlight saw ten Klansmen standing over me—hoods and all. I stood up, said, "Holy shit!" and a fifteen-foot-high wooden cross burst into flames as everyone yelled, "Hooray!" The hoods came off and everyone else leapt out from the bushes and started jumping all over each other like we'd won the Stanley Cup. The "Klansmen" were friends from the stag dressed up in authentic-looking uniforms Chin's then-wife had spent weeks making by hand.

Guys poured beer on each other and David Choe fell into the trees while trying to put Blake on his shoulders. Soon everyone was kissing. Pinky was French-kissing my dad and every other Klansman was locked in a tongue embrace. It was offensive to every possible group in the world, including gay, black Nazis. This is what I'd been shooting for since I became a teenager in 1983—no-holds-barred, asshole mayhem. This wasn't just balls-to-the-wall—we were taking our balls and lifting them up *over* the wall.

My eyes welled with tears and I looked up at the sky before quietly saying, "Thank you, God. Thank you for everything." God didn't reply. He was *pissed.* (So were the cofounders of Vice, incidentally. They refused to participate.)

The wedding the next day was beautiful and a sharp contrast to the mayhem that had come before. It was outdoors and my friend Jim Krewson's band played beautiful bluegrass music. The speeches were great despite Pinky saying something about prostitutes and my dad doing his whole insult-me shtick.

My wife looked so beautiful I was in awe. After the ceremony, everyone went to the after-party, where Chromeo played, and Blobs and I drove off in a yellow Rolls complete with JUST MARRIED on the back and bouncing cans tied to the bumper.

After tying the knot, I drastically cut down the partying, especially after the kids were born, but I never forgot my vows to the brotherhood: Never stop believing—and by "believing," we mean "being a retard."

# Hunting for Injuns (2005)

After the marriage, my wife felt compelled to learn about my heritage. Though we did invent the modern world by creating the industrial revolution and separating church and state, all you need to know about modern Scottish culture is beer and yelling.

Learning about her people was a bit more complex. American Indians remain a mystery to most people, including me, and I was surprised to see how similar they are to my own peeps. For one, I never expected them to be so funny. Like with the Scots, riffing is an integral part of almost every tribe's culture and even in the grimmest situation, someone in the room is going to bust out a gag.

What else? Their earwax is as powdery as that of the Taiwanese; they need all their body parts when they're buried, so if they have a thumb amputated they have to keep it in a jar until they die; they say "aaayyy" after every joke; and they have bigger big toes than the rest of us. You should see the big toes on these people. Nike tried to make them a special shoe to fit it but it pissed them off because they hate stereotypes—even the true ones.

It kills the white man to learn that Indians aren't looking for friends. The trusting Injuns are now extinct and the ones who have managed to stick it out tend to be dubious grumps, at least when it comes to bro-ing down with Caucasians.

My father-in-law suggested I present Blobs's tribe with a deer I killed myself. He said that the tribe would then accept our marriage as real. Thanks for telling me this *after* the marriage, Pops.

I hopped on a plane and headed to hunting hot spot Winnipeg, Manitoba, to give it a shot. I decided to go with a bow because I thought it would be more badass. After three hours at the practice range with no progress, my hosts rolled their eyes and said we had to get on with it. I was with an awesome hoser dad named Paul and a young Cree Indian named Reg.

My shirt says COMMIES AREN'T COOL with Che Guevara crossed out. That's Hoser Paul giving the thumbs-up, and Reg is taking the picture. (2005)

We were all covered in camo gear from our feet to our heads. Even our faces had camo mesh on them. Smelling like anything in the bush will frighten away the deer, so food, beer, and pissing are banned. We wished each other luck, grabbed our bows, and went to different spots along a creek. I would kill a deer, present it to my mother-in-law's family, receive some amazing gifts I'd never heard of, and be accepted into the tribe. I had already decided on my Indian name—Whistling Cheeks.

I was told I had to stay perfectly still for the rest of the day and not even breathe heavy if I wanted to bag a deer. This sounds really fucking boring but I did it for several hours and it was awesome. Sitting perfectly still as you await your prey feels like you're on opiates. It's no different from meditating, and you get into this serene zone where you're so at one with nature you feel like you could—FUCK! A deer!

The opium was gone and now I was on meth. My heart was pounding as loud as a boxing bell. I raised my bow as slowly as I could and the deer lifted his head for a moment with a "What the fuck was that?" expression. My eyeballs were protruding out of my face like a hot-rod cartoon. The whole thing lasted about three seconds. Before I knew it, my arrow had shot into the ground underneath the deer, and the animal was off like a springy rocket.

White man miss deer.

That night we went back to Paul's and told stories. They made fun of me for getting "Moose Fright."

Reminiscing about the hunt is almost as fun as the hunt itself. We were in Paul's backyard smoking pot and drinking beer when the whole—I'm talking the *entire*—sky lit up and turned into an infinitely large, undulating blanket of changing colors. I'd seen the Northern Lights, AKA Aurora Borealis, before, but not this intense. It went from slow, glowing lights to a flashing storm of lights, to huge blasts of color zipping through the cosmos like they were being controlled by a galaxy-sized kid with a flashlight. Then it went back to the undulating color blanket. Even the locals were going nuts.

"Dese are your wife's fuckin' ancestors sayin' it's OK," Paul told me, channeling the Native American spirit world through a hoser's slang. "It's like de're sayin' 'give 'er.'"

But after returning from Winnipeg with no deer carcass in tow, I knew I had to do something big to curry the Indian side of my family's favor (and these kinds of Indians don't even like curry). So when my wife invited me to her aunt's house for a sweat-lodge ceremony in January, I leapt at the chance.

The house was just outside Madison, Wisconsin, in a rural area, but it wasn't on a reservation. I was with my wife and her brother and the aunts happily introduced us to everyone in the room, which was mostly huge Indian men. The walls were filled with framed pictures of the men in the family wearing their military uniforms. Indians get a lot of flak for distancing themselves from America but they sure take the army seriously. I don't think I met a guy there who wasn't enlisted.

They asked me if I was truly prepared for the sweat lodge and I asked them why they were getting so heavy all of a sudden. "Oh, he'll be fine," the aunt said, interrupting our discussion. "We had kids in there the other day who were four years old. They loved it."

The sweat lodge was a dome made of bent branches about ten feet in diameter. The center had a small pit filled with large hot rocks that glowed red. The heat was kept in by a series of wet blankets surrounding the outside.

Blobs, her brother, me, and three Indian men crawled inside and sat cross-legged around the fire. Within seconds, I knew I was in trouble. Scottish is about as white as white gets. We invented redheads. To us, people from Wales are Southerners. I'm designed to be standing on a craggy mountain in the highlands wearing nothing but a tartan cloth as freezing rain blows sideways through my hairy beard. I'm not designed for heat. It makes me claustrophobic.

The door was a flap made by folding a blanket up, and when our host closed it he closed the door on hope. Goddamnit, it's hot in there. It's not hot like a sauna where you go, "Jeesh! Hot enough for ya?" It's hot like a live lobster being dropped into boiling water and realizing he is being prepared as food. "Has anyone died from this?" I asked nervously after introductions were made (the answer is "yes" followed by "plenty"). The Indian man leading the ceremony told me about a chief from another tribe who was in a one-person sweat lodge for so long, he cooked himself. "When they went to pull him out," our host said, "the meat came off the bone like a Christmas turkey." He was probably fucking with me, but the fact that I was putting my life into a stranger's hands made me very uncomfortable. Being burned alive wasn't helping.

White man scared.

I looked over at Blobs and she was completely drenched in sweat. Everyone was. I decided I was going to say, "Fuck this," and march out of the tent. As this tempting thought raced through my head they opened the flap and cold air rushed in. O Great Spirit, it felt like every pore in my body was chugging a glass of ice-cold water. But they quickly shut the flap again.

We were told to pray for family members who were fellow war vets suffering from various postwar maladies. One of them had some kind of lung infection and we all had to concentrate to get the poison out. This is an easy concept to grasp when you're saying grace, but I was having a bad acid trip. "We can control toxins in other people's bodies," I rambled silently, "so is it possible there are waves of energy going through the cosmos we can then manipulate and coerce into making real changes in the real world? No, it isn't! It can't be!" I was losing it. As they began their traditional songs, I started bobbing back and forth like an autistic orphan.

They could tell I was not coping so the host assured me we would open the flap after one more song. This didn't help because it wasn't a specific time. White people can take almost endless amounts of suffering; they just need to know exactly when it's going to end. Indian songs go on forever. It's not like "Louie Louie" where you get three choruses, then a guitar solo, then one more chorus and you're done. The chanting they were doing in the tent, though beautiful and haunting, kept going and going and going. Every time I thought we were done and things were coming to a close, someone else would come in with a "*Hay*-ay-aya-hey I hey-a-a" and we were off on a whole other part.

They opened the flap for what felt like a fraction of a second and then put on three more red-hot rocks for what they called the Final Round. Now I was mad. "Are they fucking with me?" I thought. "Is this some kind of joke?" The host noticed he was murdering me and he said I could put my hands behind my back and reach for some cold air outside the bottom of the tent. I did so and it was heavenly. I haven't been that jealous of my fingers since they touched Megan's beef curtains back in 1984.

As a kid, I hated roller coasters until someone explained you're supposed to yell your head off instead of sitting there holding your stomach on every turn. I tried that and realized what everyone was screaming about. Roller coasters rule. It's holding everything inside that makes you sick. I extrapolated this lesson and applied it to everything: If I wasn't a dick to people, I'd get sick. If someone's boring, I have to put my arms in the air and scream it to the world or I'll puke.

I resigned myself to surviving this steaming-hot roller-coaster ride at all costs. This was no longer a taste test of another culture's delicacies—it was war and I didn't care if they hung me by my nipples. I wasn't going to give in.

So, for the Final Round's entirety, I shamelessly increased the bobbing to head-banging proportions and said, "Uuuh! Uuuh! Uuuh!" so loud, it almost drowned out their singing. My brother-in-law was embarrassed and my wife was getting riled, but I'm sorry. You can't expect a lobster to act like Dirty Harry when you're boiling him alive. I had to shake the fear out.

After at least three hundred million hours of this, I made it to the end and when we finally walked out into the cold night air, I started to chuckle. We all had steam floating off of us like we were made of dry ice and every step I took melted everything around it. The intense suffering inside the lodge makes you appreciate how great you have it outside. A lot of Indian ceremonies seem to be about giving thanks and not taking things for granted. I was more than just happy to be out of there. Endorphins were pouring out of my brain and I felt spiritually obese. It was a rush of euphoric appreciation I've never gotten from any drug. It was almost better than sex.

We had dinner after and hung out a bit and I got the feeling I was accepted as a mate but definitely not as one of the gang. I don't think the Indian side of the family will ever accept me as one of them and I don't blame them. That's how they roll. We spent four hundred years trying to get along and it simply did not work out. I don't buy the myth that they were a serene, peaceful people who were introduced to warfare by us savages. They had war when we got here and we fought like hell for centuries. We fought with them, against them; some joined us in our battles and we joined them in others. We obliterated them and they destroyed us. Eventually, we got the land and the ones who remain have agreed to disagree.

In my children's tribal papers everyone gets a full name but I'm simply listed as "Caucasian." Oh well, at least they're politically correct.

# Underwater Pussy (2006)

The great thing about rich guys who grew up poor is they don't give a shit about money. David Cross is one of those guys and would regularly book these massive vacation homes in the Caribbean or Mexico and tell us everything was on him if we paid for our flights.

He suggested we get our scuba licenses to go deep-sea diving in Cancún, and within a week we were enrolled in a course at a tiny shop in New York called Village Divers. We took it about as seriously as Mr. Kotter's class. "Today we're going to talk about valves," the hirsute Palestinian teacher would tell us. "A bad seal can cost you your life." I held up my beer and blurted out, "I guess Heidi Klum got one of the good ones." I hadn't been in school since school and had forgotten how fun it was to be the class clown. That was my gig back in the day—so much so, I was put in a special eighth-grade class for "emotionally disturbed" kids.

I refused to learn anything during the classes. David was a little bit better, but we weren't stunned when we failed the final exam. "I know you guys don't work hard," the teacher said, staring at our pathetic results, "but this is unbelievable. I've been doing this for twenty years and have not seen one single person fail, ever. I've even had *handicapped* people pass this test."

241

We set up a rematch and I got on the computer to figure out a cheat. A week later David and I were high-fiving in front of the school after receiving a whopping fourteen out of twenty-seven correct (just over 51 percent). A week after that we were on our way to Cancún.

There were about a dozen people at the vacation house, including a skinny comedy writer named Mark Rivers and Death Cab for Cutie's Ben Gibbard. Mark, David, and I booked what's called a drift dive, where you go down about a hundred feet and the current carries you along a coral reef.

A twenty-person boat took the group about three miles out into the ocean and everyone started to get their gear on. I met a Middle Eastern dude on the way who said you didn't need a license to dive in Egypt and he saw guys spitting out blood after they came up because they didn't know about the bends. I remember our teacher saying something about the bends. What were the bends again?

During the ride, Mark started testing his equipment by putting the regulator in his mouth, which made him gag. Every time he put it past his lips, he'd retch out a crippling dry heave. I usually feel like an alpha male around comedians, especially on vacation, because I inevitably have more tattoos than them. My sense of superiority was exacerbated by the fact that Mark dyes his gray hair a kind of orangey beige (an act I passionately disapprove of). I thought his gagging was the funniest thing I'd ever seen and couldn't stop mocking him. As I snickered at Mark for continuing to gag, we all jumped into the ocean. Before I knew it, we were deep inside a crystal-clear ocean that went on forever.

This wasn't a murky Canadian lake. It was like nothing I had ever seen before. It wasn't "cool," like seeing a big painting of a dragon; it was stultifying, like seeing a herd of gigantic dragons in real life. Things were as frighteningly vivid as if I was floating in midair. I could see a football field of distance in front of me, above me, below me, and behind me. Oh, look! There's a cluster of divers floating about a mile over there. It was like being in outer space but with professional lighting. I had no file for it in my brain.

The instructor noticed my face looked like *The Scream* and made the underwater motion for "Are you OK?" I made a hand gesture that looked like I was gripping a dick, which is underwater sign language for "OK." (You can't do a thumbs-up because that means you want to go back up.) David and Mark were having a great time calmly exploring the scene about twenty feet below us.

Soon we were all a hundred feet under the surface. As my environment rapidly got weirder, I realized I should have paid attention in class. This was way freakier than looking down from the surface. The current took us deeper than a hundred feet by slowly dragging us to the right and over a mountainous coral cliff I hadn't noticed before. Over the edge was beyond deep. It was an abyss. As my mind raced with fear, David and Mark cheerily drifted along the coral cliff's edge, checking out the colorful fish hiding in the crevices. I tried to mellow out and pulled my underwater camera out of my vest to take pictures. As my jittery hands tried to work the controls, it felt like playing cribbage while falling from an airplane. At the height of my confusion, I looked up and saw a sea turtle staring at me like an angry penis in a Tupperware container. Then I looked higher and saw a huge fishing boat on the surface that was so far away, it was the size of a bedbug. My vision was starting to pinhole and I could feel my breathing get sporadic. I thought I was panicking but then I realized I'd gone way past that and was now experiencing a full-on panic attack. Then I realized this whole thing was happening underwater, where panicking can kill you. So my panic attack had a panic attack.

The most immediate problem with all this was the breathing. While using a self-contained underwater breathing apparatus, you're supposed to breathe slow and steady, like you're asleep. Us panickers don't like to be told how to breathe. We find it alarming.

I had a faint flash from the lessons back in New York. The instructor told us that if you blew up a balloon at the bottom of the ocean and then brought it to the surface, the air inside would keep expanding until the balloon popped before reaching the surface.

I was startled out of my flashback, which may have been actual death. "I'm going to pop like a balloon! I'm going to be like those bleeding Egyptians!" With bubbles exploding from my mouthpiece, I started waving my arms and signaling distress to the instructor, who

grabbed me and held me down. "Jesus Christ," I thought, "these fuck-
ers WANT me to die! It's an insurance scam!"

I shook him loose and managed to swim up much higher, but he
caught me again. He held me there for what seemed like forever before
I could shake him loose again. This happened about four times before
I finally erupted out of the water, gasping like a fiend and possibly crying. I realize now he was saving my life because the only way to avoid
the bends is to take breaks during the ascent.

When we got to the top, the instructor was livid—not at me but at
David and Mark for not sticking close to my candy ass. He held on to
my vest as I bobbed up and down in the waves like a blow-up beta male
and the two of them showed up about a minute later.

"Are we done already?" David asked.

"How dare you!" the instructor yelled with a furious Mexican
accent. "You were suppose to stay by your team! What da hell is da
matter wit' you?"

What a fool I had been. All that hubris and arrogance went crashing
into the Caribbean and when it did, my heart sank like the *Titanic*.

I didn't talk much on the way back except to ask Mark and David
not to say anything to the girls. As we opened the door to our vacation house the girls yelled, "How'd it go?" from the kitchen. Mark
said, "Gavin got scared and had to wait in the boat," before David
added, "He had a pa-a-a-anic atta-a-a-ck," and everyone laughed. It
was humiliating. I had become an underwater pussy with a vagina as
big and wet as the deep blue sea.

# I Got Knocked the Fuck Out
# (2008)

Freelance writing and making funny commercials is exactly what you'd expect it to be but working in TV is bizarre. Networks commission hundreds of pilots a year for big money, but for every eighty pilots they have written, only one will make it to air, and even then it will probably be canceled after a few episodes. It's an entire industry where people are creating content for the garbage. I'm developing a show with FX right now called *Trim* about three straight guys who become hairdressers to get laid. The odds are about 100 percent it will never see the light of day but that's just the nature of the beast. Some think it's great. I know writers here in New York who don't even want their shows to get picked up because they don't want to move to L.A. I'm not like that. I'm too much of an attention whore to let things go unnoticed.

For example, I did a pilot for Al Gore's network, Current TV, called *The Immersionist*. The pitch was, I wouldn't just go and hang out with a group of people, I'd immerse myself in their lifestyle the way George Orwell did in *Down and Out in Paris and London* or Barbara Ehrenreich did in *Nickel and Dimed*. We picked a biker gang in Oakland called the East Bay Rats as our first "tribe," and I flew out there to go live with them.

They call themselves the Rats because they live in a crackhead slum and their motorbikes were dirty pieces of shit made from scrap metal. Against all odds, I managed to ingratiate myself with the group and almost convinced their president, Trevor, to make me a Rat. Pretending to be in a motorcycle gang is fun as shit. We destroyed a car with sledgehammers and then hitched it to a tow truck and rode it around the neighborhood. We crashed motorbikes and raced tricycles down a mountain at neck-breaking speeds. And we fought.

The East Bay Rats have a boxing ring in the backyard of their clubhouse and insist every member fight. When they asked me if I knew how to fight, I mentioned years of boxing experience, so they brought in a pro MMA fighter named Meathead Eric. He was a bald Asian kid with arms that looked like they were hiding bowling balls and shoulders as wide as an ox. He was nervous before he saw me but when I walked into the room with my shirt off, he smiled and started bobbing back and forth on the balls of his feet in anticipation. I wasn't even remotely nervous because I had a plan. I was also a bit drunk.

One of the trainers at Church Street was the reigning IBF Continental Africa cruiserweight champion. He calls himself Jaffa "the African Assassin" Ballogou and yells shit like, "I AM A REAL MAN," in the changing room as his penis swings around like a rubber snake in a Darth Vader helmet. We would spar occasionally and got to be such good pals, he let me in on a secret trick that wins any fight in the world.

The trick involves standing perfectly still and acting like you're ready to receive a good right to the head. As the right comes at you, you immediately drop to your knees and nail the guy in the stomach. As he doubles over in pain, rise up off the mat like a phoenix and knock him out with a super uppercut to the chin. Bang. He's out. Then the crowd cheers and girls start excreting juices. It never fails, but Ballogou told me I could use his black magic only as a last resort.

The referee snapped me out of my Ballogou flashback and reminded me I was in the ring with a monster. We were the first fight of the evening. The referee introduced me as Sissy La La due to my less-than-fearsome presence, while Meathead Eric was allowed to stick to his real name. As the bell rang for the first round, the bikers chanted, "Sissy La La," again and again.

We sized each other up for the first round. We each threw a few loose jabs to the head to see how fast the other guy was. It became clear very quickly that this guy was a fighter jet and I was a horse-drawn carriage. He was an energized cat playing with an alcoholic mouse. I hit him in the face a few times and he accepted each blow as if it was a breath mint. I'm surprised he didn't say thanks.

When the uneventful first round ended, I went back to my corner and sat on a stool while nobody gave me a pep talk and told me what his weaknesses were. I looked around the backyard and it dawned on me that there were no paramedics. I thought, "What if things go bad?" I was starting to get nervous. "Shit, we're in Oakland. We'd be lucky if 911 garnered *any* response from *anyone*. This could be my last night on earth. Fuck. What about my kids?"

Visions of my wife danced around in my head as the second-round bell rang. This was no longer a publicity stunt. I came at the fight with a whole new mentality: survival.

I laid into the buff Chink with everything I had and got in a good five punches in a row. The footage of this sequence shows that what I thought was a brief moment of victory looks more like a puppy who's way too happy to see his owner. Eric stepped back and blocked most of my happy-dog advances until one of them managed to hit him square on the nose, which made him mad. He reached back with a wild right that dropped me to the ground like a bag of potatoes. Adrenaline and drugs propelled me instantly back up off the mat, lowering Eric's confidence from 110 percent to 109 percent.

Being strategic about fighting is like trying to play pool while someone throws bowling balls at your head. I wanted a good fifteen minutes to recover from every hit but I had less than a second. As I tried desperately to regain my footing, Meathead hit me with a one-two combo that made my world go completely black for about two seconds. The referee stepped in and asked me if I wanted to go on.

The cameras were rolling. I couldn't call off the fight after an extended blink. I told the referee I was ready to continue and decided it was time for an all-or-nothing grand finale.

Ballogou's gigantic head appeared like an African moon above the crowd. "Go low," he said in his weird Togolese accent, "then come up hard." Eric's right came at me like a meteor and I sank to my knees below it and nailed him in his twelve-pack as hard as I could. This caused Eric approximately zero discomfort so before I could deliver the deadly phoenix uppercut, I felt a left hook obliterate my head and send my whole body sprawling backward into the corner post. I was unconscious for about fifteen seconds.

"Stand back," were the next words I heard as light flooded back into my black universe, "everyone stand back." I understood English and knew that was a guy telling someone they had to get out of the way. Someone had been hurt, I guess. Then I saw a flashlight in my eyes. The referee asked me if I knew what my name was. He seemed relieved after hearing me say my name and told me to lay there for a while. Somehow it registered that I was in Oakland. I remember saying aloud, "Why the fuck am I in Oakland?" My new friend Trevor walked up to me and asked me if I knew who he was. He was a total stranger to me. "That's not good," he said.

Another strange side effect of being knocked out is you can feel your brain. You know how you can feel the shape of someone's fist on your leg when they give you a charley horse? Same thing. I could feel the exact contours of my brain pressing against my skull, and every square inch of it ached. I knew I had kids but I couldn't remember their names. I knew Blobs was an important word but I wasn't sure why.

Within forty-five minutes I knew who I was again. I was a little frazzled but still able to laugh about the hilarious romp I just had with someone several light-years out of my class. I felt like Icarus. He gets a lot of shit for flying so close to the sun but at least he pushed it as far as it could go. I'd hate to go through life with wax all over my wings wondering if I could have gone a little bit higher.

When I got back to New York, I had a neurologist check me out because my head still hurt, and he said my brain was swollen but medication would take care of it. A week after that I discovered something that hurt my brain even more—the show was canned. I almost died fighting a ninja superhero and the footage is going to sit in a dusty warehouse somewhere? How am I supposed to tell this story in a bar? It's only a beginning and a middle. I can't end a story like that. I needed an end. So, I made one.

I got the production company to send me the fight footage and issued this challenge on our website:

> *My training has finally got to the point where I can take anyone in the entire world. Therefore, I challenge you, world, to a fight. Now, this doesn't mean you can pop me in the face when I'm walking down the street. Nor does it mean I will meet you down an alleyway at 4 in the morning. What it means is, I will meet you in the ring of your choice and fight you for at least 10 rounds with a certified ref present so we don't die. I don't care how many wins you've had or what your weight class is or any of that shit. I don't even care if you are a professional fighter. I will fight anyone in America and I'll fly down to the city of your choice on my own dime.*

I received an alarmingly high number of submissions but eventually "chose" a kid from Oakland named Meathead Eric. Then I pretended to fly out there and get knocked out by him. Once I could pretend the fight happened as a result of a challenge, I could use the preshot footage as proof. A week after the "challenge" was accepted and several months after the original fight, I posted the footage with the following text:

> *Apparently I cannot beat the living shit out of anyone in the world. In fact, if the guy is much bigger than me and knows what he's doing, I'd be very lucky to get one punch in before the whole world turns to black.*

As is always the case, the press fell for it and *The Village Voice* ran a feature titled "Gavin McInnes Gets Knocked the Fuck Out," which read in part:

*After reviewing applications sent in by everyone, McInnes settled on a character, vowing to fly to San Francisco, where he would quickly make short work of [Meathead Eric]. Except what actually happened was that McInnes got knocked the fuck out. In about 40 seconds. It turns out being a tough tattooed drunk is no substitute for actually knowing how to fight.*

The story now had an end and was ready to be told in its entirety. I may have been a little punch-drunk, but I still wasn't a dumbass fact-checker at *The Village Voice*.

# The Death of Cool: Dash Snow (2009)

Dash Snow and me at Coney Island. (2002)
*Photo: Maria Schoenherr*

I wasn't close with Dash toward the end of his life but his death crushed me. He was ballsy and mischievous but also had this child-

251

like optimism that you could only get from spending your adolescence without parents. When I first met him he was still a teenager driving around the Lower East Side on a BMX bike with a huge smile on his face as if the city was his living room, which it was.

Dash was sent to reform school at a very young age, which is like sending someone to "I Don't Love You Anymore So Learn to Fight" school. When he came out at sixteen, his parents didn't seem interested in having him back, so he lived in an apartment by himself and continued life as a postpubescent grown-up.

Dash gets flak from bitter assholes because he came from money, but I'd like to see them survive abandonment at that age. That's your first year of high school. You barely have pubes. Dash handled it better than most. He took over New York and went from a petty vandal to an art superstar. Despite all the fanfare, he treated it all like a big joke and made fun of it every chance he got. He literally beat off on his paintings. Young kids looked up to him as a tough guy and graffiti star, but when I saw him, I still saw a directionless kid.

What killed me about his overdose was this ethereal sense of culpability. Did putting him in the spotlight make him feel like an icon who should go out in a blaze of glory? He died at twenty-seven, just like Kurt Cobain, Jimi Hendrix, Janis Joplin, Jim Morrison, Brian Jones, and later, Amy Winehouse. How many of my own friends had fallen for this bullshit? "Live Fast, Die Young" is just fashion. It's not real. You're not supposed to actually *do* it. You're supposed to live so fast it bruises you and then move on. Why couldn't so many of my friends move on?

Our fear of death unites us all. That's why there's religion. Heroin tricks your mind into killing yourself. It assuages the fear of death by placing you in heaven and prying you free from any awareness of your mortality. It sits on your shoulder like a little Rasputin and says, "Fuck this life. It doesn't matter. Let's leave," and your fearless bliss responds with, "Why not?" But why did these people let Rasputin sit on their shoulders in the first place?

My daughter was three when Dash died and my son was one. His daughter was two. I thought Dash was one of the guys who'd figured out there's a whole other life after cool. The party phase is fun, but it's a phase. If twenty years of getting wasted and fucking strangers doesn't sow your wild oats, it's time to give up farming.

Parenting comes after the party phase and it's like a second life. In fatherhood it's no longer about you; it's about them. Unfortunately, Dash didn't get this and I think a part of it is because he had no context. I met Dash's father once. He was doing cocaine with us at a loft party and babbling like a spoiled aristocrat who had no idea who his son was.

Nothing makes you appreciate your father more than becoming one yourself, and every day I deal with my kids, I can remember what my dad did when he was in that situation. I'd seen my dad deal with my broken wrist. He was there when I decided to move to Montreal. When I started my first business. When I got in trouble with the police and when I totally changed my mind about what I wanted to do with my life. He was always there. Both my parents were. Dash didn't have those examples, so fatherhood didn't have the same checklist. I'm not apologizing for him. I still think it's unforgivable to let heroin peel you away from your daughter, but I see how you can get lost without parents. He already built a life from scratch. Maybe he wasn't prepared to do it again.

My attitude when someone OD's is usually, "Way to go, asshole." Heroin is Russian roulette for retards. You can get plenty high from other booze/drug combinations that aren't fatal, so why risk it? For example, if I put you in a room with two girls, a 10 who had AIDS and a 9 who didn't, which would you fuck? I keep telling these junkies to fuck the 9, but they keep fucking the 10 and dying. This has been happening since I graduated university.

In March of 1995, a punk kid named Jonathan found out he got hep C from sharing needles and hanged himself. Soon after that, Melissa Auf der Maur found out her ex-boyfriend Phil had OD'd. In October of 1995, our friend Colleen died from AIDS after sharing needles. A caustic old punk named Chris who always called me out on my bullshit in college OD'd in 1995 too. A year later Melissa's roommate Sanjay, guitarist of the Montreal band the Nils, OD'd. Charles was a hilarious old queer who was never sober and always funny. He OD'd in 1997 after getting dumped by his boyfriend. That same year, a young film student named Gordon got clean but OD'd after a relapse. That's what always happens. After junkies quit, their tolerance goes down, then they get drunk and carelessly snort a line as big as the ones they did back in their junkie days. The new body can't handle the old body's habits and they die.

All the deaths I listed were in Montreal but a few years after moving to New York, my friend Ben, a bartender at Max Fish, OD'd after a relapse. Two years later, 2 Hip from a street gang called DMS died the same way. In 2008 we were going to get a kid named Jamie to play in our band but he was found dead of an overdose in his practice space. I've seen about one heroin death a year since my early twenties and almost all these kids were the same age. I've lived twenty years twice now and feel like I've barely begun living. I tried not to feel sympathy for any of them because I was mad, but Dash was the last straw. I was out of apathy.

I started drinking and getting high the second I found out he was dead and I stayed up all night crying my eyes out while writing this . . .

*The best part of living in New York is the feeling that you're in the center of everything. This feeling is like hard drugs and soon you want more. Eventually, Brooklyn isn't enough. Then certain parts of Manhattan aren't enough. You feel like you're visiting your parents when you're in SoHo or you're on a road trip when you're in Chelsea. St. Mark's is a minimall and even the East Village feels like a pale imitation of the Lower East Side.*

*You never felt like that when you were partying with Dash Snow. You felt like you were at the Ground Zero of Fun. Every night with Dash felt like The Night. He was why people move to New York. He was the first guy my wife met when she moved here and the one person who defined the city when I arrived. It was like he invited you here from your small town and felt responsible if you had a bad time. I remember coming from a club called Black & White and everyone being mildly bummed at what a mediocre evening it had been. Without warning, Dash lit a discarded Christmas tree on fire, which exploded into flames that brought down a white Range Rover before spreading onto a building. This led to an all-nighter of vandalism that we all still talk about in awe. Dash had to escape to Texas until the heat died down.*

*He wrote, "All Europeans must leave now," dozens of times all over the Lower East Side. He invented Hamster Parties, where you rip up phone books of paper for so long, the room looks like a hamster cage, and then you party in it. He had a tattoo of a spider with Saddam Hussein's head on it. I never met a guy with a stupid tattoo whom I didn't instantly love. It shows they get it. Dash Snow is also the only guy I've ever seen get into a fight with a cigarette still in his mouth. He was fearless.*

*New York has a reputation as a melting pot, but it's not. It's several totally different New Yorks piled on top of each other with people coexisting on different planes and never saying hi. I don't know any Puerto Ricans nor do I know anyone who knows any Puerto Ricans. There's an entire city of jocks who go to Irish bars up by Thirty-fourth Street. I don't know any of them but they probably have their own legends they pour some of their beer out to and do a line in memory of—which is what I just did for Dash. Then there are the born-and-raised New Yorkers who hate our guts and wear their thick accents as a badge of honor.*

*I don't give a shit about any of those scenes. The New York that interests me is these strange ten-year waves of pop-culture enthusiasts who come here from all over the world and party hard enough to define an epoch. I love the fifties beatniks who hung out with scary Negroes and got high in Greenwich Village while Jack Kerouac wrote it all down. I love the speed-freak sixties art-fag weirdoes who went to an abandoned SoHo and turned it into Philip Glass songs and Chuck Close paintings. I love the seventies CBGB's nihilist assholes with Lou Reed and Debbie Harry telling everyone to fuck off. To me, Dash Snow defines New York from 2000 to 2010. I was lucky enough to watch that unfold.*

*When I used to run around with a camera and a notepad following Irak and documenting all the mayhem, Dash asked, "Why are you always reporting on shit and reviewing other people's shit? Why don't you do your own shit?" I couldn't get it out of my head. I still can't. And neither should you. Do your own shit.*

# The Excess of Success (2010)

$\mathbf{M}$y parents are happy that I have money but they're also weird about it. I recently brought it up with Monk veteran Skeeter, who married a Paki and adopted a couple of black kids.

"Do you think they're racist?" I asked him on the phone.

"What?" he asked.

"Our parents. You married an Indian (dot) and I married an Indian (feather), and our parents both seem uncomfortable at our houses. Is it racial?" Skeeter had been thinking about this, too. He'd noticed when his Liverpool dad flew off the handle after being scoffed at for not liking Brie.

"Dude," he said, bracing me for a cold slap of seriousness, "it's *class*. They can't help but identify us as the same rich assholes who looked down on them when they were young." He was right. British people are consumed with class and no matter where the poor move or how much money they make, they'll always be paranoid about where they are perceived to be in the hierarchy. This burden is alien to those of us who were imported to a new country where nobody belonged to any class and the national anthem didn't exist.

After building my place upstate, I invited my parents down regularly to partake in its fruits and play with the kids. They did both and I was happy to see them. Despite all the mockery on both ends, I really dig my parents. They are nuts. For Christmas my mom bought my son a broken bicycle from a charity shop (he was still a baby) and she got my daughter a used Cabbage Patch doll with threadbare clothes. For me she brought a pile of *Vice* magazines several years after the split. Thanks. At the house, my father devotes his spare time to important activities like reorganizing our kitchen cupboards. The first time he did it, he couldn't believe how much food we had. "It's a bloody waste," he'd sneer while amalgamating our cheeses.

After completely overhauling every shelf in the kitchen and the entire fridge, he commanded me to stop watching movies with my mother downstairs and come upstairs for a discussion. "Look at this," he said incredulously, pointing to three large piles he had made on the counter. "You've got a huge bloody pile of these fucking corn chips," he said, "then there's this endless pile of cheese," he grumbled while pointing to two normal-sized things of cheese, "and this," he said accusingly while holding two jars of salsa. "What is salzzzza?" I told him it's a Mexican sauce and he shushed me, saying, "If only they'd invent a dish that combined cheese, corn chips, and salzzzza." I tried to tell him there is and it's called "nachos" and he acted like I was telling him pigs have blond hair, which they do.

I decided to prove my point and prepared a plate of nachos on an oven dish. As I laid the corn chips down and covered them with salsa and grated cheese, my dad started freaking as if I were burning $100 bills. "What the fuck are you doing?" he shrieked. "STOP!" he added, almost crying. I tried to convince him I was preparing a snack that exists and is often consumed, but he didn't believe me. As far as he was concerned I was pouring ice cream on spaghetti and covering it with mayonnaise to spite him. "STOP!" he yowled again like Grounds-keeper Willie in drag. I kept going because I don't give a shit about his made-up world, and he reached his breaking point.

"That's it!" he yelled while running to the guest room next to the kitchen and taking off his clothes. "I'm going to bed!" Europeans sleep in the nude so I had to watch his weird little ass bunny-hop under the covers as he tore into bedtime with a vengeance.

"You're not seriously going to bed because I made my own nachos with my own groceries, are you?" I asked while noticing old men's asses look like shaved vaginas.

"I HATE EXCESS!" my dad screamed as he threw the covers over his head.

I rolled my eyes and brought the cooked nachos downstairs, where my mother and I were watching an action movie about murder. "Mmm," she said, consuming two handfuls at a time, "these are delicious."

The next day I discovered the hater-of-excess had devoured the $60 bottle of wine my wife was saving for a girls' night with her friends. She was mad, but the thought of a cheap-ass Scotsman pissed *about* excess while piss-drunk *on* excess gives me a smile I will take to my grave.

# Turning Forty (2010)

I threw my fortieth-birthday party at my place upstate. The theme was the Great *Gavsby* and I invited everyone from Steve and Dogboy to a bunch of new dad friends who lived nearby. Everyone dressed like they were rich people from the 1920s, as was the rule.

The party went well and we drank and played badminton, but my wife is the greatest wife in the world so after she hoodwinked me into going to David Cross's next door to check on something, I returned to see she had booked the hardcore band Cerebral Ballzy to play in our backyard.

All the dads started moshing, so like any other forty-year-old man, I took off all my clothes and jumped in. Then we did keg-stands as the band played classics like "Puke Song" and "Shitrag."

At the end of the night, we all sat around a bonfire and one of the kids in the band asked me what it's like to be forty. I said, "Well, mirrors make you look old," and he laughed so I added, "I used to sing for Anal Chinook and Leathersassbuttfuk. Now I yell stuff like, 'The next person who says something is 'stupid' or calls it 'poo-poo' is getting a time-out!'" and he laughed a little less. Then I told him how pretty girls say, "Oh, excuse me, sir," when they bump into me and if

I ever get caught ogling them, they shoot back a sharp, cold look that says, "You're kidding, right?" He said he got it and tried to change the subject, but I was on a roll. "I may be an old fart," I told him, "but farts feel good and they only stink for a minute. The best part of turning forty is you can finally stop pretending to like Radiohead." I had a good ten more in me . . .

## 1. You Don't Give a Shit What People Think

In my late twenties, I asked a cab driver what it was like to be forty because that's what he was and I was getting annoyed with his talking to his friend on the phone for so long. (Why do they do that, by the way? What are they, thirteen-year-old girls?) "It's real mellow, buddy," he responded in his East Indian accent. "You don't vorry so much."

As an angry young man, I had a lot of trouble understanding how you could not give a shit what people think. "What if someone came up to your window right now and called you an asshole?" I asked.

"I vould say, 'Oh my,'" he said, "then vind up the vindow and drive off." Before I could question his manhood, he added, "Now, if it vas ten or twenty years ago I vould get out of this cab and say, 'Vat did you say, moderfucker?' and stuff like these—but now, nothing. It's not vorth it."

I finally get what he was talking about. I'm precious cargo. I can't be endangering my kids' father because some irrelevant psycho is in a bad mood. Sticks and stones still break your bones when you're forty but unless it's a peer giving constructive criticism, you honestly don't give a hamster's testicle what people think.

You also become a lot less critical of other people's work when you've actually done some of your own. *Friends* was on for ten years. I never got a show on the air so who am I to criticize? Cox does not suck. OAR makes music that sounds queer to me but they sell eighty thousand tickets a night and I can't even play the guitar. Good for them. Not to get all Baz Luhrmann commencement speech on your ass, but the more you accomplish, the less you trivialize others' accomplishments. Besides, reveling in others' failures is for losers.

## 2. Pissing Is Weird

As I think Dostoyevsky once said, "No matter how you shake your peg, the last wee drop runs down your leg." You could swing that thing around with the force of NASA's Human Training Centrifuge, but— *bloop*—a yellow drop still squirts out the second you place it back in your underwear.

I've even tried faking it out and pretending I'm done shaking to see what happens, but he waits until he's positive there's cotton around his lips and then spitefully spits out a drop. There's a generation gap between you and your dink at this age and he will do everything in his power to fuck up your shit.

## 3. You No Longer Have Game

I have run into women who I used to defile in my single days but when I talk to them now, I sound like the narrator from *The Wonder Years* holding in a fart. After you're married, women become human beings for the first time ever and it's like meeting another species. "Um, hello, do you like music?" You can try flirting but with nothing to back it up, you come across like a pugilist in a wheelchair.

This is the nature of marriage. In 1978, classmate Lee Gratton told me, "When you get married you get to see your wife's tits whenever you want." He was right, only it's your best friend's tits. You don't have any game when you're married because you're in a new universe of love, and anything else feels like a preschool reunion.

## 4. Newspapers Make You Furious

In your twenties, you have to force yourself to read the paper. In your thirties, it finally gets interesting and each article reads like your favorite book. By your forties, you're actually smarter and more experienced than most of the journalists and you catch yourself crumpling the sides going, "They're blaming the coast guard for what the pirates did? Are these journalists stupid or just trying to make their fathers angry?"

## 5. You Care About Your Lawn

Bill Hicks had a bit where he said, "What is it about men where they wake up one day caring about their lawn?" Then he talks about dads walking around in bathrobes with their balls hanging out and yelling, "Who wants sausages? I'm makin' sausages for breakfast!" These routines have gone from comedic banter to a documentary about my life. I care so much about my lawn, I wish it had a birthday so I could buy it presents. I even have nightmares about its bald spots. Scotts EZ Seed is way better for patches than that stupid pulp shit they sell but if you're in an area with a lot of pines, you're going to have to lime the shit out of it before any seeding solutions—and do it in the fall so it gets soaked in six months later when the snow melts . . . Hey, where'd everybody go?

## 6. Construction Is Fascinating

What young men consider a noisy nuisance is a giant bowl of eye candy to a forty-year-old. "Oh, they're using those planks made out of recycled bags," you think as you peer through the fence at the new community center. "Those are way too slippery for a deck." You'll also catch yourself worrying about foundations and insulation and even asking carpenters what brand of thread lock they use.

## 7. Country Music Sounds Cool

Twenty-five years ago, if you told me I'd get chills from hearing Willie Nelson and Toby Keith sing about feeding alcoholic beverages to a horse, I'd ask you why a time traveler was going to punk shows and talking to kids.

What used to sound like hillbillies yawning over unplugged guitars now sounds like a soothing pile of heartfelt stories I could listen to all night. I still like Southern rap and anarcho-punk, but it's now tempered with heaping portions of Merle Haggard.

## 8. Hangovers Become Intense

Fuck foxholes. Try finding an atheist in an old man's hangover. I have kneeled there with my head in the toilet for hours explaining to Jesus why I've never been to church and swearing to his dad I will start this Sunday. Cross my heart and hope to die, Lord, because that would be an improvement over this funeral march of head-pounding dry heaves.

When you wake up at forty with a hangover, your head feels like an inside-out Medusa. Then nausea grips your whole body like a barf snowsuit and your skin feels like a doctor accidentally gave chemotherapy to a baby on a hunger strike. This lasts, without respite, until you go to bed, and it even lingers until the following morning. I would love to party as hard as I used to, but Pavlov won't allow it, so that's it. I didn't quit drugs; drugs quit me.

## 9. Your Perversions Advance

As the Wolf recently put it, "I went out with a girl who had droopy tits when I was twenty and I wasn't into it, but I sure wouldn't mind fucking with them right now!"

For young men, it can be shocking to see how gigantic a woman's ass gets in her forties, but when you reach this age you're like, "More dessert, please." Queefs, butt hairs, blemishes, and even a faint whiff of poo are all more grist for the fuck mill, and you finally understand why Napoleon forbade Josephine from showering the week before he got home. The previous version of you looks like a vagina-phobic metrosexual by comparison. While this is happening, scantily clad twentysomethings go from sluts you catcall to young ladies who had better get a coat on or they are going to catch their death of cold.

## 10. The Party's Over

Well, it's not "over" per se. It's just drastically different. With all due respect to doing coke in the basement of Lit with Paul Sevigny all night, that's no longer my idea of a good time. I mean, it was real, it was fun, but it wasn't real fun, and although I wouldn't trade those days for the world, I just traded them for a whole new world.

I have three kids now. That means 75 percent of my roommates came out of my soul mate's genitals and I feel a much stronger bond with them than with someone who has similar tattoos and the same taste in music. I still get high but it goes like this: Getting a drawing from my daughter feels like doing a bump. Hearing my son say, "Take dat, Beezo," after punching his Bozo Bop Bag makes me laugh like I just smoked a bowl. Having a baby fall asleep on your chest feels like heroin. Seeing a little kid fly his first kite is as exciting as amphetamines, and taking all evening to build a Lego robot feels better than a Maker's on the rocks next to a perfectly poured Guinness.

I'm not saying you should skip the party stage. Just don't live there for the rest of your life. Take it as close to the edge as you can without jumping, then turn away and go for a walk through the flowers, because it's all just a lark. What really matters in the long run and what your true legacy will be is the wisdom you pass on to your kids. As brilliant old guy Horace Greeley once said, "Fame is fleeting; popularity an accident; riches take wings. Only one thing endures: character."

I'm going to pour some beer out for all my dead homies right now, but not too much, because this particular beer is delicious and I'm saving it for a toast to my dad homies. A *toast*! To the future! To life after the death of cool!

# Turning Forty (2010)

Toasting the future with Cerebral
Ballzy at my fortieth. (2010)

# Afterword

So that's it. That's my life. The party years at least. I didn't put the dad stuff in here because I don't really want my children in a book with a dozen dead junkies. I don't have any regrets. Booze was there for all the bad decisions I ever made, but it was there for the good ones too (not so much with the mediocre ones). All these choices were crucial parts of my development, but I'm not one of these existentialist types who think you can alter your destiny. Shit, Crass's Penny Rimbaud recently told me we have the power to physically change our own DNA. Hogwash. You are who you are from the day you are born. Look at identical twins separated at birth. They find each other twenty years later, and they have the same dog, same car, similar-looking husbands, similar jobs, and about the same annual income.

I didn't even want to be a writer. Not at first. I wanted to be an artist, but that shit takes forever and I simply don't have the patience. Even the work-to-reward ratio of drawing comics wasn't satisfying enough (also, I suck at it). I write because I can't not write. Like Bukowski said, "Unless it comes bursting out of you, in spite of everything, don't do it." I believe life is about figuring out what you were meant to do and pursuing that, by any means necessary. True misery is the ballerina who was meant to be an accountant or the accountant who was meant to be a ballerina. My generation has been taught that creative jobs are the special ones and everyone else is living a miserable lie, but I've got a lot more respect for a proud grout cleaner than some douchebag photographer who uses words like "lexicon."

It took a lot of trial and error to figure it all out. Selling drugs gave me diarrhea. Playing in punk bands gets old when you get old. I tried hard labor and enjoyed the satisfaction of a job well done, but I simply didn't have the stamina for it over the long haul. Besides, I was itching to tell stories. Though this vocation was set in stone from day one, I still had choices. I used those choices to peel back the layers and discover exactly what the stone said. It all comes back to that conversation with Dogboy on the roof when I asked him if he really wanted to sink his teeth into something. I knew I did and set off on this path the following day. You can't just sit on your ass and assume fate is going to tap you on the shoulder.

In high school, we chose to ignore the in-crowd hierarchy and made our own club with our own set of rules. My parents worked hard to get me and my brother away from the danger of the city, and I ran back there the day I turned eighteen. When I graduated from university, there were no jobs so I created one. When Montreal's bureaucracy started slowing us down, we moved to New York. When my wild oats were sowed, I married the love of my life and settled down. I never complained about people not giving me opportunities. The only time I got mad was when someone stood in my way.

This is where I was always meant to be and I'm infinitely grateful for that. If the reader has anything to glean from this book, I hope it's "Trust your gut." If you're an Amish sailor but you were meant to be a straight drag queen who trains dancing dogs, you're going to have to bid adieu to your bearded friends and be the Lessandra the Great you were always meant to be. That's not just something that would make you feel better. It is the very definition of happiness.

# Acknowledgments

I'd like to thank my agent, Byrd Leavell, for pushing this book as hard as he pushed *Sh\*t My Dad Says* and *I Hope They Serve Beer in Hell*. You went way beyond the call of duty and I'm forever indebted to you for that. I'd also like to thank my editor, Brant Rumble, and everyone at Scribner for their endless enthusiasm despite the raucous content. I'm confident this book will do much better than every other you've stood behind, including *The Great Gatsby* and all twenty-six Hemingways. Jim Goad inspired me to start writing back in the early nineties and has remained the gold standard ever since. Thanks for helping me punch up the manuscript, Jim. Thanks also to Patton Oswalt for taking time out of his busy schedule to give me invaluable notes on the book.

I'd also like to thank Arvind Dilawar, Benjamin Leo, and Kurt Lustgarten for their notes, as well as Matt Pisane for all those cover ideas.